WILLIAM FOOTE WHYTE is Director, Special Science Research Center, Cornell University, and has taught also at the Universities of Oklahoma and Chicago. The story he tells in this book first came to his attention at a chance luncheon meeting, and prompted him to spend two years in the study of these events, with the eager cooperation of the union, the management and the workers involved.

Professor Whyte is the author also of *Money and Motivation, Street Corner Society* and *Human Relations in the Restaurant Industry,* and a contributor to numerous professional journals.

Pattern for Industrial Peace

Pattern for
Industrial Peace

by William Foote Whyte

*Professor, New York State School of Industrial and
Labor Relations, Cornell University; Author of "Street
Corner Society," "Human Relations in the Restaurant
Industry."*

HARPER & BROTHERS, PUBLISHERS, NEW YORK

To Kathleen

PATTERN FOR INDUSTRIAL PEACE

Contents

Preface

WHY WRITE a book about the relations of Inland Steel Container Company's Chicago plant with its union local of the United Steelworkers of America? A plant of about 500 workers is hardly more than a pinpoint upon the national scene. Devoting a book to it certainly requires some explanation.

I became interested in this case study because it seemed to me that we had a chance here to discover general principles of human relations that might be applied to other cases.

In the first place, this is one of the most striking changes in union-management relations on record. After a ten year struggle of the most intense bitterness, the parties worked out of their conflict and established cooperative relations with extraordinary speed and skill. I feel that we can most profitably learn through studying such changes through a period of time. When we study a relationship that has remained in the same groove over a period of years, it is difficult to determine what factors created and maintain that pattern. When we see changes take place, we have a much better chance of studying the dynamics of human relations.

Furthermore, the skill exercised by the key men in both union and management provides many good, practical lessons in leadership. I was particularly struck with the initiative displayed by the union leadership in reshaping the relationship, for much of the literature would lead us to believe that management sets the pattern and the union leaders simply react to that pattern.

Finally, this case provided a good test of the possibilities of a human relations analysis in studying the process of negotiating a union-management contract. It seems generally agreed that human relations methods and theories are useful in explaining day-to-day relations within the factory, but it is also widely believed that human relations has no tools to cope with the "power struggle" that takes place when the parties bargain a contract. I did not see why this should be. Certainly, the discussions that take place around the bargaining table involve people and their relations with each other. We should be able to evolve some way of analyzing such behavior, whether we call it human relations or anything else.

This case provides particularly rich data upon the negotiation process, with the stenographic transcripts of all of the meetings, backed up by extensive interview data in which informants discuss their behavior and motives before, during, and after the bargaining meetings. Such data provide an opportunity to relate the negotiation process with day-to-day behavior in the plant in a manner that has never been done before. Readers must judge for themselves to what extent this opportunity has been fully exploited.

I wish to express my indebtedness to the participants in this case—particularly to William G. Caples, John Gossett, Joseph Kluck, Lucius Love, Robert Novy, and Lawrence G. Shafer—for their extraordinary cooperation in providing the full record on which this book is based. The nature of my research and of their part in it is fully described in Appendix A.

I wish to acknowledge the secretarial help I received. Dorothy Clarke transcribed my research notes. Helen Schaeffer typed the first draft of the case. Peggy Parks and Mary K. Sullivan typed subsequent drafts and helped to prepare the book for publication.

The theoretical ideas underlying the field work and discussed in Part II of this book stem from various sources. Perhaps the most important direct influence comes from the interaction theory of Eliot D. Chapple and Conrad M. Arensberg. (See their Genetic Psychology Monograph, #22, 1940, on *Measuring Human Relations*. See also Chapple and Carleton S. Coon, *Principles of Anthropology*, first four chapters.) Other influences that I am aware of come from W. Lloyd Warner, Burleigh B. Gardner, Everett C. Hughes, and Alexander H. Leighton. Readers may be interested to note how closely my theoretical statement parallels that of George C. Homans in *The Human Group* (Harcourt Brace and Co.), a book that has just appeared as my own goes to press. It may be significant that, working independently, we have arrived at theoretical statements that are markedly similar at important points.

For opportunities to discuss these ideas and to expose them to very useful criticism, I am indebted to the members of our Cornell human relations research group (1940–50): Chris Argyris, Temple Burling, Melvin Kohn, Henry Landsberger, Edith Lentz, Charles Mertens, Lois Remmers, Stephen Richardson, and Graham Taylor. While I have put together various ideas not original with me, the theoretical product, in these pages, should be regarded as highly tentative, and as my own responsibility.

WILLIAM FOOTE WHYTE

New York State School of Industrial and Labor Relations
Cornell University
October, 1950

Part I

The Story

The Story

Chapter 1

Sit-down Strike

*T*HE PAST is always present in labor relations. And the more bitter the past the more alive it is in men's memories.

The story begins in 1937 at the time of the General Motors sit-down strike in the Barrel Department of a family-owned steel-fabricating plant in Chicago.

The workers, both white and Negro, had been working beside the two long production lines on the ground floor of the plant. They were the men who took the sheets of steel and turned them into barrels, working with machines that shaped the sheets in circular form, welded their sides together, sprayed them with paint, inside and out, and welded on tops and bottoms. The barrel shells rolled along the assembly line from job to job, banging and clanging against each other. The welding machines screeched and spouted blue flame.

The men worked quietly. The din of machines and barrels smothered conversation. Then the horn blew for the night-shift lunch period. The assembly line slowed to a stop. The welders pushed goggles back on their foreheads and followed the others into the locker room.

The locker room was quiet except for the rustling of lunch bags and the snap-opening of lunch boxes. Every man in that room was thinking about what was happening three hundred miles away in Detroit, wondering how the struggle would come out, wondering what it would mean to the workingman. But at first nobody spoke

3

of the General Motors strike. Men knew that there were spies throughout this plant. Probably there was one man in that room who was paid by the company to inform on his fellows. You didn't know who it was. Might be the man who worked right alongside of you. Might even be the fellow you thought was your best friend in the plant. You had to be careful what you said. Couldn't afford to trust anybody.

Nevertheless, the sit-down strike was there in the locker room with them, as immediate as bread and butter. At last somebody broke the silence. He wondered out loud how that strike was going to come out. That broke the dam, and everybody began to talk about the struggle in Detroit.

The talk moved quickly from Detroit to Chicago—right into the plant where they worked. As the lunch hour drew to a close, men were beginning to suggest things that might be done, but nobody was agreeing and nobody knew what was going to happen. Then the horn blew to signal the end of lunch hour and to send the men back to work. The men fell silent for a moment and looked at each other. No one got up. The discussion continued, and, as the minutes passed, the men realized that they had already started something that had to go on, though they did not know where they were going or how they were going to get there. Finally, and still without any acknowledged leadership, they got up and marched in a body into the office of the night superintendent. He faced them, surprised, not knowing what to do. They stood in silence. They knew that in this company the first man to speak up was the first man to be fired. But finally one man said, "I want a raise." Then another said, "I want a raise." And then the next man said, "We want a raise," and suddenly they were all talking about what "we" want.

The night superintendent said that he had no authority to make any such decisions. He would call Mr. Squires, the assistant plant manager, and ask him to come right down to the plant. In the meantime, he suggested that the men go back to the locker room. If he had told them to go back to work until Mr. Squires came in, it is possible that, still without acknowledged leadership, they might have drifted back to their jobs and allowed themselves to be once more divided and beaten. But they were sent to the locker room and, as they kept on talking, the situation continued to develop. Word began to spread through the plant that the Barrel Department was not working. In department after department, one man would slip away from his machine and duck into the locker room to find out what was going on, and then go back to his machine and tell his fellow workers.

Still the men in the locker room did not know what they were going to do. But finally someone proposed that they go out and find out what the other fellows in the plant wanted to do. So they moved out in a body and began walking around the plant. By now the men out in the plant were waiting in tense excitement. When the men from the Barrel Department came out and began walking through, men in department after department left their machines and fell in behind. By the time the marchers had reached the stairs to the third floor, word had spread there and the third-floor workers were running down the stairs to meet them. Every worker in the plant on the night shift marched into the second-floor office space to wait for the assistant plant manager.

Before this time, a 2-cent an hour wage increase had already been announced—to become effective in two months. Squires climbed up on a desk and told the men that he had the authority to make the increase effective at once and was prepared to do so. He ordered the men to go back to work. The men stood there looking at each other. There were murmurs that 2 cents was not enough and that there was no use talking to Squires—they would have to stick together and take it to the big boss, who was then out of town. Squires waited for his answer. Someone called out, "Let's get out the cards." That set it off. The men broke up into small groups and soon were playing cards and talking all through the shop. It was a sit-down strike.

Squires called the police and told the strikers that he was not going to allow any food to come into the plant. The strikers talked this one over and replied that, if no food came in, they would hold the several members of management still in the plant as hostages and not allow them to get out. Management backed down. When the day shift came in to work, they were met at the gate by the night-shift workers. When the day-shift men heard what had happened, they immediately threw their lunches over the fence to take care of the sit-down strikers. After that, management sent in box lunches.

Gangsters called on management and offered to break the strike—at a price. Management declined.

On the second morning of the strike, a hand-painted cardboard sign appeared on the roof facing the crowd below: "Get the CIO." In this way word reached the CIO office in Chicago. A CIO representative called the plant and sought to make contact with management. After a few hours of stalling, management agreed to a meeting. On the fourth day of the strike management signed a contract recognizing the union, and accepting the union's chief economic demand, 50 cents an hour minimum wage.

Chapter 2

Building the Union

*T*HE UNION was born in that sit-down strike. But it did not come out of nothing. Management had planted the seeds and cultivated the ground even as it tried to stamp out all opposition.

The Chicago plant was originally built and run as part of a family business. Let's call them the Smith family, though that was not their name. (The people now active in the case will be identified by their real names, while those who were only part of earlier regimes will be given fictitious names throughout.)

The Smiths ran an absolute dictatorship, and they went out of their way to recruit a labor force that had no experience under any other type of management. They imported workers by the truck-load from the hills of Tennessee and Kentucky. Old-timers speak of the new recruits climbing down from the trucks with the mud of the hill country still on their shoes. Negroes as well as whites were brought in, and management played upon traditional race hostilities to keep the working force divided.

One Negro worker described the old hiring policy in this way:

If you was colored, you had to be straight from the South or they wouldn't hire you. You couldn't go in looking for work dressed up half way decent like I am now. You had to go in with an old cap on the back of your head and a torn shirt and pants and carrying a paper bag under your arm. First thing the boss asked you was, "How long you been in the city?" You answer, "I just got in," and he tells you you're hired. You tell him, "I been here all my life," and he won't have nothing to do with you.

The Smiths had the theory that discipline and productivity could best be maintained if workers—and foremen too—were constantly afraid of losing their jobs. Foreman Ed Snyder (then a worker) describes how that theory was put into practice:

Joe Smith would just as soon fire you as look at you. Art Thomas (Foreman) was so scared of Joe Smith that if he saw him coming he would dive right under those high bake ovens. The foreman had no security at all in those days.

Joe Smith fired one of our best workers on the line one day, and there wasn't anybody else who could do that job. He fired him just because he saw the man wearing a white shirt. The Smiths had an idea that nobody that wore a white shirt could really work.

I got fired once myself. Art Thomas called me over and said that Mr. Squires wanted to see me. I asked him what it was about, and he said he didn't know. I went to Mr. Squires' office, and he told me that I wasn't needed any more. I could get my check and go home. I said, "Mr. Squires, I don't want to tell you you can't fire me, but I would sure appreciate an explanation. I'd like to know what I've been doing wrong. I know you're not laying me off because there isn't enough work to go around because I see we got plenty to do. I would appreciate an explanation of what I done wrong, Mr. Squires." Well, he looked at me, and finally he said, "Somebody here don't like you, but forget about it. You might as well go back to work."

The company paid starvation wages and had a separate standard of pay for men and women, for Negroes and whites. At one time, in the early 30's, the expected starting wage for Negro women was 14½ cents an hour, Negro men 16½ cents, and white men received 18½ cents. When wages were to be raised, the company would move them up 2 cents at a time, and there would always be several weeks' notice of such a happy event. On the other hand, wage decreases of 5 cents an hour or more were announced and put into effect overnight. When NRA came in, the company was forced to raise wages, but this was only a temporary improvement. As soon as the radio brought in the news of the Supreme Court decision holding NRA unconstitutional, the Blue Eagle flag was hauled down from the top of the plant, and the workers on the next shift were greeted with a notice of a 5-cent an hour wage cut.

There was no such thing as an established 8-hour day. People were required to work at the pleasure of management; the worker never knew just what to expect. He might come in and have only an hour or two, or he might find during the day that he was expected to work for hours beyond his regular shift at straight-time pay. The NRA called for a 40-hour week, but there was no provision as to when these hours should be worked or concerning overtime after 8 hours on a given day. According to one foreman (then a worker), "Many a time I finished my 40 hours on Monday and Tuesday. Yes, I worked 20 hours a day on those days. When you came in in the morning, you'd meet yourself going home at night."

Favoritism went along with this policy of ruthlessness. In a plant of about 600 employees, there were 246 different pay rates. There was no such thing as a regular system of pay rates or job classifications. The worker received what management felt like giving him. If he wanted to get a break, he had to be especially submissive to the boss.

This lack of system in the wage structure was characteristic of the entire operation of the plant. In large measure, management knew neither what was going on nor what to expect. What records there were were entirely inadequate, and there was no communication up from the bottom to let management know what the score was. The foremen were errand boys who were neither consulted nor listened to. Management simply relied upon terrorizing the worker to make up for all the deficiencies in management planning and organization.

Such a dictatorship, naturally, gave rise to underground opposition, but management had its own way of meeting the situation. Records later showed that almost one out of every eight workers on the regular payroll was receiving at least a little money on the side from management in return for spying on his fellow workers. In this way management hoped to be able to nip in the bud any union organization drive. In fact, this is what happened in 1934 when the American Federation of Labor sought to organize.

The sit-down strike sprang up too suddenly to be beaten by a process of weeding out "troublemakers." Overnight management was confronted by a union.

Management gave in with unexpected ease, but, while the workers were still celebrating their victory, management was planning a counteroffensive. In the fall of 1937 the executives set out to break the CIO and establish a company union, which they called the United Progressive Union. Management then began laying off workers, first a few individuals and then larger and larger groups. At the same time the United Progressive Union opened a head-quarters near the plant and began signing up members. Certain workers were paid to talk against the CIO and to promote the new organization.

Management's agents threw money about with great freedom, spending many thousands of dollars. The man who asked for help from the UPU office could get rent money or have a ton of coal delivered to his house. Many workers took advantage of the situa-tion. Some people living in steam-heated flats had their coal dumped in the alley and then hired somebody to picked it up and sell it for them.

Word spread around that the worker who wore a UPU button as he went into the employment office could get back to work. The strong union men were determined at first to stay out at all costs, but the union leaders got together and decided upon a different course. Why should the good union man be on the outside while the other people were getting in? It was agreed that all workers should go in to the UPU office and sign up for membership, take their buttons into the employment office and get back to work. As soon as they were back inside the plant they were again signed up in the CIO. Since the CIO pledge cards had a later date than the UPU cards, the UPU cards had no effect. As soon as the workers were all back in the plant, the CIO brought charges against the company before the National Labor Relations Board.

The UPU episode had lasting effects upon labor relations in two important respects.

First, the company was forced to abandon its company union and the situation brought about a still further weakening of the com-pany's position in relation to the union. The union had presented 170 affidavits charging coercion to the National Labor Relations Board. When the company was caught in such flagrant and obvious violations, management's only interest was in escaping the legal penalties involved. Management, therefore, agreed to sign prac-tically any sort of contract the union wanted to write if only the union would drop its charges. The result was a loosely worded document which appeared to curtail management's powers in certain respects.

Second, on the union side, the UPU crisis brought to the fore a new leadership in the person of Lucius Love. Since he was to play a key role in all developments in this case until he became an international representative in 1948, we need to ask who Love was and how he got that way.

Love was born in Mississippi. He came to Chicago from St. Louis at the age of twenty-one. He had left school for work after the eighth grade, but even that amount of schooling was more than had been enjoyed by most Negroes brought in from the hill country. (In Chicago he went to night school and there received his high school diploma.)

Love went to work in the Barrel Department—which turned out to be the nerve center of the plant. At first his experiences there were no different from those of other workers. He had to take what they took just to hold his job. But even then there was a point beyond which you couldn't push Lucius Love. Ed Snyder, who was then Love's group leader, told this story:

We had a boss by the name of Schulz at that time. He was really tough. You'd come to him and ask him to do something, and he'd point a finger at you and say, "You stay dere. If something is wrong, I take care of it." At the time I'm talking about, we had a real hard job on some heavy barrels. Lucius had to reach down and pick them up off the floor and lift them up to push them along the line. The metal rack holding the barrel was supposed to be counterbalanced so that the barrel would lift up easy, but the counterbalance was way too light.

Lucius used to curse every time that job came up. He complained that he'd go home at night so tired he couldn't sleep and with a back so sore he could hardly straighten up. He asked me to go in and get Schulz to do something about it. I went in and talked to Schulz, but he wouldn't do anything. He wouldn't even come out and look the situation over. Well, I went back to Lucius and told him the boss had it under consideration, and maybe we'd get some action later.

The next time the job came up Love complained again, and Snyder went to Schulz again—with the same result. Finally, at the end of the day, Love said that if the same job came up the next day, and they hadn't fixed the machine, he just wouldn't work. When the job did come up, he demanded that Snyder go in to give that message to Schulz. When Schulz heard of this one-man rebellion he grew angry and told Snyder to order Love to work or else get out. Snyder went back, still trying to smooth things over. "Well," he said, "maybe they'll get to it by tomorrow. What do you say, Lucius, let's go ahead and finish it for today."

Love flatly refused. He walked off the job and right into Schulz's office. The group leader and the other men watched him go, never expecting to see him on the job again. A few minutes later Love and his foreman came out of the office together and walked over to the barrel line. Schulz was red in the face. Love was saying to him, "All right. You do the job. If you can do it just one day for eight hours, I'll do it every day after this, and I'll never complain again."

Schulz took off his coat, bent over, and went to work. He ran about fifteen barrels and gave up. And then the awe-struck onlookers saw the foreman walk away from the job with his arm on Love's shoulder. Schulz got the counterbalance fixed. And that act of defiance established Love as a leader of the men in his department —even before there was any organization to lead.

Love was in the Barrel Department on the night shift at the time the sit-down strike broke out. No one claims he organized it. It just grew. But he was there when the union was born, and he grew up with it. He became the first steward in the Barrel Department.

He felt unsure of himself at the time. He knew nothing of unions, and there were older men in the plant who had had experience with the AFL. He didn't think he was qualified, but the men chose him and he set out to learn the job. The first lesson came early. He describes it thus:

I remember the first grievance I took in. We all sat around a table with Adam Squires. We didn't know what it was all about, and there was fear in my heart. I didn't know when it came around to me if I would be able to speak up, but they all had something to say and finally Mr. Squires said to me, he says, "What's your name?" I was afraid he wanted to know my name to fire me, but I told him and then he said, "Well, have you got something to beef about?" I told him yes, I did. There were three men in our department stacking barrels and one of them was getting less money than the other two. That was a common thing in the plant at that time. So I told him that this man should get as much as the other two. The result was that he cut the rates on the other two men, so instead of getting one man an increase, I got two men a cut. That made me stop to think. After that I knew I had to study these things carefully before I brought them up. I lost my first grievance then, but I never lost one since. That is, I never lost one that was important.

Love goes on to describe his next step up:

I think I know what it was that gave me a chance to be vice-president. We were having a lot of trouble at that time, and we had a meeting with a couple of international representatives. Our president and vice-president didn't make the meeting. I came in a little late as always, and I was standing around talking to the international representatives when some of the fellows told me I ought to get up and open the meeting. I told them, "Not me!" I didn't think I was qualified to do it, but they got me up there, and I did open the meeting. I talked for just a few minutes, telling the people about the conditions we were facing, and when I sat down people clapped. I didn't know what they were clapping for. Then after the meeting some of them came up to me and shook my hand. They told me, "You done good—you done real good!"

George Micheau was president of the local at that time. He was a very smart fellow. I learned a lot from working with George. The vice-president of the local at that time didn't take much interest. When the meeting came up to elect officers somebody nominated me. I thought they were just fooling. I didn't think I was qualified. I would have got up to decline the nomination only I didn't know how to do it. I was embarrassed to stand up and talk before the people and not say the proper thing. I told George Micheau I shouldn't get the job because I wasn't qualified. He said, "That's all right. You stay in. You're a good man." So they elected me vice-president.

Micheau and I teamed up together. We were a good team. We had to work close together at that time because management was trying to play the Negroes off against the whites. If we let either the Negroes or whites get any advantage it would have wrecked our union. Micheau was 100 per cent fair with the Negroes and he could say things to the white fellows that I couldn't tell them. I wouldn't favor my own people either. The union had to come first.

Management would try to play George and me against each other. They would call George in, in the beginning, and then he'd tell me about it after. Then when I'd go into management on some other problem they'd tell me, "That isn't what Micheau told us on this thing." They were trying to embarrass me, to make me look foolish. I told Micheau after that that I thought he ought to take me in together with him. He thought I didn't trust him, but I explained to him that they were trying to split us, and I told him that suppose anything should happen to him, I'd have to take over and I wouldn't have the experience. So after that we always went in together. I would never give my opinion with management unless Micheau was there too. They'd try to get around that. They'd say to me, "What's the matter, is he your pappy? Can't you say anything until he comes?" But that didn't bother me none.

It was Love who had to lead the union in the critical period when management was trying to destroy it with the company union. Micheau had caught his hand in a machine and was in the hospital when the crisis broke. When he came out of the hospital he went on the staff of the international union. Love consulted him often on the telephone, but many decisions could not wait upon such consultation. The vice-president was learning how to lead the union.

Victory over the company union brought new prestige for Love, but it did not move him up to the top position, even when the presidency was vacant. As Love explains it:

That's the time I had to make a decision. People didn't think I should be president. They didn't say that I wasn't qualified, but especially my own people, they couldn't think of a Negro being president of a union. A thing like that had just never happened. They thought I wouldn't get the respect of management, and, of course, the white fellows didn't want me for president either. I thought it over, and I said to myself, if they don't have faith in me, the very first mistake I make they'll think that just goes to prove that I'm not qualified. So I told them I wasn't going to run for any office. I just dropped out, and that was the smartest decision I ever made.

In the following year things went from bad to worse in the union. The workers did not turn against the union but they became apathetic and dissatisfied. There were many workers who had not signed up for membership and those who were members dropped behind in the payment of dues until the union was broke and had $1,700 of back dues outstanding.

When election time came around again, two of Love's friends went to him and pleaded with him to run for president. At first he refused, saying that if he had not been qualified the year before he was certainly less qualified now after having been inactive for a year. Besides, he and his wife were busy with a small grocery store. The men talked and argued with him for seven hours and finally persuaded him to run. Love's opponent in the contest was a white man, but Love won by a margin of 40 to 1. Since Negroes and whites were then in about equal numbers in the plant, this overwhelming victory shows that the election was not a racial contest.

Upon assuming office Love felt that his first job was to make the union solid. Only then would he be able to negotiate effectively with management. He organized a flying squad to get the nonmembers into the union and prod the workers who were behind in their dues. The squad was largely made up of women who had a special talent for shaming men into joining up and paying up. They would get together at each noon hour and concentrate upon one individual, surrounding him while he ate. It got so that men were hiding out during the lunch hour, eating on top of freight cars or in other out-of-the-way places. The flying squad had indirect effects as important as direct ones. When the flying squad went through a department the loyal union members would laugh and joke with each other and cheer the girls on. This all served to build up the morale of the members and to concentrate social pressure on those who had not joined or who were behind in dues. (Such tactics brought no countermoves from management at that time, although later managements would not have allowed the union to do its organizing within the plant.)

The nonunion man got no help from union men. If he needed to borrow a tool or get some advice, he was simply out of luck. Perhaps the foreman told one of the union men to make a certain change in a job and expected him to pass the word along; but the nonunion man in the crew didn't get the word and consequently made a lot of mistakes which got him in trouble. There was at least one departmental strike, where men refused to work with the nonunion man and the man was harassed into quitting. At first the union had taken on grievances for anyone but now the officers decided that only union members would have their grievances aired.

These various tactics were effective with all but a few recalcitrant workers. A group of men then took to waiting on the corner at the end of the shift to meet the nonmembers and to escort them to the union halls, where they were advised to sign up.

The union's policy at the time was frankly that the plant had to be organized down to the last worker. As Love expresses it:

I told it to the people in the union meeting. I said to them, "Nobody is forced to belong to the union here. If you don't like our union there's a thousand and one other places you can work in Chicago, so you don't have to belong to the union. But we like our union, and we want to pay dues. If you don't like your union and don't want to pay dues, you can just get out and leave the union to the people who want to support it." We got rid of some people that way. That way we finally got the plant 100 per cent signed up, and then we got some more respect out of management.

The membership has remained 100 per cent down to the present writing. That drive was a turning point for the union. There were many bitter battles with management ahead, but from this point on, management had to contend with a united union.

There were still difficult problems to be worked out within the union. With about an even balance of white and Negro members who were not accustomed to working together—and who served under a management which sought to divide them—the officers faced a delicate race relations situation from the beginning. But they met the problem firmly, and it caused them surprisingly little trouble. The Micheau-Love team set the pattern: an executive board half white, half Negro, working together on a strict, no-discrimination policy.

Even in later years when the membership had become 65 per cent Negro, this even balance of officers was maintained. Love was once quoted by a fellow Negro officer as saying, "We'll keep our executive board half white even if we have to paint somebody white."

There were some who opposed this policy, but Love had an answer for them:

I used to get men to come up to me and ask me why I didn't do something special for my own people. Maybe there was some job they weren't really entitled to, but I could use my influence to get it for them before the white man. I'd tell them, "Well, I'm just the president of the union and I'm carrying out the laws of the union. If you want those laws changed you go before the meeting and make a motion." I knew they wouldn't have the nerve to do that. Then I'd tell them, "Look at how bad it was for us before the union came in. Then the Negroes didn't have no chance at all. If you want to favor us ahead of the white man, that will just break up our union and we'll be back where we started from."

Chapter 3

Inland Steel Takes Over

IN 1939 the family owners sold out to Inland Steel Company, which set up the Chicago, New Orleans, and Jersey City plants as a subsidiary later named the Inland Steel Container Company.

The plants had produced a large volume of steel containers over a period of years. The purchase assured the parent corporation of an important outlet for its steel production. But Inland Steel Company was also buying an organization of men and women—an organization shot through with discord, confusion, and bitterness.

It was to take years to establish an efficient and harmonious organization. Perhaps the process was slowed by the extraordinary demands put upon management when the war came, but, in any case, the struggle went on, and at first there was no progress to report.

The years 1939–1944 were marked by strife, confusion, and rapid turnover within the ranks of management. The Chicago plant had six managers in that period. Foremen turned over much more rapidly, and in one 2-year stretch the plant had ten personnel managers.

At the top level, positions were more stable. Mr. Worth came in as president in 1940 and appointed Mr. Jessup, former purchasing agent, as assistant to the president, and Mr. Craig as general factories manager.

These changes did not improve matters. Worth, the president, was completely out of touch with the factory situation. His only channel of communication with the factory was through his assistant, Jessup. Jessup, in turn, did not get along with the factory people and therefore was not in a position to serve as a useful channel of communication.

This left Craig, the general factories manager, in an exceedingly difficult position. He felt that he had neither backing nor understanding from his superiors. In his infrequent contacts with Worth he was simply ordered to keep the factory running, without receiving any advice as to how this should be done. Craig did not like the union but these instructions meant to him that he could not go too far in opposing it. The result was that he would take a position and try to maintain it in discussion with eloquence and ingenuity that sometimes confused the opposition. But always, when the showdown came, he would give in. This situation is well stated by a union official who made this comment: "Until this recent change in Mr. Gossett, I think Mr. Craig was the best manager we ever had. He would try to pull some fast ones all right, but when we'd catch him up on those we could get him to back down."

This policy—or lack of policy—on the part of management encouraged union men to feel that their main and almost exclusive requirement for winning their points was a show of strength.

The plight of lower management, under Craig, was hardly improved over the family regime. One man who served under Craig reported that there were only superficial differences. You couldn't get a hearing from top management before; you could get a hearing from Craig. He would listen to what you had to say and talk with you pleasantly, but you got nothing out of it except a conversation. The foremen simply could not get action from their superiors.

Frequently workers or the union steward would go to the foreman to ask for action on some problem. The foreman would go to his superiors and get turned down; or else be put off so that he had no real answer to take back. Then when the situation got sufficiently irritating for the union members, they would organize a demonstration in their department and march into Craig's office to demand action. In such cases management usually gave the union what it had refused to give the foremen. Such behavior undermined the position of the foremen.

This does not mean that the union was satisfied with its position and its relations with management during the Craig period. The guerrilla warfare being waged between union and management gave rise to new problems faster than the old ones could be adjusted. Nevertheless, through work stoppages and delegations into the general factories manager's office the union was able to get action on certain issues.

Management faced a complicated and difficult situation. In such a situation it would have been good judgment to make a painstaking effort to clear up the existing problems before introducing any new elements. This was not Craig's way of proceeding. He was a firm believer in piecework and felt that the introduction of incentive rates would clear up many of his problems. And, so, into this already overheated situation he threw the most explosive package that any management can handle.

Up to this time in certain departments, the workers had been under a system whereby group bonuses were paid on an average production over a 2-week period. The bonuses did not amount to much and the workers paid little attention to them. Craig felt that a piece-rate system with an attractive daily pay-off would motivate workers more strongly to produce.

At that time (1940) the union did not take kindly to incentive systems and sought to resist their introduction into the plant, although the general factories manager promised that the system would enable the people to make more money. When Craig seemed determined to go ahead, at least on this particular issue, the union leaders felt that opinion would be sufficiently divided within their ranks so that they could not afford to fight management's decision. Instead, they would go along and wait and see.

Management began to introduce incentives into parts of the plant, with the view of making it possible for the men to earn 20 to 30 per cent above their base pay. As the incentives came in, in certain places, so that particular workers were making additional money, other workers not covered by the incentive demanded that they also should be included. This led to the rapid extension of the incentive system. In fact, management was pushed so fast in certain cases that it was not able to carry on the careful studies usually involved in rate setting. For example, on one occasion the men in the Steel Storage Department, who are responsible for unloading the steel coming in from the mill and distributing it to the various departments in the plant, called upon Craig in a body and demanded that they be covered immediately by an incentive plan. To establish rates, on the basis of time and motion study in this department, would have required several weeks of work, and the men were not willing to wait. When he was thus pushed into a corner, Craig established a rate based on past tonnage. The men were satisfied, as well they might be, since this turned out to be the "loosest" rate in the plant, and the men in this department are still making a much higher bonus than those in any other department.

The introduction of incentive rates did, indeed, stimulate production in certain departments but gave rise to still further and, perhaps, more acute problems between union and management. There was constant wrangling over the rates with the union seeking to pressure management to put in rates where they did not exist or loosen up allegedly tight rates.

However, these problems were simple compared to those that arose following the 1942 union negotiations. The union came into these negotiations demanding a 10 cent an hour increase for all workers. The company was not making a profit at that time and top management had issued orders to Craig that no increase was to be given. Nevertheless, something had to be given or there would be a strike. In consultation with his factory superintendent, Craig hit upon a compromise. He felt that the workers not covered by the incentive were entitled to a 10 cent an hour flat increase. But he proposed to give the increase in such a manner that those who were on incentive would receive nothing at all. In other words, there would be a general 10 cent an hour increase for all workers, but there would be no change in incentive rates. This meant, in effect, that the workers on incentives would have a higher guaranteed minimum and higher earnings on daywork, but their incentive earnings would not be changed unless they put out more production.

How this scheme worked out can be illustrated by an example from the Barrel Department. There base rates were increased from 62 to 72 cents an hour. Incentive rates remained the same at $3.65 per thousand, class #1 drums. Let us assume that the men were putting out 1,800 drums in an 8-hour day. Their straight-time earnings would have been $4.96 before the increase. The incentive earnings were then $6.57. They were then earning a bonus of $1.61, or 32 per cent. This seems enough to have been rather attractive to them. When their base pay was increased, straight hourly earnings would have been $5.76 per day, and if they continued to produce 1,800 drums they would continue to receive only the $6.57 of incentive earnings. This meant a bonus of 81 cents compared to the $1.61 they had been earning, or a bonus of 14 per cent over their base rate compared to the 32 per cent they had been earning.

This was a way of seeming to give away money without actually giving anything. The move proved terribly costly to management. Originally, Craig had tried to make the incentive system attractive by providing for a bonus of from 20 to 30 per cent. He believed that only a bonus of such magnitude would be an effective incentive. Up to the 1942 change, incentive earnings from department to department had run between 15 and 35 per cent, and, with technological changes, the trend was upward. A 10-cent an hour increase, on a 62-cent an hour base rate, is an increase of approximately 16 per cent. In effect, this would wipe out the bonus earnings in certain departments and lower them so substantially in others that the workers would hardly feel it was worth the effort to get out extra production. That is, in fact, what happened.

There is some difference of opinion as to whether the union officials were misled in this case. According to a view expressed by a union official, the negotiators realized that they were not actually getting anything for the people on incentive. However, they still did not believe in incentives and felt that after the war was over the system would be thrown out. The main objective for the union should, therefore, be to raise the base rates, which were considered far too low. Furthermore, if management refused to give 10 cents on top of the incentive to the people on incentive, the union could find other ways to get it back. They felt that they could make matters so difficult that management would have to chage the rates to assure higher earnings. Whatever the view of the union leaders, it is certain that the workers in the plant did not realize what was taking place. At the time the agreement was signed they thought everybody was getting 10 cents an hour and when the people on incentives found that they were getting nothing, there was hell to pay.

When the nature of the settlement became clear to them, the

workers generally felt that management had cheated them and therefore that it would be all right for them to cheat back in order to get even with management and get "a fair day's pay for a fair day's work."

The first crisis arose in the Barrel Deparment. Up to that time it had been the practice for the men to absorb all periods of down time up to 15 minutes while management paid them day rates for all periods longer than 15 minutes. The men now claimed that, with the change in day rates, they were not able to make any money. They claimed that the equipment was in such bad shape that they were getting much more down time than was originally allowed in the rates. A delegation from the Barrel Department went in to argue with Craig on the matter. He finally agreed to give them day-rate credit for all down time beyond half an hour in any given day (the rates had been set originally on the basis of an estimate of an average down time of half an hour in 8 hours). Furthermore, he agreed to figure the down time for the entire Barrel line on the basis of the amount of time that one of the machines was down.

The workers immediately began to utilize this agreement to their advantage. One Barrel Department worker described the situation in this way, beginning with a comment on Craig's decision on the 10-cent an hour increase:

He really screwed us on that one. We thought we were going to get the 10 cents on top of the incentive but instead he took it away from us. The way it turned out we couldn't make any money on those rates. The only way we could make a lot of money was by getting extra down time. At that time, the down time was figured on the double seamer and that's the fastest machine. We had a lot of people then who didn't know how to figure their rates. I was always good at figures and another fellow and I figured out how to operate the double seamer so we got plenty of down time. At that time you could check in and check out yourself. Sometimes when the timekeeper wasn't looking, we'd check out and keep running barrels, then when he'd come back we'd check in again. We would let the seamer go down until we had barrels stacked off on the floor beside us and then we'd start it up and run them through. Of course, that was cheating, but we were only asking for a fair day's pay for a fair day's work. When they wouldn't give it to us, we had to get it some way or other.

A management representative described the resulting situation in the following way:

At the time, management was very lax in recording the down time, and we were letting people get away with things, recording their own time. It got so that some days they were claiming so much time that they would have from 380 to 400 barrels an hour of running time going through that double seamer. We argued with them on that. We told them that we knew just exactly how fast that machine could possibly go and it was impossible to run through 380 to 400 barrels an hour. They said to us, "All right, what is the maximum speed?" We told them 360 an hour was the fastest possible speed. After that they always had it figured out so that they'd have 360 barrels an hour of running time. It was easy to tell how much time they worked each day. You just took the total production of the day and divided it by 360. That would give you the number of hours running time and you could be sure that the rest was down time. For a long time there they were running 5½ hours and getting 2½ hours down time. That was a bad situation. We had no incentive upon production at that time. We just had an incentive on down time.

This procedure worked out relatively well for the workers. The double seamer being not only the fastest machine but toward the end of the production line, it was possible for the double seamer operators to have their machine down a large part of the day without slowing the total production of the line very much. This got down-time credit not only for the double seamer operators but for every worker on the line, even though the other workers might have been working much more of the total time.

While the machines involved were not particularly delicate instruments, the workers could readily manage to jam them or to get them out of adjustment without any possibility of management's detecting the offense. The foreman could not be everywhere at once to prevent this tampering.

Once the workers had developed this system for getting down time credit, they had no incentive for getting out further production. Perhaps, if they had worked at maximum speed and minimized down time all day long, their total earnings might have been greater (for the 8-hour day), but each hour of down time eliminated lost the men 72 cents in hourly rates and they felt it was not worth the effort.

The problem in the Pail Assembly Department was equally difficult and was not resolved satisfactorily for the union. The workers in this department had been making only approximately 15 per cent bonus and a 10-cent an hour increase in base pay ate up this entire bonus. Perhaps with extraordinary efforts the workers might have been able to make a 10 per cent bonus, but, to show their hostility to management and to put pressure on management, they held their production down to around 10 per cent below the guaranteed day rate. The Pail Assembly Department problem was still being argued when a new top management came in.

While these departmental issues were being thrashed out, the union developed a highly effective strategy for meeting problems wherever they occurred in the plant. The first moves would be made against the foreman, who would find himself spending hours of the day talking and arguing with individual workers, the union steward, or with a delegation from his department or the whole department. When this brought no action from the foreman, who was rarely in a position to make any decisions, the workers resorted to a work stoppage which would immediately bring top management into the picture.

There were two types of work stoppages: one was organized by union officials themselves, the other arose spontaneously without the sanction of the union officers. In the first case the union would find itself blocked in getting settlement of a problem through the grievance procedure, and the officers involved would pass the word around that at a certain specified hour there would be a "spontaneous work stoppage" at which time they would go into Craig's office and get action on their problem. A top union officer could not, of course, acknowledge having a hand in such stoppages but, as a matter of fact, the stoppages were the only technique they had to get action and it was hardly to be expected that they would not make use of this weapon. On the other hand, the weapon itself was not easy to handle. As workers in one department observed people in another department getting action through a stoppage, they sometimes went right ahead and organized a stoppage without having any union officials involved in it. Such behavior was frowned upon by the union officers, who made every effort to keep it under control. When the union officers were called in to discuss such an issue with management, they would not know in full the facts and feelings involved in the case and therefore would not be able to negotiate effectively with management. The only thing they could do in such a case would be to advise the workers to go back to work. In one such case, when the men refused to go back to work under union orders, the union was able to persuade management to allow the union to handle the discipline case and the men were brought to trial before the union body and subjected to fines. Those who refused to pay the fines were discharged.

In this disorganized struggle management tried one tactic after another to hold the union in check. The most remarkable policy of all was put into effect by one of the many personnel managers. He had a theory that it was impossible for management to work with the union leaders. Therefore, management should try to get to the people directly. Where before management had been pressured by union officers and delegations of workers, it now became common practice for whole departments, if not the whole plant, to stop work and march on the top-management office. There were times when workers were packed into the office so thickly that there was no space for anybody to move, and people were lined up and down the hall outside and waiting in groups in the general office space. These mass demonstrations only served to increase the general tension and confusion.

While management floundered through this period, the union became stronger and more effectively organized.

It had grown up on a personal basis, with Love as the center. When workers asked him to handle their problems, he couldn't say no. Besides the time he spent on union business during regular working hours, he found himself staying after work for two or three hours every night to work for the people on the second shift.

All the union's problems had become Love's personal problems. The strain began to tell. Finally, in 1941 he came to the end of his rope. He was plagued by headaches, he lost weight, and could not sleep. A doctor advised him to get away for a rest and warned him that he would have to cut down on his work.

Love took two weeks away from the city to think out his future.

He came to realize that his willingness to handle anybody's problem any time was not only bad for him, it was bad for the union. A sound union does not rest upon one man alone. It depends upon an organizational structure in which authority and responsibility are shared with all the officers, right down to the shop steward.

When Love returned, he remained an active president—but with a difference. He now insisted that workers take their problems first to the stewards, and he would not come in on a problem until it had been first referred up to the grievance committeeman and handled by him.

There was a steward for each department and a grievance committeeman for each floor. Love worked with these men and with the members of his executive board so that the union became a real organization instead of a mass of people pivoting around one man.

The union was strong in that period, but it could hardly have been called a well-disciplined union. The rank-and-file members were so militant against management that the leaders were under constant pressure to take aggressive action. Many times these pressures fitted in well with what the leaders wanted to do. Sometimes they were able to block a course of action they did not believe in, but at other times they felt that the situation was so hot that they had to go along whether they liked it or not. This was no time for a careful mapping of long-run aims; the union leaders had to run fast to stay ahead of the membership.

The recurring strikes and slowdowns and protest demonstrations brought no effective countermeasures from management at that time, but they did produce one penalty. The union had petitioned the War Labor Board to direct the company to grant "maintenance of membership." The board at first declined to issue such an order. (Maintenance was directed in response to a later petition, but it was not embodied in a contract, since the parties were deadlocked in negotiations at the time.) Throughout the war it was almost a routine matter for the board to order maintenance of membership upon such a petition. Such an order was withheld only if, in the opinion of the board, the union in question had shown itself to be flagrantly irresponsible. The long record of wildcat strikes and slowdowns in the wartime emergency was cited by the board to justify the withholding of its order.

Since the union was 100 per cent organized at the time, the board's first decision was not a serious handicap. But such governmental censure was a blow at the self-respect of the union leaders and at the prestige of the union. The union leaders were not only interested in having a militant organization. They also wanted to build one which would command the respect of management, government, and the community. On that score, there was still a big job to be done.

Chapter 4

Management Takes Its Stand

*F*OR SOME years Inland Steel Company has been one of the most profitable organizations in its industry. Yet here was a subsidiary, at the peak of wartime prosperity, consistently losing money. Such a situation could not be tolerated.

In 1943 a new man was brought in to take the place of Craig as general factories manager. Craig himself had long been disgusted with his situation, and he moved on to success in another management. When the new general factories manager brought no improvements, more sweeping changes were carried through a year later.

The president of Milcor Products Company, a profitable subsidiary, took on the presidency of Inland Steel Container Company in addition to his other duties.

The new president appointed John Gossett as vice-president and general manager and Robert Novy as general factories manager. The president was then available for consultation, but he made it clear that he expected these men to work out the problems on their own initiative.

It was Gossett and Novy who were to lead management out of the wilderness—but only after many months more of conflict. To understand what they did, we need to know more about the men themselves.

John Gossett supported himself from the time he finished high school. When we got into World War I, he enlisted in the navy and served as an ordinary seaman. When the war was over, he spent some months moving about the country, trying his hand at one job and another. He found that selling was what he liked to do.

Gossett was successful in sales from the beginning. People liked him, he had a quick mind, and he was adaptable. He came into this organization in 1937 as manager of eastern sales. In 1939 he became vice-president in charge of eastern operations.

Up to that time he had had no experience in production. As he stepped into this strange job, his superior gave him just one piece of advice: "You ought to walk through the plant once a week—and fire somebody. That's the way to maintain discipline and keep people on their toes."

Gossett shook his head and said he just could not manage that way. The president warned him he would soon find out that that was the practical, businesslike way of doing things.

Robert Novy came in as production manager, Gossett and Novy began working closely together, and in a short time the situation began to improve. Gossett spent time in the plant learning production problems at first hand, but he delegated the responsibility for that area to Novy.

The two men made an effective team. Production steadily increased. Relations with the union (International Chemical Workers' Union, AFL) were reasonably harmonious.

On the other hand, there were only seventy-five workers in the Jersey City plant compared to almost ten times that number in the main Chicago plant, so the problems were comparatively simple. There was a bigger job ahead for both men.

Novy had had to leave college to go to work in 1931. At that time his father was a shipping clerk in the Chicago plant. Young Novy was offered a job at 20 cents an hour. He held out for 25 and got it. It was little enough, but still it was well above the regular beginning wage at the time.

In the succeeding years Novy worked in every department in the plant and moved up, first to foreman, and then to production manager. According to the standards of management, he was a good man. Novy himself said later:

It was altogether different at that time. I had to fit into the old pattern. At that time you just gave orders, and, if things didn't go right, you fired people. I fired people myself. I wouldn't do it right away like some of them. I'd always give warnings and maybe suspend a man first. But I was tough myself. I had to be.

It was only later, when he went to the Jersey City plant in 1940 that Novy began to see things differently. His office was right next to the production line and the work force was small enough so that he could know every man well. He began working with the men instead of cracking the whip. He found it worked better, and he liked himself better for it.

Novy's success in Jersey City led to an assignment in the New Orleans plant. He was sent down for ten days to get that plant in proper working order. He spent eight weeks, working twelve to sixteen hours a day, getting right into the production line himself to study the problems at close range. In that time he was able to reorganize men, machines, and processes, set up new controls, increase productivity, and effect tremendous economies. It was that assignment which won him the Chicago job.

Gossett was at first reluctant to take over the Chicago plant. He had recently been married, and he and his wife had bought a farm out in the country. He enjoyed his work and his friends in Jersey City and New York. He was happy with life in the country. He was making enough money so that a salary increase would mean little to him. And he knew that the Chicago situation was in a mess —though he had no clear idea of its nature. Still, this was a bigger job and a more challenging assignment.

Gossett's first contact with the plant after he had accepted the job was anything but reassuring. He visited the plant several weeks before he was to assume his new position. He came to talk the situation over with Worth, who was then still in charge. Before Gossett could get in to see the president, he had to wait downstairs for ten minutes while everybody in the plant marched upstairs ahead of him. At the end of the procession, came the personnel manager, who explained that there was going to be a meeting with the union upstairs. When he finally got upstairs into the president's office, Gossett received an appalling impression of the extent of top management's demoralization. It was clear that the president of the company could not have the faintest idea of what was going on in the plant and, furthermore, he was afraid that violence was about to break out. A few days earlier Gossett was told that a woman employee had complained that someone had stolen her wrist watch. Management instituted a search of the particular locker room where the workers in that department dressed. In going through the pocket-books, the nurse found knives, razors, and revolvers. To top this off, Worth had received an FBI report predicting that race riots would break out in plants in Washington, Detroit, Kansas City, and Chicago as soon as the war ended. Worth was afraid his riot would break out at any moment, war or no war.

When Gossett returned to take over his position officially, he got together with Novy to analyze the situation they faced. They found management constantly being pushed around by the union. They found the organization disorganized and demoralized, practically every member of it being on the point of quitting his job. They found no records or written precedents on past performance to guide them or let them know what was going on. Such records as there were had been removed or destroyed by the outgoing general factories manager. They found that the factory was being operated with few controls, in the systems of accounting, production planning, or industrial relations. Everything was done according to past practices, but the situation was so confused and there were so many changes in management personnel that the management people had no clear idea of what they were doing and how they were supposed to do it.

The magnitude of the job facing the new men was appalling. This was a situation which seemed to require extraordinary measures. This is how they diagnosed their problems.

They felt that the first requirement was for management to wield its authority firmly. They felt that the union had been making serious inroads upon management's powers; these inroads were to be stopped. Management's prerogatives were to be defined in discussion with other members of management; and an invisible line was to be drawn beyond which the union was not to be allowed to push. Top management could not pursue a firm policy toward the union with a lower management that was demoralized by constant defeats at the hands of the union. Therefore, the job was to put some backbone into management all down the line. Foremen and higher management officials were to be assured that once management's policy had been determined, whoever stood for that policy would be backed up to the limit. Foremen and people in middle management were to be given greater authority in dealings with the union. Lower management people were to have a more active part in management. Top management would seek to understand their problems and act upon them.

Finally, management would begin the job of setting up systems and controls for carrying on its operations. The best way of doing things would be determined and reduced to writing so that everybody would know where he stood and what was expected of him.

The campaign to revitalize management began immediately. Twice a week Gossett held meetings in his office of his top staff, including Novy, the treasurer, the sales manager, and the purchasing agent of the company. Once a week Novy held meetings of his staff, including floor supervisors, foremen, and the heads of maintenance, engineering, and industrial engineering. These were sometimes attended also by Gossett. In addition, the floor supervisors met weekly with their foremen to discuss problems.

In so far as production was concerned, Gossett and Novy played two quite different roles. With his background in selling, Gossett did not feel comfortable in his new situation, but he was convinced that the situation required that he become the autocrat who laid down the law and rode roughshod over subordinates who sought to raise questions. It was Novy's role, on the other hand, to work more closely with the production men to carry out policies, to get complaints and suggestions from subordinates, and to smooth over troubled situations.

In explaining the relationship between the two men, Gossett compared it to his selling experience. It was common in selling, especially where large items were involved, for the salesmen to operate in teams of two. One man played the role of the "friend of the buyer," while his partner was out to drive the most hardheaded bargain possible. The buyer's friend tried to work out an advantageous deal for the buyer, while the other salesman undervalued anything the buyer had to offer and was cold and calculating throughout. The buyer was so offended at the behavior of the "hard" salesman that he was ready to sign right up when the "friend of the buyer" persuaded his partner to make the deal.

In this situation Bob Novy was the "friend of the buyer," so far as his subordinates in management were concerned. Remembering Novy from his earlier Chicago experience, they at first expected no sympathy from him. But, as Gossett applied the pressure and they struggled to adjust to the new situation, they found that they could go to Novy and get a hearing. Novy knew the plant thoroughly. He understood their problems and tried to take action upon them. They turned to him more and more.

In that period Novy played a difficult and important go-between role. He was loyal to his superior, and he and Gossett discussed policy problems at great length and frequently. But when Gossett's stern manner of implementing these policies gave rise to antagonism in the ranks below, Novy was able to step in and smooth over the difficulties. This job had to be done if the organization was to be held together during the difficult period.

It did not take long for the union to discover that the new regime meant many changes. The first clash came on Gossett's second day on the new job when he was in conference with the president of the company and the retiring president. Gossett's secretary came in to announce that a union committee was waiting outside to see him. He said he was sorry that he could not see them. She said that it would not do any good for her to tell them to go away; he would have to speak to them in person.

Gossett asked the retiring president, "Have you ever had a delegation up in this office before?"

Worth shook his head.

Gossett said, "Then I'll see to it that they never come up here again."

He stepped into the outer office to find President Lucius Love, Vice-President Tom Beal, and two others waiting for him. Love moved forward and extended his hand. Gossett put his hands behind his back and leaned back against his secretary's desk.

"What is your business here?" he asked curtly.

"We want to discuss the general situation," Love explained.

"There is nothing to discuss," Gossett said.

Love cast about for a different approach. He started to say that there were many problems in the plant that needed attention, but Gossett cut him off, saying that grievance meetings were set up for that purpose.

Love tried again. The plant was in war production; its products were vitally needed. "Mr. Gossett," he said, "aren't you patriotic?"

"Is that a subject for negotiation?" Gossett countered.

Still the union men tried to argue, but Gossett would have no more of it. Furthermore, he said, "This is the last time I will ever see you in this office, unless I call a meeting myself."

That was all. The men went out, stunned and boiling mad.

Gossett followed up this rebuff by seeking to pin down the union still further. He wanted no delegations to the general factories manager's office either. All problems were to be thrashed out first at lower levels of management. There would be no more departmental, group, or plant meetings with workers.

Middle management, consisting of the personnel manager and the floor supervisors, was to have no contacts whatsoever with the union except in the officially scheduled grievance meetings. (This policy was continued when a general production supervisor and his assistant took the place of the floor supervisors.)

In order to get a firsthand view of problems of the plant, Gossett took to sitting in on the grievance meetings at the third step, in the personnel manager's office.

Up to that time all grievances had been presented orally. Now Gossett required that everything be reduced to writing—a common requirement in labor relations. Finally, there were to be no discussions between union and management concerning a work stoppage until the men had gone back to work. Management was determined not to allow stoppages of production to pressure it into ill-considered decisions.

"Give respect and demand respect." That was the oft-repeated statement of one union officer to his fellow members as he advised them how they should deal with management. It had not been easy to carry out in the past. For one thing, the plant up to that time had not had a management which the union people could genuinely respect; and the previous management had only respected the union's strength. There had been no respect between the parties on the basis of intelligence and character.

But if the respect problem had been difficult in the past, it now became the focus of all activity in union-management relations. When John Gossett refused to shake hands with Lucius Love, he performed a symbolic act of the greatest consequence. By that gesture Gossett meant to indicate that he did not recognize the right of the union officers to demand a hearing from him at that time and place and under those circumstances. He did not mean to challenge the right of these men to represent the workers— through what he considered to be the proper channels. And it certainly made no difference to him whether the union leader who extended his hand was white or colored. (He also had not shaken hands with Vice-President Beal, who was a white man.)

But the meaning John Gossett intended to convey by his gesture does not help us to explain what grew out of it. The important question is: what did the gesture mean to the union representatives, and how did they interpret it to their followers?

Love and his committee concluded that Gossett had no respect for the union officers. This meant that management hoped to destroy the union. Since it was Gossett who refused the proffered hand, he became the most hated symbol of management to the union. One worker expressed forcefully the union reaction to the new boss when he made this statement in a union meeting:

I'd like to take a rope and put it on Mr. Gossett's neck and hang him out of that second-story window of his office. I'd let him hang there and I wouldn't even let a fly touch him until he promised and agreed to respect our union officers.

There was another explosive aspect to this respect problem. When Gossett refused to shake hands, Love asked himself, "Can the man be prejudiced?" Did Gossett refuse to shake hands simply because Love was a union officer or was it because Love was a Negro? Love was not inclined to weigh that question objectively. He felt that he had been hit personally, and he was out to make a case against his enemy. A few days later the union met with management to discuss grievances at the third step in the procedure. Love heard that Gossett was to attend the meeting. Before Gossett came in, Love remarked casually to Mr. Kluck, the new personnel manager, that he had already met Gossett but the grievance committeeman (a white man) had not been introduced. Love suggested that Kluck take care of that introduction. When Gossett came in, Kluck made the introductions, the committeeman rose with extended hand, and Gossett shook hands without any hesitation. Love said nothing at the time but he told the whole story later at a union meeting. This story stirred up further antagonism in a membership now 65 per cent Negro.

An incident at this same grievance meeting added fuel to the fire. In the midst of an argument with Love, Gossett said, "I know all about you. You're out to make a reputation for yourself. Well, I'm going to see that you don't do it here."

"I know all about you too," Love replied, "and I'll see to it that you don't stay here long."

As Love said later, "I thought to myself: Is that man really going to keep me from making my reputation?" The challenge made it a personal issue to Love. The meetings became a struggle between the two men.

Gossett had come down to the third-step meetings with the hope of getting in close touch with the problems and convincing the union officers of his honesty and sincerity of purpose. Instead, his presence merely strengthened the hostile feelings of the union men.

Having been slapped down so abruptly in these initial encounters, the union leaders fought back with all the bitterness and resourcefulness they could command. They found themselves suddenly faced with a whole new series of management requirements. They felt that they must either block or sabotage each new requirement.

The demand that all grievances be in writing seemed to place the union at a disadvantage. Managers came and went, but the union leaders stayed on. Love thus became the leading authority on past developments in union-management relations. When no agreements were reduced to writing, no one could question his interpretation of past events. When the new management sought to take action that the union wished to block, Love would bring up a so-called "gentlemen's agreement," that he had entered into with a previous manager. Sometimes these oral agreements had actually been made, and sometimes the stories were just invented for the occasion. But, whether real or imaginary, the new management had no way of checking over the past history and felt compelled to insist that everything be reduced to writing.

This not only took away from the union an advantage it held, but also laid new burdens on the union in the processing of grievances, for there were a few stewards who were not sufficiently literate to handle grievances in writing.

When management was adamant on this point, the union officers held a strategy meeting and decided to counter with so much paper work that management would get sick of the new ruling. Orders went out to bring in all grievances that could possibly be imagined by the stewards and grievance committeemen. From that point on, and for a long time, at least half the grievances presented to management were of this imaginary variety. The management men no doubt knew that grievances were being manufactured but it was difficult for them to distinguish between the grievances the union believed in and those which were introduced simply to harass management. The contract called for a third-step grievance meeting each week, and additional meetings in case the existing grievances could not be cleared up at that time. For a period of many months, management was meeting with the union three days a week and arguing for long hours on each occasion. At the time, the contract called for management to pay for the time of union representatives in these grievance meetings, and this included time-and-a-half for overtime after the regular shift. The union officers took particular pleasure in dragging out the meetings far into the late afternoon or evening. It pleased them to think that, while they were getting their time-and-a-half, the management men were losing out on dinners and other social engagements. Finally, Gossett refused to carry on any meeting after five o'clock, but still the meetings continued on a three-a-week basis, and the arguments went on interminably.

While the arguments with top management continued, the union intensified its harassing efforts against the foremen. Management's refusal to meet with delegations or discuss problems during work stoppages necessitated a change in union tactics. One popular move was described in this way by Love:

We weren't supposed to hold any more demonstrations on company time, so we would wait until lunch hour and then everybody in one crew would crowd into the foreman's office. That was on our own time you see. We would make sure that we took all the rest of the lunch hour telling the foreman what we wanted. By the time he was able to say anything the lunch hour was over, and we were still there waiting for an answer. So you see, the foreman was keeping us back.

If the workers could not meet with the foreman in a body, they could at least go to see him individually. So, one by one, every worker in the department would go in to lodge a complaint, or they would call to the foreman when he was out on the factory floor, and keep him walking back and forth for hours up and down the production line trying to keep up with their complaints. All the foremen were harassed in this manner but the union was particularly aggressive with those who were loyal followers of Gossett's leadership.

The Personnel Office also experienced its share of harassing tactics. At that time it had been a company policy to let a worker see his personnel record any time he asked for it, so the workers suddenly became interested in their personnel records and went down one after another demanding to see them. This threw the Personnel Office into confusion and stopped all other work. Management countered by withdrawing the privilege of looking at the personnel records.

The war between union and management was carried on, primarily, on a local basis. But on certain occasions the union brought in its international representative or other members of the international staff. By this time Gossett had acquired an unflattering reputation in the circles of the international union, and the international officials who came into the situation were only able to give vent to their outraged feelings. There were two such occasions in the first year of Gossett's tenure; each time the international representative made no effort to discuss the grievances in question, but simply issued a bitter denunciation of Gossett and predicted that the union would drive him out of his position. Before this happened the first time, Gossett had felt that some progress was being made and that it might be possible to work out certain problems with the union. After the explosions with the international representative, the war went on with undiminished vigor.

Since Gossett, who was the chief management representative at the fourth step of the grievance procedure, was sitting in on all third-step grievance meetings, the union could expect only a rehashing of old arguments at the fourth step, unless it planned to push on to arbitration. Thus, in effect, the grievance procedure bogged down and the union had no way of adjusting its problems with management.

The union leaders felt that the union needed some way of putting pressure upon management so that some of the problems finally would be solved. The harassing tactics were important to the union in that they gave the members a field of activity and a way of expressing antagonism toward management but they alone were not enough.

The real battle had to be fought on the production line, where management could be hurt most severely. There had been slowdowns and breakdowns before, but now the union embarked upon an intensified campaign. Over a period of four months production was slowed to the point where the people were just making 100 per cent, in other words, making no bonus. This involved serious losses to the people but it also hurt management severely and that was the point. The slowdown did not bring production below 100 per cent, as a matter of union policy, for Love always considered the possibility that if things got too bad management might actually shut the plant down. He thought that as long as the workers gave management a shade over 100 per cent, management would be making a little money and would continue to operate.

Management recognized that the slowdown was a matter of deliberate union policy. Several times Gossett called in the union committee to argue with them that the slowdown was a violation of the contract. Love would reply that he had no cause to complain; if the people were making 100 per cent and didn't feel like doing any more, there was nothing he could do about it. Finally Gossett announced to the union committee that he was going to force a showdown on the issue. Somebody was going to get fired for loafing.

To consider this new move, Love called his committee together. If a worker was fired for loafing, the union would have to carry the case right up to arbitration. Love did not know of any arbitration cases on such a matter. He was afraid that the arbitrator might rule against the union and set a precedent that would cause difficulties for his own local and other unions. It seemed time, therefore, to change tactics. The union shifted from slowdowns to breakdowns. The machines would start off at top speed and everything would look rosy for management, but then they would begin to break down. It was a simple matter for an experienced worker to persuade a machine to break down without any danger of having the foreman detect his action. When the breakdown came, everybody on the line would simply sit down. Even if it was only a question of picking a nut up off the floor and screwing it back on the machine, no one would do it. The workers would just say that it wasn't their job. They wouldn't let the foreman do it either because he wasn't supposed to do any work on the line. If the foreman didn't happen to be in the department when the line went down, nobody bothered to notify him. The workers just sat and waited. When the foreman found out what had happened, he had to call up the Maintenance Department to send a man down. Maintenance men, being union members also, were never in any hurry to get to the breakdown. It might take the man fifteen or twenty minutes to get down and begin working on a repair job. Perhaps it was an easy job for one maintenance man but just for a few seconds in the middle of a job he needed help from a second man to hold a bar for him while he worked on the machine. None of the production workers would give such help, so the maintenance man would have to call for a second man from the Maintenance Department. That man, in turn, would be in no hurry to get the line back in action, and it would be some time before he showed up. Each maintenance man was also technical in interpreting what was or was not his job, so several men often had to be called in.

While the line was down, the production workers would be on

their relief period scattered around the plant. They wouldn't know when the line was going to be ready again, so the foreman had to round up his crew and that took time too.

The union took full advantage of any management inefficiency. Sometimes the schedule sheets given to the workers did not contain full instructions for the job. In such a case it had been customary for the workers to point out the missing items to the foreman, who would quickly get them filled in. But now, if the workers did not have the exact specifications, they did not work. Before, when one job was running out they would let the foreman know and he would be able to tell them what to put on next. Now he might be out of the department when the job ran out, and they'd just sit down and wait until he came back.

The breakdowns and stalling tactics continued, and management had great difficulty coping with them. When workers or union officers were criticized, they would simply argue that the machines were in bad shape or else that management was inefficient. In certain cases, this was true. There were machines that needed improvement and the new management had a far-reaching job to improve on the inefficient practices of previous managements. But in this overheated situation management found it difficult to distinguish between the claims that had foundation in faulty machinery or management practices and those which arose simply to harass management. In this situation it was natural for some management men to conclude that the workers and union officials were constantly "bellyaching" and that there was nothing to be gained from listening to their complaints. Such attitudes further stifled effective communication between union and management and added steam to the problems that were already close to the explosion point.

The explosion came on August 27, 1945. The issue involved a payment of time-and-a-half for hours worked before or after the regular shift, even though the employees in question only worked 8 hours on a given day. There were a number of men who regularly came in an hour early to set up the lines for production and also left an hour before their fellow workers got out. There were also men who came in an hour late and stayed on for an hour after other workers went home, to shut the lines properly. The company argued that the contract called for time-and-a-half only for irregular hours worked. Since these men were on a regular shift, the fact that they started an hour earlier or an hour later than other workers didn't entitle them to time-and-a-half for the early or the late hour. The union argued that it had been management's past practice to pay people for the hour worked before or after the regular shift even when the men were on such a regular schedule and worked only an 8-hour day. Management argued that overtime had not been paid in such cases except on two occasions when there had been a clerical error. Gossett informed the union that no overtime would be paid in such cases. The union officers met to discuss the matter. They felt that this was a crucial issue; if Gossett got away with this particular move, there was no telling how far he would go. Therefore, they had to block him immediately. They advised the workers who were to come in an hour early to report at the regular time for the regular shift in protest against the company's refusal to pay overtime. When the setup men reported to work an hour late, they were given two days' suspension.

The company sent a telegram to each suspended employee directing him to return at the end of the two days' suspension and stating that failure to do so "will have the result of your having automatically discharged yourself." When the suspended employees returned to work they were to report to the Personnel Office and were asked to answer the following question:

Are you willing to go back to work and follow the foreman's instructions which will be given in a just manner and not stop work but go through the grievance procedure if you feel you have been given an unfair order?

Employees who answered yes were returned to work and those who answered no or qualified their answer by saying "Yes, if they are in accord with the contract" or "Yes, if they are fair and just," were fired.

As soon as the union discovered what management's procedure was to be, Love took a leave of absence from the plant in order to handle the situation from the union office. Workers were advised to refuse to answer the question in the Personnel Office unless represented by the union. Therefore, when each of the suspended

employees returned to the Personnel Office, Kluck had to telephone
the union office to notify Love, who would then come in to argue
the case. Love saw to it that the company did not get a simple
yes-or-no answer; each case was argued at great length in the
Personnel Office. Consequently, the hearings were drawn out for
days.

When men were discharged, the company sought to move up
other men to take their positions. These men, in turn, refused to
follow management's orders and were suspended and fired according to the same procedure. The process went on and on until, by
September 12, the company had discharged 53 employees. While the
firings went on, management made every effort to keep the plant
operating, but was finally reduced to devising make-work projects
for the remaining employees. On September 12 this was finally
abandoned, and the plant was shut down.

This was a period of great nervous tension for both management
and union. Neither party realized at the outset how one step would
lead to another until both had become much more deeply involved
than they had originally planned. For management, the case was
exceedingly costly, not even counting the August 27 to September
12 period of highly inefficient operation. The plant was shut down
for nine weeks while the case was argued before the arbitrator, and
while a rehearing was held on the company's petition to the
arbitrator.

The union had even more at stake. The power and prestige of
the union and the jobs of almost one-tenth of its members hung in
the balance. A decision against the union would have been ca-
tastrophic.

As the case turned out, the arbitrator did not award a clear
victory to either side. He ruled that neither the contract nor the
past practice required management to pay time-and-a-half to the
men in question. Futhermore, the workers had been in the wrong
in refusing to follow management's orders. The proper course was
for them to obey orders under protest and process the case through
the grievance procedure. On the other hand, management was
ruled out of line on the question that was asked of each suspended
employee as he went back to work. The arbitrator held that this
constituted an effort on the part of the company to require an

individual agreement with workers, where the collective bargaining agreement was the only one that had any standing. This he held to be a violation of the contract and he therefore ordered that the company reinstate the 53 employees with back pay up to the closing of the plant on September 12 (this cost the company an additional sum of approximately $2,500).

While neither side won a clear victory in this case, the arbitrator's decision was received much more happily by the union officers, who perhaps realized hòw close they had come to disaster. Furthermore, they felt that they had administered severe punishment to the company.

Management was outraged at the decision and felt that the only way of maintaining its position in relation to the union was to utilize the arbitrator's ruling regarding insubordination, and require all workers to follow orders to the letter, firing them if there was any evidence of resistance.

Here again the union officers felt that management must not be allowed to crack down too hard. To meet this situation, a second arbitration case was put into the works. At that time there was no stipulation in the contract as to the time period allowed to elapse between a fourth-step grievance and notification that the case would go into arbitration. Six months earlier, a woman employee, returning from a leave of absence, had claimed that she was not well enough to go back to work and had asked an extension of time. But management did not believe her story, and claimed that it notified her over the phone that she must return. When she did not return she was discharged. The union lodged a grievance in the case, but the woman in question was not seriously concerned as to whether she went back to work or not; so the grievance was not appealed beyond the fourth step until six months had elapsed. Then the officers threw it into arbitration. The arbitrator ruled that the company had no evidence that the woman was actually able to return to work at the time management claimed, nor was there any evidence beyond management's unsubstantiated word concerning the telephone call to the woman ordering her back to work. Therefore, management was ordered to reinstate her with $400 in back pay. Back pay for the total amount of time she was out would have been $600 but the arbitrator scaled it down to $400, observing that the union had unnecessarily stalled the case along. This was a happy outcome for the union. It was $400 of found money for the woman in question, and the union leaders were cheered at having won a victory over management and having thrown another road block across Gossett's path.

Following the settlement of the large-scale insubordination case, the plant reopened in November, only to shut down again with the general steel strike on January 21, 1946. As far as management was concerned, there was no reason for a strike in this plant. When the industry-wide strike loomed up, management announced to the local union officials that management would accept whatever wage settlement was worked out in the general industry pattern, and the workers were invited to stay on the job until the pattern developed. Meanwhile, there was an ample supply of steel on hand to keep the plant working through a strike of several weeks' duration. However, the workers seemed ready and even eager to go out, and the strike was under way.

When the strike came, management and union had already been negotiating at frequent intervals for over a year and a half on the contract. The old contract had expired in mid-1944, and management and union had met more than twenty times seeking to write a new one. While the war was on in the plant, little headway had been made.

The impasse continued for five months of the strike without a single negotiation meeting. In that period the top union and management people met several times in a vain effort to establish a basis for negotiation. Meanwhile, there were serious discussions in top management of Inland Steel Company and of its subsidiary on the possibility of permanently closing the Chicago plant. Management called on its legal counsel to prepare a detailed report upon the legal questions involved in selling the plant as a bare plant and moving the machinery and equipment to some other location where a complete new working force could be recruited. Except for the legal difficulties involved, the Chicago plant might have been sold at that time.

When the parties finally did resume negotiations, it was management that was pressing for the most far-reaching contract changes. William Caples, industrial relations manager for the parent corporation, had gone over the contract carefully and had noted fifty changes which management should seek to make. Of these, twenty were considered of a major nature, so important that management people felt they could not run the plant effectively without getting the changes written into the contract.

It may not be necessary to detail these twenty changes here, but some of them can be outlined in order to show the problems as management conceived them. Management sought to strengthen the management clause of the contract, so as to state specifically that management had the authority to schedule work and men. Management insisted upon a strong statement in the contract prohibiting work stoppages and slowdowns. (Such clauses were then common in steelworker contracts, but, since there was none here, to concede the point could appear to workers as a sign of union weakness.)

In meetings before the strike, management had been proposing the elimination of the two 15-minute relief periods allowed workers each day. Now management was willing to allow the relief period to continue, but demanded a statement that workers who overstayed their relief periods could be subject to discipline, including discharge.

The old contract had contained a provision that inequities in rates could be negotiated by union and management at special meetings. Management now sought to eliminate this provision, holding that any alleged inequities should be settled at the regular bargaining session; otherwise management could be forced to negotiate all year round.

Management demanded a clarification and strengthening of its rate-setting authority. The old contract had contained a statement concerning the setting of "fair rates." Since the contract provided no standard for determining what was fair, it seemed to management highly ambiguous.

The old contract had provided that union and management must agree concerning the way layoffs were to be carried out. Management demanded that it have sole authority in layoffs.

Management also sought to limit the union's freedom in handling grievances and arbitration cases. It demanded a time limitation between the fourth-step grievance decision and the union's notification of an arbitration appeal. Management also sought to tie down stewards and grievance committeemen, insisting that they could not move about from department to department without having a grievance written up on the regular forms.

Finally, management was willing to give the union a revocable checkoff, so that a member could resign from the union and cut out his dues deductions at any time. The union was insisting on an irrevocable checkoff.

The union had been accustomed to submitting its own contract demands and coming in to negotiate upon those demands. From 1944 on, management insisted that negotiations be conducted on the basis of management's draft, since it was management that was proposing the major changes. At first this was resisted by the union, but finally the officers agreed to go over management's draft, and the heated arguments that followed were conducted within this framework.

The 20-odd negotiation meetings, spread over two years, were a considerable strain upon the international union. Before an agreement was finally reached, five officers of the international had tried their hand at negotiating. In several of the meetings the international was represented by the subdistrict director, as well as by the regular international representative.

All the union officers, local or international, were bitterly antagonistic at this time. It seemed to them that management was trying to use the contract as a club to hold over the workers and the union in every sphere of their activity. The union officers felt that management had all the powers it needed when they agreed to a management clause which read as follows:

Subject to the provisions to this Agreement, the management of the works and direction of the working forces, including the right to hire, suspend or discharge for proper cause, or promote, demote or transfer, to schedule working hours and shifts and the right to relieve employees from duty because of lack of work or other legitimate reasons are vested in the Company. The Company will not, however, use the provisions of this Article for the purpose of discrimination against any member of the Union.

The union men were alarmed at management's efforts to attach disciplinary clauses to certain other provisions of the contract. The union's viewpoint was rather explosively expressed by the subdistrict director when he discussed management's proposal concerning the 15-minute relief period. He spoke standing up, banging his brief case on the table to emphasize his points.

"Abuse of this privilege by employees shall be cause for discipline including discharge." For Christ's sake, who ever heard of contracts being written up in such a manner as that. It can do anything it likes in that clause; a man might come in here and something might happen to that man that he would not be able to get back amongst the other employees. He may be in a position that he would have to go to the toilet or something like that. He comes in here and has to go to the toilet. He stays too long in the toilet and he's fired.

It says here for discipline, including discharge. I am not going along with such truck as that. That kind of stuff in a contract is not going to go with me. I am going to be reasonable with this contract all the way through, but I am not going to take this thing on the chin like that. It is a lot of foolishness and you know damn well it is a lot of foolishness. It is about time we get our feet on the ground and talk sense around here and talk about clauses in the contract rather than state every time we bring up a clause that you bring them up and state your reasons for it and you tie a tail on it where you're going to discharge or discipline some employees. Well, you're not going on with that. You might just as well understand that we are not going to operate the plant where we are going to be restricted every time we turn around or be fired or disciplined. We can't do it. I'm telling you that I am not going to go along with that. I want to go along, but I am not going to go along with that kind of truck, and that's what it is—pure truck!

A brief interchange followed this statement, whereupon the subdistrict director picked up his hat and walked out of the meeting.

In late July of 1946 the parties agreed to end the 191-day strike. Even though the strike had come at a time of full employment, it was beginning to involve sacrifices for the membership. When it became evident that this was to be a long strike, the union officers had turned the union hall into an employment and social welfare agency. In this way most of the workers were able to secure jobs elsewhere, but there were some who had to go on relief. Furthermore, few of the workers were able to get jobs that gave them anything close to the earning power they had enjoyed on their regular jobs. This was partly due to the relatively high level of earnings at Inland Steel Container Company, and also partly due to the fact that other employers, knowing the workers were on strike and would return to their former jobs when the strike was settled, had no interest in putting them in anything except the lower positions. The strike was particularly costly to the officers of the local, who accepted responsibility for the welfare of the membership and were thus unable to seek employment elsewhere. They received some financial support from the international but it fell far short of the earnings they would have had on a regular job.

In spite of these pressures, the union was by no means unanimous in its decision to accept the contract. In the final negotiation meeting, two of the local officers openly charged that the international representative was giving too much to management. Then, when the contract was presented to the membership, one member of the negotiating committee spoke against accepting it. President Love endorsed the contract, but with some reluctance. He argued that there were always ways of getting around the tightest contract, and if the people went back to work they could still win the victory in the day-to-day activities of the shop. This view finally prevailed.

The union's gains were limited to a maintenance-of-membership clause. (An irrevocable checkoff except for the standard escape period at the time of negotiations.) The 1946 contract showed that the company won all its major objectives, as seen by management at the start of negotiations. There were compromises on minor points, to be sure. For example, management had proposed that abuse of the 15-minute rest period should be "cause for discipline, including discharge." The final draft of the contract retained the phrase "cause for discipline" but dropped the words "including discharge."

The provision concerning arbitration of wages will serve as an example of a point considered of major importance on both sides, and on which the company gained its objective. The contract provision reads as follows: "The arbitration provisions of Section 2 [concerning grievance procedure] shall not apply to determination of wages, wage rates or job classifications." Up to that time there had been no arbitration of such cases, but the union officers had assumed that they had the right to put cases of this nature into arbitration.

The new contract specifically took this away from them. It meant that grievances concerning the setting of incentive rates could be taken up as far as the fourth step, but there management would have the final decision without any possibility of appeal. This was a bitter pill for the union to swallow, and it deserves special note here because it was to come up again as the major issue of the 1947 negotiations.

While the management negotiators thought they had made important gains in this new contract, there was no jubilation when it was signed. They simply felt they now had an agreement they could work with, and they went back to work hoping for the best—still worried, but a little more confident of the future.

Chapter 5

Between War and Peace

*E*VERYONE was happy to be back at work when the plant reopened early in August, 1946, but still no era of good feeling was immediately apparent on the horizon. There were significant changes here and there, but there was as yet no solid foundation upon which to place them.

For the first time top management began making adjustments to the union. The contract appeared to limit discussions in grievance meetings to written grievances, submitted in advance and placed on the agenda. Love asked if management would be willing, following the grievance discussions, to consider other problem situations. He argued that often a difficult situation could be cleared up before it gave rise to grievances if the parties were able to get together and discuss it. Gossett agreed to see how this would work out. In that way the union-management meetings took on a flexibility not possible when discussions were nailed down strictly to contract clauses. But, even so, this change did not go far. The nongrievance discussions came in only incidentally.

Top management also took a new line in the case of discharge for refusal to obey orders. The 1945 arbitration decision clearly established management's right to make such discharges, and several were in fact made in order to show that management meant business. It was then decided that this was not the best way to handle the problem in all situations.

Some of the jobs of setup men on production lines were quite heavy and disagreeable work. When the regular setup man was not present, management had the right, under the contract, to assign another man to the job. The foreman could then select a man from his department or call for one from another department. A man could be fired for refusal to follow such an order. Instead, management ordered the foreman to take the matter up first with the shop steward in his own department or with a foreman in another department, who would in turn consult his own shop steward. The foreman was to put it to the steward that, unless someone set up the line, production could not begin and the workers as well as management would lose out. The steward would then help the foreman to see to it that a qualified man took over the job. In case steward or worker failed to co-operate, management reserved its right to issue a direct order, but this never happened. In this narrow area, the parties managed to work out a better adjustment.

Some adjustments were made at the middle-management level also. Personnel Manager Joe Kluck and General Production Supervisor Al Short were old friends and had always worked closely together. Some time after the 1946 strike, Short and Kluck were talking over their mutual problems and sympathizing with each other upon the impossible job they had to do. They had no love for the union at the time, but they did not believe that management's firm policy would ever accomplish results, and they felt that they, as middle management, were in an intolerable position while the battle was going on. Life did not seem worth living in the plant, following out the orders of top management. They therefore decided to try out something different. Instead of avoiding all contact with the union, except in grievance meetings, according to orders, they would invite Love and his grievance committeemen to confer with them on certain problems. They would make any adjustments that were within their power and did not have to be passed on by top management. They recognized that this was a violation of top-management policy but by this time they set a low value upon their jobs and the possibility of being fired was not a serious threat.

This middle-management decision was announced to Love and the grievance committeemen in a regular grievance meeting.

According to Love's recollection, Short began by exhibiting his pipe, which had a broken stem. He said he had bitten a piece out of it in the previous meeting when Love had been in the process of cursing him out. He had decided that things could not go along further in that direction. From now on he was going to try to get together with the union.

The union men welcomed this overture and agreed to try to get together with middle management.

Three years after this beginning the participants could not recall any specific points on which they were able to get together, but the testimony on both sides seems to indicate that this adjustment with middle management was real, however limited its scope. It took the problems of the Barrel Department to enlarge the scope of give-and-take activity.

Management returned to work following the strike determined to eliminate the slowdown in the Barrel Department. To understand what took place here, we must go back in time to 1945 and look in on the Pail Assembly Department. There management had, in effect, given the workers the 10 cents an hour they had thought they were getting from Craig in 1942 and, at the same time, management introduced what it called its "5-minute down time feature." In this department workers had been absorbing down time up to 15 minutes, but if the down time went 15 minutes or beyond it, management paid hourly rates for the entire period. Under such a system the workers might have been able to get the line back in operation in 5 to 10 minutes, absorbing that time themselves. There was a natural tendency, therefore, for them to string out the down time periods to at least 15 minutes so that they would be paid for those periods. In the new 5-minute feature, workers were required to absorb the first 5 minutes of down time due to almost any cause and management paid hourly rates for any minutes beyond 5. (Management agreed to pay hourly rates for the entire time in cases where lines were down due to failure of supply from other departments or similar problems completely beyond the control of workers.) This provided an incentive to get the lines back operating in less than 5 minutes, if possible. It discouraged the manufacture of down time. (Management had sought to introduce a 10-minute down time feature, but negotiations had reduced it to 5.)

In the fall of 1946 management wished to introduce the same 5-minute feature to the Barrel Department. According to the contract, such a change in rates could be introduced only in case of major changes in the nature of the job. During the strike the Engineering Department had worked out elaborate plans to improve the production lines in the Barrel Department, and these plans were now put into effect.

During the negotiation period there had been several meetings between President Love and officers of management to discuss the down time problem in the Barrel Department. At these meetings management had made clear its plans for that department and asked for Love's support. In fact, Love's agreement was required before management would sign the 1946 contract. This put the union president in a difficult position. He felt that the manufactured down time was simply cheating (which could be justified only on the grounds that management had cheated labor in the past). He did not feel that he could take a strong position in defense of this down time. On the other hand, he knew he could not eliminate the down time simply by telling the workers to go to work. Therefore, he agreed to accept management's plans in principle, but at the same time made it clear that he could get the workers to accept the new rates with the 5-minute feature only if it was possible for him and management to show them that the new system was fair and reasonable and would not cut down on their earnings. Rate setting in such a department is a complex problem. The Time Study Department carried on thorough studies over a period of weeks, and it was not until November 16, 1946, that the new rates were formally instituted. Up to that time the men had been on "average earnings," which meant that they received the average pay they had earned in the last 2-week period preceding the strike. Since the earnings for those two weeks had been unusually high, the workers were well satisfied, and the pay provided them with no incentive to get production up.

When the new rates were introduced, November 16, there was immediate protest that they were far too tight, a common reaction to an incentive system. The men claimed that it would be impossible to make any money on these rates. They also said to each other that there were serious mechanical defects in the lines which would have to be straightened out before production could be stepped up much. However, the question of the bugs in the lines was not pressed with management at this time. The objective was to get the rates changed first and then to work the bugs out of the lines so that maximum earnings could be gained. Between November and February several meetings were held between union and management to discuss and argue the rates.

Before we go on with the story it is necessary to take a closer look at the situation in the Barrel Department, and especially at the relationship between Ed Snyder, the foreman, and Lucius Love. The two men had worked closely together over a period of years. We may recall Snyder's story of Love and Foreman Schulz, when Snyder was a group leader. They had always got along well. Snyder was relatively new as a member of management. The foreman's job was not a particularly attractive one when Snyder took it up in 1945. There had been considerable turnover in the position, previous foreman having fallen before the cross fire in the struggle between union and top management.

The job that he had to do would have broken a foreman of less endurance than Snyder. This is how he describes it.

I used to be on the go all day long. I had an office but you'd never see me there. There was always trouble somewhere. A machine would go down on one end of the line. It might be only a little bolt dropping out on the floor, but do you think they'd pick it up? No, not them. I'd only have time to get that thing fixed up when there would be a call for me at the other end of the line and I'd walk back. I was going and coming all day long. Sometimes my feet were bloody at night. And then there was that tension in the air. You could feel it when trouble was brewing. You knew it was coming, but you didn't know what you could do about it. It wasn't only trouble in my department. If there was trouble anywhere else in the plant the word would get around and you could feel it in the Barrel Department, too. Even when we got things straightened out in the Barrel Department I could see trouble coming when there was trouble upstairs. But I worked that out with Lucius. I'd call him in and I'd say, "Look, Love, I know there's trouble upstairs, but that doesn't concern the Barrel Department. Let them take care of it and let us take care of our own department." He'd tell the boys then and things would calm down.

I wouldn't have missed having those experiences, but I can tell you

I wouldn't be able to go through it again. I don't know how I lasted as long as I did. I think the only thing that saved me was that I had an understanding wife. When I'd come home worn out at night she wouldn't get after me to go out with her. She'd just let me sit there quietly by myself thinking about things while she went out to a show with the daughter. Then I could turn in early and get some rest so that I'd be ready for the next day.

Harassed as he was, Snyder was always willing to listen to what any worker had to say. While many complaints were simply moves in the larger struggle between union and management, there were some he considered justified and some that he could do something about. In those cases he took action.

Snyder did not get production up in his first months on the job, but at least he had the good sense to recognize the limitations of power of a foreman in such a situation. Lucius Love points out that many foremen, when faced with such a difficult situation, will allow their exasperation to get the better of their judgment and seek to take punitive action against some individual or group of indivduals on a problem that is really plant wide. In such cases the workers make the situation increasingly unbearable, until the foreman is finally forced out. Snyder, on the contrary, followed a rule which makes good management sense: When there is nothing you can do, don't try anything.

When Snyder did take action on a disciplinary matter, or some change in working procedure, he always talked things over first with Love or with the departmental steward or both of them. For this consideration the union leaders paid him back in kind. The foregoing description of the hectic life of Snyder may make it appear that the union was unrelenting in its pressure against him. Love insists that this was not the case. He says that he and the other union officers considered Snyder a good foreman. Since he was a representative of the hated management, they had to be rough on him, but they always recognized the values of having a "good fore-man" around and would not subject him to the extreme pressure that was used against some of the unpopular men.

In working so closely with the union officers in his department Snyder felt that he was strictly on his own. Gossett had issued a memorandum saying that foremen were to give full consideration to complaints raised by individual workers, whether or not they might be taken up later as grievances. But I have found no record of a policy indicating that the foremen were to consult stewards before taking action on any problem—except in the case of the set up man situation, described earlier. Snyder's recollection is that foremen were not forbidden to consult stewards—but neither were they advised to do so.

As a matter of fact this was the only way to make life bearable for the foremen within their departments, while the big struggle was going on, and the foremen who survived this period seem to have developed such informal, cooperative relations with their stewards. But at the same time they feared top management's disapproval if their relations with stewards became known. Consequently, they felt their way in anxious uncertainty on all fronts.

In a situation such as I have been describing there is no possibility for the foreman to establish thoroughgoing cooperative relations with the union. The major problems have to be worked out at the top, and he can make only minor adjustments. The significant thing to watch in this case is the way in which the cooperation between Snyder and Love led to further and wider cooperation between union and management.

On February 2, 1947, almost three months after the introduction of the new rates in the Barrel Department, a final union and management meeting was held on the rate problem, and management made its decision. There was no change in the rates; there management stood firm. But management agreed to add two men to each production line, so that it would be possible to increase production without extra pressure on any man. There were also minor changes in job classification, so that men at certain points in the line received a few cents an hour more money. Management also agreed to assign a maintenance man to the department so that all mechanical problems could be taken care of quickly.

Gossett and Novy then talked the situation over with Production Supervisor Short, who arranged to have Snyder give management's decision to Love and try to sell him the idea that the rates were fair and could lead to high earnings.

Snyder reports that he himself was now satisfied with the situation, and he readily undertook the job of persuasion. He says that Love was not pleased with the decision but felt, nevertheless, that the rates might prove to be fair providing management could work the bugs out of the production line.

Love called a meeting of the men in his department to give his point of view on the situation. By that time the men had been working for almost three months without making any bonus, and the slowdown was a heavy sacrifice to them. Furthermore, management had now ruled that in case of a breakdown workers must remain by their machines. This restriction made time lost boring and burdensome to them. Love thought, therefore, that they might be willing to try the new rates out if he could convince them that management's decision was final. This he was able to do. While the workers were bitterly hostile to Gossett, they had come to recognize that when he said a decision was final that was indeed the case, and he would take untold losses in order to maintain that position. The workers had, therefore, to find some other avenue of building up their earnings. Love assembled their criticisms concerning the operation of the production line and said that he would see what he could do about them.

Up to that time it would have done no good for Love and Snyder to sit down to discuss production because the problem was really out of Snyder's hands. Now, however, they did get together and discuss the situation thoroughly. The two men walked up and down the lines together as Love pointed out the complaints that the men had been making. Snyder felt that many of these criticisms were well founded and agreed to see what action he could get from higher up.

Snyder went to his immediate superior, Production Supervisor Short, to discuss the complaints. Short's first reply was "They're always bellyaching." He refused to take any action.

Snyder returned to Love and reported that the matter was under consideration and he was still hopeful of getting action. After this Snyder went to his boss several times, argued that at least some of the criticisms were justified, and pleaded for action. Finally Short agreed to look the situation over in person.

Short and Kluck now got together on the Barrel Department problem, and went down to go over the lines with Love. They felt that some of the complaints were trivial matters, but others were well founded, and they decided that even the trivial matters should be taken care of so that the workers would have no possible excuse for failing to step up production.

When Kluck and Short agreed to cooperate with the union in clearing up the Barrel Department problems, they had to take one further and seemingly hazardous step. Up to that time, although they were both on the friendliest terms with General Factories Manager Novy, they kept their cooperative activities secret from him. Now the necessary changes in the Barrel Department required the attention of the Engineering Department, and neither Kluck nor Short was in a position to bring the engineers into the situation. This was one question that would have to be brought before Bob Novy. Short and Kluck kidded each other about how they had enjoyed working together and about the jobs they were now about to lose, and then went in to tell their secret to the boss.

They reported that Novy seemed momentarily surprised but then, after giving the matter some thought, replied that he had noticed things were improving throughout the plant. Perhaps they were on the right track. He suggested that they proceed with caution, since he did not yet trust the union leadership. He furthermore promised to have the Engineering Department come into the Barrel Department and put forth every possible effort to satisfy the union complaints. They were to recheck everything—even points where no complaints had been made. Short and Kluck asked him to promise that their undercover activities would not be revealed to Gossett. Novy said he would keep the matter secret as long as he could.

As the technical problems were cleared up, production began to improve. But Snyder still had one serious problem.

A few weeks earlier the plant had been visited by Mr. Sykes, president of Inland Steel Company. As Gossett showed him through, from department to department, it seemed that wherever they went they encountered Lucius Love, transacting union business. While Mr. Sykes made no comment on this—he had no way of knowing who Love was—Gossett was exceedingly annoyed. He issued orders that Snyder should tie Love down to a particular job just as closely as possible and keep track of his whereabouts at all times. Up to this point Love had been classified as a utility man, which meant that he filled in on all sorts of jobs but had no regular assignment. He was now given a job spraying paint. This required his full time, and he could not move around at all without getting someone to relieve him.

Snyder described his problem in this way:

I was responsible for keeping him pinned down. I had to account for his time every minute of the day. Besides all the other things I did, I had to keep that record. I'm telling you that was a headache. Sometimes Love would be off and I wouldn't know where he was and when he'd come back I'd tell him, "Now, look, Love, I don't want to get in trouble on account of you. It's only fair for you to let me know," and he was pretty good about it. I was supposed to keep Love tied down as tight as I could. I didn't like it. He'd come to me and ask to get off on union business. He said he had to spend a couple of hours on it one time so I went up to Al Short for him and I told Al, "Look, Al, Love is taking care of some problems for me. He's helped me out. Now I want to help him. How is he going to keep on working good with me and helping me if I can't do anything for him?"

Short thought it over. He had noticed that while Love was tied down troubles seemed to pop out all over the plant in the most unpredictable manner. When he was freer to move around, the troubles were organized in a more orderly and less explosive fashion. He agreed that they should loosen the reins—and just hope that Gossett wouldn't see Love too often when he was out of position.

Sometime later a situation came up in which Novy had to tell Gossett about the new developments in middle and lower management. Gossett himself had been noticing that Love was again moving around more, but he had also noticed that the general situation seemed to be improving, so he was willing to go along with these changes.

Through this same period there was a decided change in the nature of the grievance meetings in which Gossett participated. Gossett had felt that the 1946 contract provided ironclad protection against insubordination, and the foremen had strict orders to lay off anyone who refused to do what he was told. The union officers had felt from the outset that the contract was unworkable if applied literally, and had been attempting to loosen up its interpretation. They felt that they gradually accomplished this in cases involving discharge for insubordination. They report that following the institution of the 1946 contract there was a series of cases in which workers claimed they were unable to do the work demanded of them by foremen and were fired. In some of these cases—especially in those involving women—the union was able to show that problems of health were involved. In such cases Gossett had to reverse the foreman's decision.

As Love describes it:

So Mr. Gossett finally began to give some to the union and that was the time I had been waiting for. I knew things couldn't go on like this forever. If we kept on fighting, we just would kill each other off. I was hoping to see the day when we could live like people, so when Mr. Gossett began to give a little, I gave some too. That was easy to do then because half of the grievances we had in there didn't mean a thing and was just put in to make things hard for management.

The elimination of the union's political-pressure grievances was a great gain in itself for the union-management relationship. Up to that time, while management had been aware that many grievances were put in simply for pressure purposes, it was not always possible to distinguish between such grievances and those in which workers and union leaders genuinely believed. Therefore, a large part of the grievance meetings had been devoted to arguments in which management was unable to get at the actual issues involved. Now, as the union discarded its pressure grievances, management and union at last began to be able to get together and talk about the actual situation underlying the grievances. This provided management with much better information upon developments within the shop and made possible a more realistic handling of shop problems.

While these changes were taking place in union-management relations, equally important changes were going forward within management. Up through the 1946 strike and the months immediately after it, Gossett had been running the company in a manner which his subordinates considered highly dictatorial. In part, he was aware of the reaction. In fact, his original diagnosis of the situation called for a stern policy in relation to lower management as well as in relation to the union. Not only did he lay down the law to foremen and members of middle management, in meetings, he also seemed irritable and unfriendly in other contacts. When he walked through the plant he seemed preoccupied and rarely gave any sign of recognition to the foremen.

Gossett had put his organization under pressure, but he too was under pressure—under the pressure of an exceedingly difficult situation. He estimates that in this period about four-fifths of his time was taken up on union-management problems. It was not just a matter of dealing with each issue as it came up; there was always the problem of trying to think a step or more ahead. As Novy expresses it, he and Gossett might think of nine possible moves that the union might make in a given situation and the only thing they could count on was that the union would make the tenth move, which they had not anticipated. Gossett was working in a state of constant tension and anxiety. It is surprising that Gossett had no serious difficulties with his health in this period, although he did lose twelve pounds, and for a man of medium height and slight build that was an indication of the effect of the nervous wear and tear.

It is easy to understand how the big boss should be irritable and snap at his subordinates under such conditions, but this behavior had to be halted for the building of a harmonious organization. The showdown on this issue came quite suddenly one particular morning, which, according to the memory of the various participants, must have been in December of 1946 or in January or February of 1947. Unfortunately we cannot place the date exactly, but it is clear that the vital change within management came along at approximately the same time that things began to turn for the better in union-management relations in the Barrel Department.

The immediate impetus for the move against Gossett apparently came from Al Short, the general production supervisor. The memories of the men do not agree as to what particular grievance Short had against Gossett on that occasion, but that is not important. He had an accumulation of resentments against Gossett, and he went to Novy to ask permission to go over his head and tell the big boss off. Novy said he would seek to make arrangements.

For some time Novy had been concerned over the hostility of members of middle and lower management toward Gossett. He was afraid the situation might explode if it was not met skillfully and firmly. This seemed to be the point where action was called for. Novy, who had all along been smoothing over the troubled relations between his superior and his subordinates, now undertook what was, in a sense, the biggest job of his career.

He walked into the boss's office and spent about an hour and a half laying out the problem with complete frankness and in full detail. Novy added that there were other people in management who were looking for an opportunity to tell the boss off.

In spite of the close relationship they had enjoyed up to that point, Novy went in for this discussion with some apprehension. It is not customary in management for a subordinate to tell the boss off. But there was no cause for concern in this case. Gossett listened attentively and expressed his appreciation for what Novy had told him. Furthermore, Gossett decided that a situation as serious as this must be given immediate and thoroughgoing airing. He asked Novy to arrange to give everyone who was waiting to tell him off an opportunity to do so.

Short was the first man to go in and he too talked for almost an hour and a half. He was followed by the treasurer of the company, the purchasing agent, and the assistant sales manager, and people in management at lower levels also.

This series of talks had a remarkable effect upon the entire management organization. Some of Gossett's key subordinates were able to get long pent-up complaints off their chests, and the atmosphere of tension and frustration was immediately eased.

At the same time Gossett was able to accept the most drastic criticisms without becoming emotional about them himself. They hurt, to be sure, but they also provided him with an opportunity to take stock of his position. He decided then that the stern policy he had been pursuing in relation to his management had served its purpose and outlived its usefulness. He would have to ease up on his dictatorial practices and build up friendlier relations with his subordinates.

Gossett went about carrying through this decision at once. That same afternoon, as he walked through the Barrel Department, he came upon Ed Snyder, slapped him on the back, gave him a pleasant smile, and said "How you doing, Ed?" It was only a small gesture but it represented a great deal. Snyder was stunned. He went to his superior, Al Short, and asked for an explanation of the sudden change. Short told him simply that the friendly greeting was just an example of the fact that Gossett was really a fine fellow when you got to know him.

Nor was this an isolated gesture. The same men who spoke so bitterly against Gossett in the earlier period, now look upon him with respect, loyalty, and cordiality. The man who once rode rough-shod over all potential opposition or criticism and seemed to show no interest in the problems of subordinates is now highly sensitive to criticism and suggestions from those same men and seeks to consult them on important policy matters. The man who was curt and irritable now seems to have an unusually large supply of patience and tact.

A foreman summed up the change in the big boss in this way:

It's remarkable. It's as different as night from day. He never used to smile at you going through the plant. He never had anything to say to you, but after he went through and got back to his office, you'd hear of it. He'd have plenty of criticism. Now he'll smile at you and ask how things are going, and ask how much you're making today. He's very pleasant to us now.

Such a profound change coming about so suddenly is seldom found in any organization. The importance of the change to management organization and to the union-management relationship could hardly be overestimated. In fact, the change within management was a necessary accompaniment to the changes in the union-management relationship, and neither could have carried through to the present point of cooperation without the other.

These changes within management and between management and union brought about far-reaching changes in the position of the foreman. Before Gossett and Novy came in, he had been little more than an errand boy for top management; he seldom had any clear idea of what was going on; and he was rarely able to get any action from his superiors on his problems. The new management immediately took steps to keep the foremen informed on important developments affecting them. They were also backed up in their decisions as they had not been before. They were able to get somewhat more action from their superiors, but here there were still problems during Gossett's dictatorial period. The change in the vice-president and general manager opened up communications all up and down the line and enabled foremen to get action on their problems with far great frequency than had ever been possible before. The foreman's job was at last becoming a good job to have.

Few men are able to make such a drastic change in behavior as we have seen in the case of John Gossett. How could he do it? A fully satisfactory answer to that question would require an intensive personality study of the executive. That is beyond the scope of this report, but at least we can give certain tentative leads.

Toughness did not come natural to John Gossett. His whole earlier career in selling had taught him to be sensitive to the feelings of others and adjust himself accordingly. When he came into the Chicago plant he decided that the situation called for a firm, dictatorial line of action. He recognized the hostility building up against him in union and lower management, but hostility often gives rise to counterhostility, and that tends simply to confirm a man in his line of action.

Then, when the showdown came, the pressures of the situation were already easing slightly. No basic problems had been solved, but there were tentative evidences of improvement all through the plant. The tension was somewhat relaxed when Novy came in to lead the protest movement.

In explaining what happened in his office that day, Gossett harks back to his experience as a seaman in World War I. It was customary in the navy, he says, for the master of the vessel to make himself available on the quarterdeck at a certain time of day to listen to anyone—even the lowliest seaman—who had a complaint to make. Just how free men feel to take advantage of this opportunity in other situations we have no way of knowing, but apparently, in John Gossett's experience, this really meant something. On the ship where he had served, he knew men who had gone in to complain and protest. He knew that the captain had listened attentively, had taken action when he could, and—above all—had never taken it out on the man who had nerve enough to come in and speak up.

That made an impression on Gossett. He felt that an executive should be able to take criticism and profit from it. And profit he did.

Chapter 6

Bargaining for Cooperation: I

*A*S THE 1947 negotiations approached, the two parties looked upon their situation quite differently. The management people saw signs of improvement, and were hopeful. Considering the long 1946 strike, they did not think another strike was to be expected.

On the union side the workers seemed full of fight and expecting a strike. In fact, many workers felt that the union had been losing ground to management. The local union officers therefore approached the 1947 negotiations prepared for a showdown fight. They called for a contribution of $5 per worker for a strike fund and raised over $3,000. There was every indication that the workers would back their officers strongly if another strike was called. Even before the first negotiation meeting, all the necessary committees had been set up so that a strike could be started at a moment's notice.

The problem of incentive rates was most troubling to the union. This problem had come to a head in what we may call the air-hose case. This involved a grievance concerning a change in rates on two jobs on a particular punch press. This punch press blanked out covers from sheets of steel to be used on the pail line. When the job was first run, there was a tendency for the cover pieces to stick to the machine; the operator then had to tap them loose, which slowed up the machine considerably.

It is not known now just who made the change in this case, except that it was a worker and not a member of management. Perhaps it was a die setter who connected an air hose to a compressed-air connection so that the hose would blow air upon the covers from above to push them loose onto an inclined plane out of the machine. This change had been in effect for some time without any change in rates when a time-study man observed it and consulted the operator about it. The time-study man reported the matter to the Engineering Department, which installed a metal pipe to blow air on the underside of the punch press. Management claimed that this was a major improvement in machine and method justifying a revision in the piecework rate, and the price was thereby reduced by 9 cents a thousand pieces on one job and by 11 cents a thousand pieces on another. The worker in question and all the union people were incensed at this change. One of them said, "They held us up on that just as if they had stuck a gun at us. That's what I thought then and I still think so."

The union claimed that blowing the air from the bottom instead of from the top was simply an excuse for rate cutting and was therefore not justified. Furthermore, the original idea had come from a worker and not from management, and the job already had been run with an air hose for some time.

Management argued that the rubber air hose never worked properly and had been disconnected for some time before the metal air hose was put in the new position. Therefore, this constituted a major change, which justified a restudy of the job. Furthermore, management claimed that earnings on this job had increased since the rate change.

The grievance was written on November 11, 1946, and had been processed through the third step (the personnel manager's decision) by November 26. Then, because the union was changing international representatives, there was a long delay and the fourth-step appeal was not taken until after the 1947 negotiations.

After the first steps of the grievance procedure had been taken on this case, it was evident what management's final decision would be. It seemed that the union officers had no effective way of appealing the decision. They interpreted it to mean that management could cut rates anywhere in the plant at any time and they would have no recourse. They did not anticipate any wholesale cutting of rates, but it then seemed possible that management might take an inch here and an inch there until the whole rate structure was in jeopardy. Therefore, it seemed a matter of the utmost importance to write in the new contract a provision that rates would be subject to arbitration.

Management was equally determined that rates should not be subject to arbitration. The executives recognized these union fears of rate cutting but felt that they were unjustified, since top management was firmly opposed to rate cutting.

Whatever the basis of union fears in actions of earlier managements or of the current Time Study Department, those fears were real—and compelling enough to make this the crucial issue of the 1947 negotiations.

With some exceptions, management was reasonably well satisfied with the 1946 contract, but a number of aggressive demands were expected from the union, and the management officers had to prepare themselves to meet this attack. Gossett and Novy had several long meetings with William G. Caples, industrial relations manager of the parent company, and Charles Kaufman, the company's legal counsel, in order to work out their strategy.

They developed several points that they felt it was important for management to achieve. For example, they wanted to change the practice on the installation of new incentive rates for new or changed jobs. At the time, the employee going on an incentive job, for which a rate had not yet been set received the average earnings of his previous two weeks' work. Thus he had no financial interest in producing until the rate was installed. Management wanted such employees to be paid hourly rates until the new rate was installed, at which time the incentive earnings would be paid retroactively to the beginning of the job. Management also wanted a provision that would make clear the foreman's right to do production work in instructing workers or in an emergency.

Management also developed a number of minor points—clauses it really hoped to achieve but which were certainly not worth taking a strike for.

With four men intending to participate for management, it was essential for them to plan carefully the roles they were to play. They decided that, to begin with, Novy and Gossett would negotiate alone, in order to give the impression to the union that they were not professionals who were trying to outsmart them with technical points. They hoped to create a favorable atmosphere for negotiations by the time the specialists came in to help them.

Novy was to lead off in the bargaining, being as friendly as possible—without giving anything away. Gossett was to be the man who said NO, the last man to agree on any point. Kaufman would take over the leadership of the negotiations when he entered and would be especially responsible for handling questions of phraseology. When Caples came into the negotiations later on, he was to be the man who finally gave the union what Gossett and Novy agreed management could afford to give. Caples could make no offer without Gossett's approval. Before each meeting with the union, they met among themselves to decide which clauses of the contract were to be discussed by which man.

They agreed to try to keep negotiations on a calm, unemotional plane and not make personal attacks on the men across the table. They were to discuss problems in which the union negotiators might have been involved without seeking to pin personal responsibility on them. But that did not rule out a little needling of Lucius Love by Gossett when the union was pushing hard on a sensitive spot, and management wished to distract attention from the issue.

This account of management strategy and program should not imply that the decisions were reached easily. There were several long and heated arguments before management reached agreement on the contract it wanted.

The negotiations brought a new international representative, Lawrence G. ("Jake") Shafer, into the picture. Having struggled with five international men over a period of three years, management feared the worst, and Shafer's stormy background would have provided them no reassurance had they known about it.

Shafer was born in 1914 in the Pennsylvania mining community of Huntingdon, the son of a small store owner. He grew up in the bloody era of the coal and iron police. He went into the union when he was still in his teens and quickly won a position of local leadership, being recognized for his courage, eloquence, intelligence, and the formidable power of his fists.

When the Steel Workers' Organizing Committee was formed, Shafer moved in to help organize the new industry. He first achieved widespread notice in the spring of 1941 when he was one of the leaders of a brief but hard-fought campaign to organize the main plant of Bethlehem Steel Company in Bethlehem. He gave the signal for the strike and helped bring it to a successful conclusion against the opposition of company guards, local police, and state militia. The newspapers of the period carried stories of street fights between strikers and forces lined up against them. They did not report the years that followed, in which relations between the company in that plant and the union developed a reasonably stable basis.

Shafer's problems in Inland Steel Container Company were not limited to the management relationship. He also faced a difficult situation in relation to the union local. This was an exceedingly well-knit local, and the officers took great pride in it. The previous international representative had brought about the signing of the contract but in the process he had put himself into a precarious position with the local officers and the membership. Love and his associates had seen a lot of international representatives and were not easily impressed by them. They would not have hesitated to appeal to the district director if Shafer had not seemed suitable to them. Shafer, therefore, had to establish himself with the local union before he could negotiate freely with management.

The first meeting between Shafer and the local union officials took place in the Chicago West Side subdistrict office of the union several weeks before negotiations were to begin. Love and his committee outlined the plant problems and Shafer spoke about his experience in union work and his general ideas of procedure.

The committee left the meeting with certain misgivings about Shafer. His story of developments at Bethlehem Steel was impressive and suggested that he was a well-qualified man. But, on the other hand, he had emphasized that it was his policy to show respect for management in order to get respect for the union in return. The local officers felt that this was a highly impractical outlook. They still did not believe that management would ever respect union officers, and they feared that a respectful attitude on Shafer's part would be considered a sign of weakness.

This was the only face-to-face meeting before negotiations began, but in between Love had some long telephone conversations with Shafer and submitted to him notes on desirable changes in the contract. Shafer incorporated these suggestions with some of his own ideas and prepared the draft that he submitted to management. The local officers were pleased with the draft, and they began to feel that perhaps Shafer knew what he was doing. At least they decided that they must withhold judgment until they had observed him while coming to grips with management.

Shafer sized up the situation in this way: He knew he had a determined management to deal with; he had heard that long before this local became his responsibility. Other international representatives had told him that he would never be able to work with John Gossett. He was also inclined to agree with the local officers in their opinion of management. However, it was evident that previous relations of union and management had become highly charged with personal antagonism. The clash between Love and Gossett was especially sharp. If Shafer allowed them to get into an argument, it might well blow up all his negotiation plans. On the other hand, if he could soft-pedal the personal antagonism and keep the emotions pitched in a low key, it might be possible to find some basis of adjustment. This seemed a long shot. Shafer felt that he must insist upon substantial changes in the contract, and a strike seemed a much more likely outcome. He was fully prepared to call a strike. He was also determined to make every effort to find a basis for agreement first.

Shafer worked with a committee of six. Besides himself and Love, there were Don Hanes, the vice-president, Ernie Rose, a grievance committeeman, Irene Jones, and Al Wagner. Miss Jones was the committee secretary and Wagner, who worked in the Maintenance Department, was the committee's statistician, with the special assignment of working up figures to compare the maintenance rates in this plant with those paid in other plants.

To carry through his strategy, Shafer exacted a remarkable pledge from the local members of the negotiating committee. No one except Love was to feel free to come into the discussion and, at critical points, even Love was to check first with Shafer. If a local officer wanted to raise a question or make an observation, he must first whisper it or write it on a note to Shafer, who would then decide whether the member should have his say at that particular time. Shafer explained why he made this demand. He said he had no wish to be dictatorial. He would discuss his plans with the committee both before and after negotiating sessions, and in any recesses, and they were always free to veto any arrangement he made. He argued that negotiating in this situation was a delicate problem which must be handled primarily by one man. In view of the strong feelings involved on both sides of the table, any free-for-all discussion would disrupt negotiations. The committee agreed to go along with this stipulation. According to Love, their point of view was that a strike could not be avoided. However, when they had a man who thought there was any chance of reaching a peaceful settlement they did not want to assume responsibility for fighting until that possibility had been fully explored. They felt that they had nothing to lose if they sat back and let Shafer take charge until he had convinced himself that a strike was necessary.

Shafer also persuaded the committee to agree that the development of negotiations would be kept strictly confidential until there was definite progress to report to the membership or else they had gone into a deadlock. He argued that in a situation such as this the committee needed a maximum freedom of action and should not be hampered by the pressures that would come from a membership stirred up by fragmentary reports of developments. This was accepted both by the committee and by the membership in a general meeting.

Shafer was anxious to impress management with the idea that his committee knew what it was doing and had the power to act, and therefore he resolved to cut recesses for consultation down to a minimum and carry on the discussions continuously so far as possible.

Shafer did not plan to confine himself entirely to discussion of specific contract provisions. It was his practice to spend some time in expressing his general point of view on problems of negotiation and the union philosophy behind certain points. This was not done in an argumentative manner. Shafer gave the impression of a man thinking out loud in a group of friends.

When discussion became heated, he had a tactic prepared. An ardent hunter and fisherman, he carried with him into the negotiations a large number of photographs taken on hunting and fishing trips. When a cooling-off period seemed in order, he could interrupt the negotiations by throwing some of the pictures on the table and having a discussion on hunting and fishing.

When he found four men participating for management, he made every effort to bring them all into the arguments in the hope of getting from one a commitment he had been unable to get from another. But, while he tried to play one man off against the others, at no time did he question the good faith of management or attack management directly.

The first four meetings, on March 25 and April 9, 14, and 15, were primarily devoted to jockeying for position and sizing up the opposing parties.

Shafer led off on the first meeting with a statement as to how he wished the negotiations to proceed:

> I would like to make a general statement . . . . I do not know what the policy, the experience of management has been, but I do know this, that usually and particularly the first meeting, which is a matter of formality, that I have found dealing with various managements, particularly of the magnitude of such as yours, that oftentime it is advisable to have somewhat of a gentlemen's agreement of how we expect to do the job in order to expedite the situation. I am just as anxious to get these negotiations rolling systematically and to have as little waste motion as we possibly can. Concerning the gentlemen's agreement, there are certain understandings I'd like to have. I have had a little experience in negotiating basic steel and a few others in the past eight or ten years and I have seen situations that have gotten out of hand. By that I am not referring to management alone—to the union as well. Sometimes we are sidetracked by the fact that we let personalities enter into the picture. Insofar as the personalities are concerned, our admiration for each other may not be too great, but it is a known fact that we have a mutual problem confronting us. I expect my committee, along with myself being a party to it, to cooperate and command all the respect that is humanly possible throughout these negotiations. You probably view the wording "humanly possible" with skepticism. At times whenever we are negotiating points you just cannot keep the blood pressure from rising, but then if we check that point and cool off and renew our negotiations I certainly believe we can do a much better job.

Novy responded by expressing management's firm intention to negotiate in the same manner.

The rest of the brief first meeting was taken up in discussion of procedure. Shafer promised to submit the union's proposed contract before the second meeting. He explained that the draft had been delayed so that he might have further time to "check or recheck" it with his committee. (Actually the union draft was ready but Shafer wanted to hold it until the last possible moment so that management would be caught off balance when negotiations got under way. Also he intended to worry management by a little stalling as contract termination time, April 15, was already uncomfortably close. For the same reason, Shafer agreed to have the second meeting on April 4 and then postponed it to April 9.)

The second meeting also was devoted largely to questions of procedure. Using the argument that management's draft contained fewer changes from the existing contract, management was able to persuade the union negotiators to use that draft as a basis of negotiation. Then Novy proposed that, as they went through the draft, they initial the clauses on which they seemed to be in agreement. Shafer refused to initial and held out for simply checking the clauses. This seemingly trivial point was important to the union in this way: The initialling would seem a firm commitment so that, if negotiations broke down with only one or two clauses uninitialed, management could announce that everything was agreed to except those particular points, which might have the effect of dividing the union membership and making some of them feel that their committee was being unreasonable to refuse the settlement that was apparently so near. Shafer felt that it was important to keep everything tentative until everything was agreed, so that, if they deadlocked on one clause, they could announce to the membership that they had not agreed on anything.

After an extended argument, management agreed to the checking procedure. But later in this same meeting Shafer was even reluctant to check clauses, and the following discussion took place:

Novy: Article VI, Hours of Work, Section 1. I don't think that can be any clearer and I don't think you can expect any more than that. Shall we check it?

Shafer: No, we are just looking it over. As I previously stated, I thought
we were just going over this.

Novy: I think you are confused as to what we are attempting to do. We
are using our draft as the base. We have to get this done—time is
running short. We are negotiating now, is that correct?

Shafer: Then let's start back at the beginning and take section by
section.

Novy: I thought it was clear that that is what we are doing, we are
negotiating this contract. Don't you know the procedure?

Shafer: I resent that statement. It so happens that I appreciate management's position. I have been in a few negotiations myself where we
agreed to something tentatively and set it down by the wayside and
got into the crux of the situation. I certainly am sorry that I was
working under some illusion here—that would take us back to
page 2.

Novy: You say we are just reading over the agreement, haven't we
tentatively agreed on some of the sections?

Shafer: Oh, yes, tentatively agreeing.

At this point it seemed to the management representatives that
either they were confused or else Shafer was confused—and probably it was Shafer. But, actually, most of the confusion at this
time was deliberately injected into the negotiations by the international representative. He felt that he had to fight shy of any
significant commitments for some time, for two important reasons.
First, the wage pattern for the industry had not yet been set by
Big Steel and the union, so the local officers were awaiting developments. Of course, management was similarly situated on this issue.
But this was not the controlling reason for holding back, for there
were many other issues that had to be negotiated strictly on a local
basis, and some of these were to prove much thornier than the
question of hourly rates. Second, Shafer did not want to show his
hand until he was satisfied that all of management's big guns had
been brought into play. He had heard impressive accounts of the
past performances of Company Counsel Kaufman and Industrial
Relations Manager Caples, and he was waiting for them to get into
action. Consequently, some of the time in the second and third
meetings was taken up with discussions of who had the power to
settle what. Both union and management negotiators insisted they
had the power to commit their organizations and to bargain on

anything at once, and neither party took quite seriously the statements on this subject coming from the other side of the table.

When April 15 came both parties were still jockeying for position. They had explored some of their differences but had tentatively agreed on practically nothing except those clauses in the old contract which neither party was seeking to change. The fourth meeting, therefore, had to be devoted to reaching an agreement on the extension of the contract. Although both parties were eager to make the extension, it took almost three hours of vigorous argument to come to an agreement on this point. The union was pressing for a clause stipulating that retroactivity on any wage increase that might be granted should be "a proper matter for negotiation," and the union also wanted to be able to terminate the extension to call a strike on 10 days' notice. Management did not want to make any commitments regarding retroactivity, and was asking 45 days' notice for a strike.

Agreement was reached on the basis of the union's retroactivity provision and a 30-day strike notice. Since this seems a natural sort of compromise, it might be asked why such strenuous argument was necessary to reach the point. The answer is that both parties were anxious to avoid any impression of weakness in their bargaining. Although the retroactivity clause did not commit management to any formula and only stated that the subject could be brought up later—which the union could be expected to do with or without such a clause—Gossett and Novy were afraid that if they gave in on this point they would appear to be weak and would have more trouble on later issues. Consequently, they were willing to give in on that point only when they had pushed the strike notice period up from 10 to 30 days. On the union side, the issue had a similar symbolic value. The committee could now tell the members that the extension showed they were able to get some action out of management. The fact that there was never any reference to the terms of the extension in later negotiations does not invalidate the symbolic value it had for the union at the time.

Immediately after this meeting the union gave its 30-day strike notice. The management people were disturbed by this apparent lack of faith in a peaceable outcome, but Shafer simply wanted to be free as soon as possible to exert maximum pressure for a settlement.

With the fifth meeting, on May 23, we find the parties making real progress. But this suggests that more progress was made in earlier sessions than appeared on the surface, and the impression is confirmed by later discussions with the participants. The arguments were vigorous, but with restraint shown on both sides, plus Shafer's hunting and fishing trips thrown in to ease tension, there were no emotional explosions. One has only to review the bitter arguments of earlier negotiations to appreciate the magnitude of this improvement.

By the time that Counsel Kaufman came into the situation the tension was already somewhat eased, and the lawyer continued to build this atmosphere. For example, management proposed a new vacation clause, which rewarded faithful attenders over workers who had bad absence records. This led to a discussion of the absenteeism problem, in which management and union representatives found themselves in effect on the same side of the table, facing a common problem. We have Shafer calling management's proposal

A good benefit from our standpoint in that it gives more vacation pay to the fellows who work more. Those are the people we are primarily interested in. We are not interested in the fellows who lay off—and we have many of them in the shop—and I think your own people will tell you that. In this way his pay will be cut and it should be cut if he does not want to work. . . . Our absentee record is pretty lousy.

Gossett replied, "It is greatly improved over last year, but it still could stand a lot of improvement." Kaufman then went on to say that union and management had discussed the problem before, and he added: "Absenteeism has improved, and we imagine that Lucius and the rest of the boys have been keeping after them about absenteeism."

A little later this interchange took place:

Shafer: Incidentally, the question of absenteeism was considered by the union, I can assure you that the union brings that up at their meeting. For example, last Sunday there was one of the things that was discussed and I might say a very fine job was done for management by Lucius and his executive committee.
Gossett: We are very happy to hear that.
Shafer: Of course, I concurred with the chairman of the local committee

and the chairman of the executive committee because I personally feel where absenteeism has a tendency to hamper production in any way whatsoever, when we are a party to an agreement we are partially responsible where our union people are at fault.

Out of this discussion came an invitation from Shafer to management for a joint effort in this field. No commitments were made at the time but, following the close of negotiations, we will see action developing further in this direction.

As discussions of the company's vacation plan continued, questions by Shafer led Kaufman to discover that the proposed new clause was so worded as to deprive all workers of a vacation—due to the time lost the previous year in the strike. He then withdrew that clause and discussion moved on to consideration of a substitute clause that would meet the objective both parties had in mind.

It is significant to observe how the union negotiators met this situation. This could have been interpreted as a management attempt to "pull a fast one"—if Shafer had wished to assume that management was (1) unprincipled and (2) stupid enough to try to slip in a completely unworkable clause. Instead, he accepted the application of the clause for what it was, a management oversight, and went on with the business of the meeting.

The vacation issue gave rise to another interchange whose significance can be appreciated only against a knowledge of the background of the case. Here management was arguing that employees who quit should not receive vacation pay, and the union was arguing that this was a part of their earnings. Note here the fencing between Shafer and Kaufman:

Kaufman: We give a vacation because the employee comes back to work a better workman and that is our benefit. We do not get that if a fellow says, "I'm through," and that is why we do not want to pay him a vacation.

Shafer: By being a good employee he has earned a vacation and in being on the job. It is an economic problem and he has earned his vacation and he is entitled to it.

Kaufman: I admit there are two sides to it, but the way we look at it is this: when vacations were first brought in, I don't know whether they were earned vacations or not.

Shafer: That is the way we say now.

Kaufman: They were sold to the employer on the ground that you say we get a benefit out of it. We get a benefit because we get a worker back who has had some time off and he is more physically fit. We are not interested in the fellows who do not come back. If a fellow wants to quit, we do not think he is entitled to any vacation pay. Is that a fair statement?

Gossett: I think so, yes.

Kaufman: We do not regard a fellow earning it or not, but the only way we get any benefit out of him is if he comes back to us a better employee. I know a fellow can take his vacation and never return and say, "I will be back," and never show and he can beat us that way if he wants to. I understand that, but we do not think we will run into too much of that. We do not think if a fellow is quitting us to take another job that he needs the vacation or the vacation money.

Shafer: Let us just reverse the picture. The vacation plan is also an inducement to have employees report to work rather than lay off or what have you. He takes a vacation over a specified period in order that he may be on the job to keep up production. We say that that vacation program is a problem of an economic nature.

Kaufman: It is a cost to us.

Shafer: Therefore, it can be computed as earnings, and so on the basis of that I ask you as management's representative why you would like to deny a man something that he has earned. Would you take it from his pay envelope?

Kaufman: With this business of earning a vacation, to my mind that is a lot of bunk so far as I am concerned.

Shafer: Let us throw all these out then.

Kaufman: I cannot remember any employer, and I say this in all frankness, who ever got credit for an improved vacation plan. This is substantially improved over what it was four or five years ago, is that right?

Novy: Yes.

Kaufman: The employees never regarded that as a wage increase. The War Labor Board, if they were figuring the Little Steel formula, never gave the employer any consideration for giving the employees a more liberal vacation plan.

Shafer: May I ask a question there? I am not attempting to interrupt you, but in the Little Steel formula under the War Labor Board plan, if management wished to improve the vacation setup, are you saying they could do it without the approval of the board?

Kaufman: I did not say they could do it without the approval of the board, but what I said is the increased amount which the employees made by reason of their vacation was never counted by the board as an offset reducing the amount allowable to which employees were entitled to under the Little Steel formula.

Shafer: The conception of the Little Steel formula was that vacations should be given no consideration.

Kaufman: Look at the economic end of that, and we were in the Little Steel case as well as the basic steel case and you will find out that they considered vacations.

Shafer: They did not improve the vacation plan because of the economic problem but they applied the 15 per cent under the formula.

Kaufman: They put the base rate here and the vacations off behind the left-field bleachers.

Shafer: And they did not touch it.

Kaufman: No, they did not touch it. They touched it later on.

Shafer: Because of the cost factor.

Kaufman: They did later on. The War Labor Board granted a different vacation in the basic steel case even though there was nothing more allowable under the formula. We do not even think you people should be interested in that. After all, you are interested primarily in the people who work in the plant.

If a fellow wants to go to another job and is quitting, let him worry about it.

Shafer: However, it is computed as a part of his wages.

Kaufman: No, it is not.

Shafer: Or earnings?

Kaufman: It is not.

Shafer: Why not?

Kaufman: It does cost us because anything that the worker gets costs us. The fact that a plant may keep up and maintain better facilities of this kind, or that kind, that is done for the worker and that is the cost and it comes out of what the worker takes in income, but from the worker's standpoint I do not think he counts it as an earning.

Shafer: He must earn it.

Kaufman: He has to earn it and he has to be an employee of the company to get it.

Shafer: You are saying that now.

Kaufman: That is what I think.

Shafer: We say he has earned it and he is entitled to it and so why deny it to him.

Kaufman: That is our opinion.

Shafer: That is definitely an economic problem and certainly if an employee has earned it under the requirements of any plan he should be entitled to it.

Kaufman: One of the things, or there are a lot of things, to say that the company computes as a part of its cost and I suppose they could compute my fee as a part of the cost and that is no part of the employee's earnings.

Shafer: That is granted. I noticed Mr. Gossett shaking his head.

Gossett: I hate to have that thing coming up all the time. We get it two ways every time we sit down.

Shafer: I cannot agree with you on that. I am afraid we do not see eye to eye on that.

Novy: Would you say two or three a month quit?

Kluck: There may be that many quitting but they would not be eligible for a vacation because a lot are here only a few months and then they quit. Those eligible for vacations are very few.

Shafer: Thank you.

Kaufman: That works both ways.

Shafer: That is correct. That clears the air in my mind.

Kaufman: That would not make a lot of difference and, as I say, we are not citing to the contrary. However, from our point of view we are not interested in the fellow and giving him a vacation because he is going to work for somebody else.

Shafer: Are you arguing this on the basis of a principle, Mr. Kaufman, or what?

Kaufman: Largely principle. Sometimes I cannot get people to agree with them, however.

Shafer: I cannot agree with you.

Kaufman: I say this in all honesty. I do not think you people ought to be interested in the fellow who is quitting to take another job.

Shafer: If an individual has earned something he has a right to it, and he must earn his vacation in order to receive pay for it.

Kaufman: I will mark on section five that you want the same provision or the old provision on that, is that correct? The old sentence of old four which reads: "Employees eligible for vacation who have not received their vacation and have voluntarily quit shall be entitled to vacation pay"?

Shafer: Right.

When this interchange was concluded, Shafer noted that his committee members were following with obvious interest and appreciation, and Love passed him a note saying that this was the first time he had seen anyone outmaneouver Charles Kaufman. Shafer had stuck right with him through the technical discussion of WLB policy, and then had seemed to turn these complicated matters to the union's advantage.

Now here was a point that was of only minor importance to management. Nevertheless, the effect upon the union was highly important. Up until now, the committee members were just hoping for the best but were not at all confident that Shafer would be able to meet management on even terms. Shafer had to prove himself to his own group. When that was accomplished, he gained much greater security in his dealings with management, and increased his influence with the union committee.

The outcome, paradoxically, was as beneficial to management as it was to the union. It was to management's advantage to have Shafer in a strong position. If Kaufman had appeared to "win" the argument but management had then "given" the point away, the effect would have been far different. In that case the committee members would have lost confidence in their negotiator and would have felt the need to strike back strongly.

We are making no judgment as to who actually won the argument in this case. Such a judgment would be irrelevant. The payoff is in what developed out of the argument. Here the union people felt they had won, and that feeling contributed significantly to the progress of the negotiations. Since management had not considered this argument important, no "face" was lost in the process, and the management men felt no need to fight back to even the score.

The negotiators then turned to discussing the grievance procedure. Here the union was pushing to get certain clauses clarified, to bring other clauses in line with established practice in the plant, and to shorten the time used in processing grievances up the line. Management here showed basically the same interest in improving the procedure, and attention was focused upon practices rather than upon principles.

The first point discussed illustrates the approach taken. Article XII, Section 1, of the old contract read:

"Grievances are defined as differences as to the meaning and application of the provisions of this agreement."

Love made this statement:

First we had to define the grievance as to the violation of the contract. In the grievance we had to specify the clause in the contract that was violated or the section that was violated for it to be a grievance. In fact, it was turned down at least a month before we could get a grievance into the personnel office that would be acceptable because the foreman was interpreting what section was violated and that section was not violated according to the definition and the application of the provision and so we did not have any grievance.

It was several weeks before we were able to break through that barrier. I see no sense in having words in here that you have got to argue about when Section 2 takes care of everything that might happen. That is something I think should be deleted.

Management agreed that Section 2, dealing with "differences . . . as to the meaning and application of the provisions of this Agreement," covered the situation adequately and agreed to drop Section 1, providing the union accepted a clause later in the grievance article stipulating that an arbitrator should not have the power to alter the contract in any way but could only "interpret, apply, and determine compliance." The union accepted this familiar sort of provision, and there was no further argument on the point.

The negotiators then went on to clarify certain understandings that were not to be written into the agreement. Shafer was assured that if he asked for additional time after the fourth-step grievance decision to determine whether or not to submit the case to arbitration such an extension would be granted.

Similarly, at the start of the sixth meeting, May 26, Love raised the question as to whether anything beyond official grievances could be discussed in grievance meetings. The point was that sometimes the union officers wished to anticipate problems that might later result in grievances. Or there might be problems which fitted no specific clause but were nevertheless threatening to disturb union-management relations. Love said that the union had previously had trouble in getting management to discuss such matters. Gossett and Personnel Manager Kluck said that for the past six months management had been accepting such discussions and there was no current difficulty on that point. Love agreed but said he just wanted it on the record that the practice would be continued. This was agreed.

Up to this point the negotiators were still skirting around the major issue, but they were making progress. For five and a half meetings, they had been able to avoid emotional explosions and personal recriminations. On some problems they were beginning to find common ground. However, they still had a long way to go.

Chapter 7

Bargaining for Cooperation: II

THIS WAS the tensest series of bargaining meetings that had ever been experienced by the men who faced each other across the long table in the conference room. In the first four meetings they agreed on practically nothing, and it seemed they might not even be able to get together on extending the contract in order to keep the discussions going.

The 30-day strike notice of April 15 provided a reprieve for both sides, but the parties were then not able to get together for the next meeting until May 23. The time had run out. Now a strike could legally be called at any moment, on any issue.

Rumors ran through the plant. The strike was coming. People were even naming the day and the time of day. The workers feared and dreaded a strike, but they were ready for it. When their negotiators walked out of a meeting, reporting the deadlock, the word would spread immediately through the plant, and the workers would walk out behind their committee.

The management people could feel the tension in the plant. They argued, with the realization that, if they talked their way into a deadlock, they would see the men across the table get up and go out—and that would be it. All the painstaking efforts of many months, all of that long struggle to find a basis for agreement, would be swept away in another strike. Thousands of dollars would be lost, day after day, but there was something more important than that. They had tried, they thought they were making progress, they had begun to hope for a way out—and now a strike would dash those hopes. If not now, when could they ever hope to find a really stable basis for agreement?

The union negotiators also were under pressure. The last strike had lasted 191 days. Jobs were hardly worth having in a plant that had a strike—perhaps a long strike—every year. No one, and least of all the local officers, could afford a strike. And yet everyone was expecting a strike, even thinking a strike was inevitable. Everyone, that is, except Jake Shafer. He kept trying and kept hoping right to the showdown.

The specter of that threatened strike was in the room with them, on the conference table before them. The men were playing for high stakes. It takes steady nerves to play your cards skillfully when you know that one wrong move may mean disaster.

The men at the conference table were moving ahead slowly—but very slowly. The fifth meeting showed some evidences of the give-and-take spirit that leads to agreements, and the sixth meeting had begun in the same way. They had learned that they could talk across the table, for hours on end, and still keep their emotions under control. That was a gain.

But so far, in five and a half meetings, they had not yet got their teeth into the rate-arbitration issue. By now they all knew that was the key issue to the negotiations. It had already come up several times, but each time the parties had circled around it, tested out each other's positions, and then moved on to other clauses.

Now, in the middle of the sixth meeting, they clashed head on. Instead of waiting for the union challenge, management began by stating its case in strong terms. The argument opened in this way:

Kaufman: All right. "The arbitration provisions of Section 2 shall not apply to the determination of wages, wage rates, or job classifications."

Now, that is one that I believe we are going to have to insist on. I don't know how familiar you are with the history of our problems in this plant, and I can imagine, without knowing, what the union has said about it. If the union wants to explain why it wants that change, maybe we had better hear from them first on it.

I want to tell you at the outset that that has been in there several years, I think, and we think that that provision is what has enabled us to beat several programs—when I say programs I am not mentioning a program that Lucius or Don or Ernie or anybody else are involved in—several concerted efforts which were pretty clearly slowdowns.

Is that a fair statement of our position, Bob?

Novy: That is putting it very mildly.

Kaufman: I am a mild fellow.

Shafer: I am interested in Mr. Novy's statement. You say, "That is putting it very mildly."

Novy: That is right. We have had not several but a good many conditions here which, because of the inability of people to recognize at the time they were put in whether or not rates were fair, became slowdowns in an attempt by that means to force management to revise or change the existing conditions in relation to those rates, and it was not a healthy condition from either side. Everybody lost by it and since that time, in many cases, after the rates were in for a period of time, I am sure that the people found that they were not as unfair as they originally thought they were because they made out very amply on those rates.

We have no reason or method behind setting the rates other than setting them up fairly and equitably for everybody concerned on the basis of the way rates have always been set in this plant.

Gossett, Novy, and Kaufman went on to state that employee earnings in this plant were "substantially the highest in our industry."

Shafer replied simply, "I am very happy to hear that."

Kaufman then began to go into more detail on the history of slowdowns in the plant. Love objected, "Let's not negotiate that," but Kaufman felt it was important to management's position to have this summary of recent difficulties put before Shafer. He mentioned the Pail Department slowdown briefly and then went into more detail on the Barrel Department problems, discussing the old premium on down time, the changes on the production lines, and the agreement with Love that new rates designed to discourage down time should be introduced. Kaufman pointed out that the employees had held back their production for several months, trying to convince management that the new rates were unfair. Only when they finally had to recognize that management would not budge did they really try to find out what was possible on the line. And then, Novy added, they began to make an average of 12 cents an hour more than they had made under the old rates (not counting the 18½-cent increase).

Gossett then came in with this comparison:

Gossett: I would just like to add to that this statement, that with the identical equipment plus superior equipment, with the identical number of people, the production at this plant is so far below either the Jersey City or New Orleans plants that there is no basis for comparison, yet these people here are getting more money in their pay envelope—and I am talking about the Barrel Department specifically now—than those people either at New Orleans or at Jersey City.

You know, we are going to recognize it, I am confident before the next year has elapsed. The only way we can hope to pay more money is to get more production. We try to contribute to greater production by technological progress. If we don't get more production we are not going to stay competitive, or as an alternative we are going to operate at a loss, and it is going to be far better from our standpoint to ship the steel to Jersey City or ship it to New Orleans and absorb that higher freight rate and still make more money than we can make operating this plant at the rate of production we are getting.

Those are facts that we can prove without any question in the world, not for a flash period but over an extensive period of years.

That is the situation and it is not healthy for the people and it is not healthy for management. As things become tighter economically, it is going to be bad for both of us. There isn't any doubt about that. We are just going to lose business. That is all there is to it.

As long as things were going out and we were in a seller's market, we didn't have to worry. That picture is changing very, very rapidly.

Only after management had laid out all its arguments did the union begin to state its case. Love led off in this manner:

Love: I would like to make some comments. First, I hope that Mr. Kaufman isn't going to say, "Now, look, Lucius, we are not part of old management so why always throw that in? How many years do we have to live that down?"

By the same token, I say the same thing.

A lot of things happened that maybe shouldn't have happened. Those things have rapidly eliminated themselves. I can't see and I can't believe that with the equipment that you have here with the breakdowns how any management can expect to get any more production than they are getting in this plant. Cooperation and friendly relationships add to this picture.

When we first came back in after the six months' strike there was no such animal existing in this plant and it took the officers a long time to convince the people that management was just as tight in all their dealings as they could possibly be.

I know any number of times where these things have been brought to my attention even in the Barrel Department where Mr. Kluck and Mr. Short brought it to my attention that something has to be done and we have to sit down and talk this thing over, and get this bad feeling out of the department and get some more production, and I think they can speak as to what happened in that department.

You say the pails are tops. Okay. Just like we sit down and spend a day or two, a few hours during that time in getting some of the bugs out—I am no part of management. It doesn't take very long to tell that, but we stand ready at all times to assist in these things wherever management will permit us and that is one of the instances where production was increased, and we still stand ready to do the same thing.

I can point out any number of cases, and I think there is any number of people in the plant that can do the same thing. It isn't the people's fault. The people work like hell down there but there is certain equipment, certain things, certain methods being used that just doesn't permit you to get production there.

I went over some of these things, attempted to go over some of these things a week or so ago. Mr. Short went on his vacation and we didn't finish talking about it. The union isn't responsible as far as that is concerned so I don't want the union to take all this responsibility about it not getting done.

As I started to say a moment ago, it wasn't two or three months that caused all of the delay for a better rate. It was a question of management not recognizing certain facts that were brought to their attention when the rates were put into effect before the equipment was ready to go, and there are still certain rates, still certain jobs that you run in a department, in my department, which you run on the old system, since you streamlined the plant, and you made very few changes in your complete setup which I don't want to go into here, which causes the people to have to work harder to make certain barrels.

No consideration at all is given that particular matter. In other words, you bring it to management's attention, they look at it or they consider it or they don't consider it, and they see the work and you tell them, "Now, here it is, here is a picture," and they will look right in your eye without cracking a smile and say, "There is no more work involved in this," when the man perhaps is working time and a half as hard as he was previously.

Those things are visible to the eye and those things are things that management has not given consideration to, certain jobs and other things, certain equipment that is holding people back, and the help situation which has been pretty bad, especially during the vacation season, is partly responsible, and this equipment that you put in was supposed to work and it didn't work.

All those things have added to the fact of not getting consideration in the way of getting these grievances in.

In the new contract it will be different. Where you had a grievance previously and you couldn't get it in on a Friday and it would go over to the next week, and there would be a delay, and all those things have added to this rate of production, and that is why it caused so much confusion in the department which, to me, should have no bearing on whether or not we have a clause in there that we should have no slowdown, but which should also have no bearing on whether the rates should be in there.

Gossett: We don't make any drum here, Lucius, that we don't make at Jersey, or New Orleans and what I said before still holds. There isn't anything different in this plant in materials or the type of product that we make than is the case of those made at the other two plants.

Love: What about your equipment in the placing of work?

Gossett: I say the identical number of people, identical equipment, except superior ovens here.

Love: You might have superior equipment and not superior ovens.

Gossett: I said the identical equipment, the identical number of people with the advantage of better ovens, more troublefree ovens.

Love: I might have a car but—

Gossett: Let me just go on here about this thing. We make everything in those plants that we make at Chicago, everything that you talk about where somebody works one and one-half times as hard, which I seriously question in my own mind.

We do all those things and yet there is no comparison between the production in Chicago and in the other cities. It is something that I am constantly trying to explain, something I am constantly trying to find out what the trouble is, because to me, I can't understand it. There is no way I can understand it. I know conditions here and I know conditions there.

Now, you talk about the cooperative attitude of the union. We suggested a change in the clause that relates to supervisory help. If you want to know the real difference in my opinion between Jersey and this plant, it lies right in the requirement of that clause. We are going to suggest another change on that before we are through.

Another thing about rates is that we suggested a new clause in this draft which met immediate objection on the part of the union. The clause provided that in the case of a new job where no rate has been set, the operator goes on the job, and so that he doesn't work on average pay as has been the past practice here, making it very difficult to get an entirely clear picture, we suggest that he go on the job and then the rate is made retroactive to the date on which he starts on the job, which is absolutely fair.

Kaufman: Not only fair but usual.

Gossett: Absolutely fair. You object to that. You objected strenuously to that on the first reading. We are going to work hard to get that Lucius. We think it is important, and we think if you are sincere in what you say, and I am inclined to believe you are, more this time than any time in the past, that you are going to think about that clause. It is going to be important to everybody.

Shafer: We have been thinking about that, Mr. Gossett, but where that is in existence certainly is a matter subject to arbitration, where you set rates up in that manner.

Kaufman continued to argue against arbitration on the grounds, first, that the company's rates were unusually generous and, second, that incentive rates were a highly technical problem that could not be satisfactorily handled by an outsider who would be unfamiliar with the plant.

Love countered by saying that the union's record of taking cases to arbitration (only two in ten years) showed that management would not have to fear a flood of rate arbitrations if the way for them was once again opened. Rose added that the only two cases on the record had had nothing to do with rates. The union, nevertheless, did not want to close off the possibility of an appeal in such cases.

Kaufman challenged the union men to show specifically how they had been hurt by the prohibition of rate arbitration that had been introduced into the 1946 contract. How had management cut the rates?

The union men replied by arguing the air-hose case.

Rose: In the punch press department there were several incidents of it, and there were statements made by representatives of management that the job was paying too much, which I had proof of.

In order to protect ourselves on that kind of condition, that is one of the main reasons why we feel that we should have arbitration of wages.

Love: I might add for Mr. Kaufman's benefit—I don't know what he considers a major change—that we had one case in particular in the press room where they just changed the air, where the air used to blow from the side and they had it put up from the bottom and called that a major change and cut the rate. That was a major change.

Now, the operator had been using this and it was his own idea in order to speed up production, so that these little pieces would fall out of the machine faster than they did. He got an air hose and would blow the material out.

Management just changed it and had the air put through the machine and said that was a major change, and cut the rate.

Gossett: What happened to the earnings of the man?

Love: I am not talking about—

Gossett: What happened to the earnings of the man?

Love: I didn't follow the case through.

Gossett: I have, because I heard this case before. I read the grievance on it. You had better complete the story. The man is earning more than he was before?

Love: The man is working harder, too, than he was. That might be true.

Gossett: To cut the rate means to cut earnings.

Kaufman: Do you know that case Bob?

Novy: Yes.

Kaufman: What happened was this. The rate was originally set for operation without the air hose.

Novy: Right.

Kaufman: Then when the air hose was put on as you said yourself it made the job faster.

Love: That isn't true. The air hose had been on there ever since the rate was set.

Novy: It is possible, I don't know. If it was done that way, there was no authority to put an air hose on. We have air ejectors that are mechanical for that purpose. Nobody in the plant should take an air hose and attach it.

Love: I might say for your benefit, Mr. Shafer, that this went on for three or four years, and the foreman approved it. It must have been approved by management. There was no objection to it. I guess it was even longer than that, so more than one foreman approved the thing. Two or three foremen were in there who approved it, and it was on at the same time that the rate was set.

Novy: Were the employees' earnings cut?

Love: Your production was increased.

Novy: I didn't ask that question. I said, were the employees' earnings cut? You mean to say the employee was earning less after the adjustment than he did before?

Hanes: For his efforts, yes.

Kaufman: There have been some jobs where a fellow can—there always are some soft jobs where a fellow doesn't put out much effort and goes along, particularly in the group situations, correct? There shouldn't be any kick because his job is changed so that he puts out a reasonable amount of effort, even if it is twice what he put out before. It should not be done if it is a reasonable amount of effort and he makes good money at it. I don't see where there was any room for grief there.

Hanes: There wasn't a group situation.

Kaufman: Yes, I know. I don't know the situation, I don't know what the individual case was, but I think that the facts of the case alone will pretty well refute Lucius' claim.

Now, look, this was a piece-work case, wasn't it, that is what it was for all practical purposes? It was an individual case so he made what he could, so we have to assume he put out substantial effort on the job. That is what the piece work is there for, to induce employees to put out substantial effort.

You say even after we reduced the rate he is making more than he did before. This guy hasn't suddenly become a superman. He is undoubtedly keeping somewhere at the same piece work rate he was before, and he is making more money, so how the hell can he say he is prejudiced by the change in rate?

It seems to me you are ignoring the actualities. Either the rate before was ridiculously soft, or the new rate is even more fair, or both, because he is now making more than he did before. Do you think he has got a basis for grievance?

Love: That is just one example.

The argument had become more heated at this point than at any previous time in the negotiations. Having remained in the background to let the local men argue the union's case, Shafer now came in to make a concluding statement. He accepted management's point of view to this extent:

Shafer: In the final analysis, the important factor in the making of a wage agreement, whether we are kidding ourselves or whether we like it or not, it is based on production.

Then he went on to state the issue in this way:

Certainly this organization of ours, the Steelworkers Union, is as interested in production as management, because we are well aware of what it means, but the proposal has been made, and I say that naturally we are considering it, but certainly we can't consider where we are setting up a method on the institution of rates or what have you—in fact, I don't feel as though I can talk about methods and what we have presently, because that in itself will require some discussion, mutual discussion, but certainly we can't be in the position of saying, "Now, here is a method we are going to introduce but any factor that may arise from this in no way whatsoever shall be arbitrated."

I am sorry, gentlemen, I just can't go along with you on that basis.

The negotiators now passed on to other issues. The conflicting points of view had been strongly stated, and there was not yet the slightest sign of any way out of the impasse. Nevertheless, there was one hope. They had gone thoroughly over the toughest issue and had still kept their tempers below the boiling point. Following a lunchtime recess, it was possible for them to come back and face less explosive issues in the same objective and conciliatory fashion that had characterized the adjustments made before the rate question came up.

Shafer objected to the provision that a grievance committeeman, upon entering another department to consult with a steward, had to show the foreman a written statement of the grievance in question. Shafer pointed out that a grievance committeeman should be able to investigate a problem before filing a formal grievance. Strict enforcement of this clause would put into the machinery some grievances that might be considered unwarranted by the grievance committeeman if he had the chance to investigate first. It was, therefore, of mutual advantage to allow some latitude for investigation. Actually management was already allowing some latitude on this point, and the negotiators readily agreed with Shafer's position. Several minutes were taken up with a search for proper phraseology, but there was no conflict in aims here.

Toward the end of the meeting management brought up its proposal to cut the twice-a-day 15-minute rest periods to 10 minutes. The purpose here was to point out the abuses of the rest-period time by certain employees who were not back at the end of 15 minutes and to get the union to take some concern in the matter. Shafer, of course, objected to the cut in time but accepted management's objective as a mutual one. After some discussion of the problem, management agreed to go along with 15 minutes and the union agreed to a new provision spelling out the employees' obligation to be at their posts on time and to have a supervisor's permission before going on relief. In Shafer's opinion, the new section simply confirmed certain powers management already had, but management welcomed this explicit statement as a means of highlighting the problem.

In the discussion of the grievance procedure and of the relief problem, management and the union were building up a pattern of meeting problems that augured well for the peaceful settlement of the contract. First, the discussions brought out that management had not been adhering to a strict, legalistic interpretation of the 1946 contract. There were some signs of the growth of unwritten understandings that must inevitably be a part of any stable relationship. These were still tentative enough and the situation was still tense enough so that the union men felt the need to be reassured that these understandings would be continued in future relations, though no new clauses were demanded or given. There were also cases here and in later negotiations where the contract wording was changed to bring it in line with existing practices.

The negotiators here did not argue principles but instead worked on problems which they could agree were of mutual concern. Management brought up a new clause in order to raise a practical problem, and the union's acceptance of joint responsibility on this problem had a favorable effect upon management attitudes as well as contributing to the solution of the problem.

In the seventh meeting, June 3, Caples joined the management negotiators for the first time, and Shafer had a new problem to size up. The sparring period did not take long in this case. Shafer had been led to expect a stiff, egocentric character. Instead, he found an easygoing, relaxed individual, who was not given to emphasizing his own importance. Quite early in the session, we find this interchange:

Shafer: Naturally, I am not in a position to read your mind nor are you in a position to read my mind.
Caples: I am not in a position to read my own sometimes.
Shafer: I guess we find ourselves in that position sometimes, too.

This was more than idle banter. Such a light touch tended to relax the tension of negotiations and promoted a more friendly, informal relationship. Shafer decided that he could get along with a man who could kid himself occasionally even while hammering away at serious issues.

Later in the meeting the handling of the furlough clause provided another example of the pattern the parties had evolved for the adjustment of their differences. First they stated the issue: the old contract allowed for a 90-day furlough period with one possible extension of 30 days; the union wanted to liberalize the extension period to provide for employees who might suffer a serious illness and be unable to return within the extension time. Then they agreed that they had the same objectives; both parties wanted a liberal policy and at the same time wanted to guard against its abuse. They talked in this way:

Novy: It is hard to determine when a case needs an extension. They bring in a doctor's certificate and we may even know from the bare facts that that is not the case.
Shafer: An employee that would do that is not a good employee and we don't want him in our organization. If they are not a good employee, they are not good for us.

Love: That is right.

Caples: Take any group of people and you will get a small percentage of them. I do not care how good or how bad a group is. You are going to have a certain percentage. You know in the Army there were a bunch of dogs and no matter how much you changed a company, you had the same thing.

Shafer: One of the pet things I said to Mr. Gossett is that the Good Lord himself picked twelve men and He got one son of a b and we are only human beings, and we are dealing with hundreds. You see what happened.

Kaufman: Would it be satisfactory, and I agree with you, Lucius, all right that it has been working better since the last agreement—

Shafer: It has been working much better since our negotiations, isn't that right?

After a brief mention of several pending cases, the discussion went in this direction:

Love: The committee took it upon themselves to investigate also because we do not want the privilege abused because we realize when they come up here you are going to talk about more restrictions when a small group of people abuse it.

So, I have issued instructions to the committeeman in the department to get the names and addresses of all the people who work in the department so whenever we want to investigate a case we take it upon ourselves to investigate that because we get a list of the people who are on leave of absence and if we find that there is no justification for it, which we have in some cases, they did not come back and were discharged and the union did not present their case. But, thirty days or sixty days you don't know. It does not cover it.

Kaufman: You got ninety to start with. What aggregate are you aiming at? You got ninety to start with and we suggested two extensions of thirty days each, and that is five months. You probably have one case in the history of the plant and you could take that up on a special basis. When you get into that sort of a situation that could be handled differently, but one hundred and twenty days is a tremendous lot of time.

A lot of contracts have thirty days for a leave absence. I understand, and we all appreciate that you have been working with us on this and the problem is a lot better than it ever was before, isn't it?

Novy: Very much so. We can take those up as a special case.

Here the union was assuming joint responsibility for the problem and management was giving the union credit for that cooperation. The parties agreed that no conceivable clause could cover every contingency, and they were willing to go along on a gentlemen's agreement as to how special cases would be handled.

The negotiators were finding it possible to find common ground on one issue after another, but, while the rate arbitration issue was deadlocked, there seemed little hope of reaching a settlement. Between the seventh and eighth meetings, Love got together with the local members of the negotiating committee to discuss this impasse. Love told them that he personally was determined, at all costs, to get an arbitration clause. On the other hand, maybe Jake Shafer didn't feel the same way. If he wanted to get an agreement without that clause and try to sell it to the membership, Love wouldn't stand in his way. But neither would he be a party to such an agreement. Rather than go along, he would withdraw from the negotiation committee.

The other members argued that Love should tell Shafer how he felt and what he planned to do. Love insisted that the information be kept from him. He had nothing against Shafer; in fact, he was developing a warm admiration for him. But he did not want to make a threat that would put pressure on Shafer. He told them that he would go along until he felt there was no hope of getting that crucial clause—and then he would do what he felt he had to do.

The eighth meeting, June 6, brought the parties right up against the deadlock. The argument was brief this time but sharp. There were no lengthy explanations or justifications of the positions taken —just short, flat statements. For example:

Shafer: . . . we won't go along with the agreement where new rates will be established where we say that they are not arbitrable. That we cannot do.
Kaufman: You have done it before. This is the same as it was in the old agreement.
Shafer: We are not going to do it now.
Kaufman: We are not going to change this one either.
Shafer: We are not going to go along with you on that.
Kaufman: We have been burned too often on these.

Shafer proposed a "diligent effort" clause so that, when a rate went to arbitration, if management could show that workers were not trying to get out production on the job, the arbitrator could throw out the case without passing on the rate. Management found no protection in this.

Here Shafer called a recess to consult with his committee. There was no question of giving in on this point. The real question was: Could the union benefit from any further discussions with management? Wasn't this the time to walk out of the meeting and touch off the strike? Love was ready for action. He saw no point in going on. Shafer was not optimistic, but he wanted to keep trying. He suggested that they pass over the arbitration issue and see if they could clear up all the other points of disagreement. If they could reach agreement on other issues, it would be worth while to come back to the arbitration issue for one more try.

Love agreed to go back in, but he felt that, unless management suddenly became much more conciliatory, further discussions would be a waste of time.

When Shafer announced that the union was adamant on its arbitration demand, management called a recess. Kaufman came back to announce that there would be no change in management's position and asked Shafer if they could go on with other clauses. Shafer agreed.

Without a pause, the parties then plunged right into another deadlock. This was on the safety-and-health clause. Management had set up a Safety Committee to meet twice a month to advise management on safety measures. The worker members of the committee were selected by management. The union was demanding that it choose those members.

The argument went this way:

Kaufman: Your point is that you want representation on the committee, is that right?

Shafer: Yes.

Kaufman: I think we pointed out that actually some of your people are on the committee.

Shafer: That is not what we call representation. We want to know who they are and we want to have some opportunity of selecting those people.

Kaufman: What do you mean you do not know who the people are? You don't know the Safety Committee, Lucius?

Love: I don't. I don't think anybody in the plant knows or not anybody, but a lot of people do not know them.

Kaufman: We have no objection to telling you who they are.

Shafer: We are just as interested in that as management, and we want participation.

Kaufman: What kind of participation?

Shafer: The naming of our people.

Kaufman: You want to name all of the people on it?

Shafer: The union committeemen.

Kaufman: They are all of the union people, aren't they?

Novy: Yes.

Shafer: Well, we want to be able to select them.

Hanes: Don't you have representatives on there by management?

Shafer: We cannot hold our people responsible under the setup now.

Kaufman: Who?

Shafer: The members of our organization because they are selected by management.

Kaufman: Why not?

Shafer: Because we cannot; because we don't participate.

Kaufman: I don't understand that frankly. I can see why if you had a situation where the company was picking people who were not union members on a safety committee, you might feel there was some discrimination being shown and you had no voice in it, but when we do not do that and the men picked from production and maintenance are union officers or members, I do not see how you can say you have not representation and participation.

Shafer: We want representation and participation. We cannot hold them responsible otherwise because they are selected by management.

Novy: What do you mean by responsibility?

Shafer: They should report to the union.

Novy: What do you mean by being responsible? Is there anything wrong with the program established now?

Love: What is the point of selecting people if they do not make a report at the regular meeting?

Novy: We have no objection to their making a report. They come to the company meeting and they make a report.

Shafer: I hope we are not insulting anyone's intelligence.

Kaufman: What sort of a report?

Love: What good is it for the committee to talk over the unsafe problems

unless he is going to convey it to the membership and report at
the regular meeting what is necessary. We do not have any voice
in this thing now and we don't know who they are.

Love was satisfied now that it was useless to go on. He got to
his feet. Shafer stood up also.

The management people saw the negotiations on the point of
breaking up. Caples got to his feet. He took a deep breath and began
talking to Shafer. He wasn't prepared to yield the point, least of
all under such obvious pressure, but he cast about for a possible
adjustment.

Caples suggested that management furnish the union the names
of worker representatives on the Safety Committee and also the
minutes of each committee meeting.

Shafer asked what would happen if the union felt that one of the
worker representatives was not doing a good job. Caples passed the
question to Novy, who said that management would weigh the
charges carefully and make a change, if good evidence were
presented.

Kaufman asked if the union felt it was not getting consideration
on safety matters. Novy pointed out that Love had brought some
matters up to Personnel Manager Kluck and had got action on them.
Love argued that such matters should not be handled on an individual basis. The union should have representation and responsibility.

Shafer said that, if the union had representation, the committee
members could report at regular union meetings. Caples suggested
that the worker representatives could well report at union meetings,
as matters then stood, and management would arm them with copies
of the minutes of Safety Committee meetings.

Shafer said, "What are we arguing about then?"

Shafer sat down. Caples sat down. Love was left standing alone.
Shafer phrased the agreement in this way:

"Our understanding is from here on out these people will be
requested to make a report to the local union, and they will be
armed with the minutes of the previous meeting. What is to prevent
them from accepting suggestions at that time."

Kaufman said, "We will be glad to have them."

Love hesitated a moment longer. Then he too sat down. The immediate crisis had passed—although there was still no agreement in sight.

Shafer was by no means satisfied by the outcome on this issue. The union had wanted representation, and the union had not achieved it. Still, the union had got itself in a position to exert more influence on the safety program. Furthermore, since the safety record was good, as it stood, the issue was hardly worth a strike. In fact, Shafer had said, right in the middle of the argument: "For your record, we feel that the record so far as your safety setup, it is magnificent, and you are to be congratulated."

The parties moved on to less controversial issues, and the temperature of the meeting went down.

Toward the end of the session management made its general wage offer: 12 cents across the board plus ½ cent to be allocated to clearing up inequities in the Maintenance Department.

Shafer asked how the increase would affect the incentive system. Gossett replied that the increase would be added on top of the incentive and would not cut the incentive—as it had in the 1942 contract. He went on to give a full explanation as to how the increase would be applied. When he had finished, Shafer nodded and said, "That's it." Gossett felt that it was at this point that Shafer began to feel he could trust him. Shafer agrees that the incident did make a favorable impression. But it was not the money, he says. That was never directly a problem in the negotiations. Rather it was the frank and open way in which Gossett stated the case. At least, they would not be tricked into an agreement.

In the ninth meeting (June 9), the union accepted management's wage offer after only a brief discussion period. The negotiators were satisfied that this fitted in well with the pattern then developing in steel fabricating.

Now there were few issues still unsettled, and the parties were faced again with the arbitration issue. Shafer proposed that the no-strike clause be amended to leave open the possibility of a strike on a rate case. This was unacceptable to management.

Shafer noted that they had reached a deadlock and would have to take the issue to the people. He said that he would present the progress they had achieved in some detail and then would outline the disagreement on this final point. The committee would also recommend that the membership reject the contract on this point, and he was confident that their judgement would be sustained by the rank and file.

Following a luncheon recess, the negotiators reviewed the whole contract and found themselves on agreement on every other point. Then, in spite of the fact that both sides were expecting a strike, a remarkable interchange took place. It began with Shafer's assuring management, in this way, of the union's determination to discharge its responsibilities:

Shafer: . . . By the same virtue we are making an agreement here in good faith and what has been said or what has transpired in the past we are going to live up to and I for one have to be the representative who will be servicing this particular local Union, and I can assure you, and you can incorporate that in the record, that any time a situation like that comes up I will be available. It would not be the first time I did that, not with your company, but with other companies. Right is right and wrong is wrong. Labor in assuming it is in a correct position and in assuming the proper attitude, certainly cannot condone any ancient history, but it has been our experience that as long as we have situations as have existed that leave a foul taste, not only in the mouths of management, but in the mouths of labor as well, as long as we hold that in the picture, it certainly does not heal any breach.

I also feel that our action in spite of the fact that we did not consummate an agreement, certainly that should have indicated to management that we are sincere and we have gone along. The local union has been charged with this responsibility and the officers of the local union have assumed their responsibility and in their last meeting the executive officers of the local were virtually taking the hides off some of the people. They were assuming the position of supporting management.

I believe that the record in itself will indicate that and not only that, we intend to improve on it. You may have had some lip service in the past, but you will get some actual service, now Mr. Kaufman, and you will continue to get it. That is not only the understanding between the local executive committee and myself, but it is my understanding with other people in our International Union.

If I happened to get banged by an automobile this afternoon or tomorrow, then my successor in this particular picture will take over with that understanding because there will be a book of rules and here is what we agree to and here is what it means, and here is what we are going to do.

Of course, if that precedent has not been set up before, that is no responsibility of mine and you certainly can't condemn the international union for that.

Kaufman: We don't.

Shafer: We have had many situations as Mr. Caples knows very well, on wildcats and what have you that happened and as we grow older and we live with each other longer we can exercise more control than we have exercised in the past. Of course, the history in the organization itself will explain some of the reasons why occasionally fragments have gotten out of line, but now we are more coordinated than ever before and with a two year agreement our position, so far as the Union is concerned, is much better so far as coordinating is concerned.

I will be quite frank with you; I feel that management and the union have been quite frank in our deliberations and throughout all of the negotiations they have been fine. The Union feels there have been no cards dealt under the table and we respect management's representation for that to the highest degree, but on this question we must do something about it. We feel that in view of the action and the things that we have done, we hope to indicate to management that we are sincere and we are going to assume our responsibility.

We can see the justification of management being somewhat skeptical, but if we are going to live in the past, then certainly, we are not going to get along too well.

Kaufman: Do you want to take one more crack at the prohibition to see if we can wipe that out?

Shafer: I am interested in the main issue which is the arbitration clause. Let us stay on that.

Gossett: Do you have an idea?

Love: I was going to say something.

Shafer: I am hoping we can reach an agreement.

Gossett: Certainly we want to reach an agreement. I think that everything you said is true. We can sit here with pride and believe that we have done our part on this thing in an upright and forward manner.

Shafer: That still stands regardless of whether we consummate an agreement here today or not. That is for the record.

Caples: What we want is very obvious. We want not promises, but a
  year or two of action.
Shafer: You are getting it already.
Caples: I would say this: I think our relationships out here have improved and I don't know if that is the union's feeling, but it is
  management's feeling, but we still do have problems.
Shafer: That is understandable.

Here was a group of men, deadlocked, facing a strike and yet able
to express the firm respect for each other that they had built out of
the hard but cleanly fought negotiations.

There was no formula for settlement yet in sight, but perhaps
they had already won something more important than a formula.
They had created an atmosphere favorable to settlement. Both sides
were willing to stand a strike on the one remaining issue, and yet
they were determined to do everything possible to seek a way out
of the deadlock. In fact, Shafer commented, "This is the most
peculiar deadlock I've ever seen."

Following this session, Shafer went over the situation at length
with his subdistrict director, Oakley Mills, District Director Joseph
Germano, and with the general counsel of the CIO. They were
surprised and pleased to hear of the progress that had been made,
and the CIO counsel urged Shafer to settle with management even
without rate arbitration. He argued that management could not be
expected to yield on that point; the union should stand pat on the
gains it had already achieved and not risk a strike only a year after
the 191-day strike.

Shafer was adamant: no rate arbitration, no contract. He insisted
that he would stand on that platform before the membership
meeting. The argument went on, but Mills and Germano backed
Shafer. If the members were prepared to strike on that issue, they
would have the backing of the international.

Shafer found the membership meeting unexpectedly stormy. The
big trouble came from a leak of information.

Management had agreed with the union to keep the progress of
negotiations strictly secret—except that the foremen were to be kept
informed. Now, several days before the union meeting at which the
first open discussion of progress was to take place, the foreman of the
Maintenance Department let some of his men see the inequity rate

adjustments that were tentatively agreed upon for certain classifications in his department.

To appreciate the seriousness of this leak we have to look at the relations between production workers and maintenance workers within the union. In many unions there tends to be a cleavage between maintenance and production workers. This is especially likely to be true when the production workers are on incentive and the maintenance men, who consider themselves the most highly skilled people in the plant, find they are not earning as much as the semiskilled incentive workers.

That was the case in this plant. The maintenance workers had been clamoring for "inequity adjustments" and, between the fourth and fifth negotiation meetings, a three-man delegation called on Gossett. He met them in his office, with Caples. As soon as Gossett and Caples discovered that the men wanted to discuss wages with management, they called in Lucius Love to sit with them. The session then came to an abrupt end.

The production workers all knew of this incident, and they felt that such irregular behavior should be rebuffed rather than rewarded. The production workers also considered themselves far more active in the union than the maintenance workers and were not sympathetic with special benefits in this direction. Furthermore, there were rumors at this time of a separate union coming into the Maintenance Department.

On the other hand, the new figures gave rise to as much resentment as satisfaction within the Maintenance Department. Some of the workers who were to get increases felt that those increases were still not enough to bring them in line with prevailing rates for those jobs in the industry. Certain workers had been receiving "red circle rates," several cents above the bargained rates, which had their origin years before in the old days of unsystematic management. The new management had been trying to eliminate these nonstandard rates, and they were to be finally wiped out in the inequity adjustments, which meant that workers on red-circle rates would not advance quite so much as those in the same job who had been on standard rates. Of course, those who had been in the favored position resented losing this advantage. Finally, there were classifications which management and the union agreed were in line with rates elsewhere and hence were entitled to no inequity adjustment. Naturally the people who were thus passed over could not be expected to be happy about it.

As anyone with experience in labor relations well knows, inequity adjustments are touchy problems at best. In the membership meeting, the committee had planned only to mention the 12-cent general increase and the ½-cent inequity figure, without giving any particulars as to who was going to get what. The excuse for this reticence would be that the inequity matter was still wide open for negotiation —and indeed several changes were agreed upon later. The political reason for this action was compelling. A committee that has to sell a contract clause by clause is in a disadvantageous position. No matter who writes the contract, there will always be particular clauses that seem to work a hardship upon certain individuals or groups. If such a clause is debated out of context with the whole contract, those who feel particularly aggrieved may be able to rally considerable support to their position.

Since the inequity adjustments were the most delicate problem from the standpoint of internal union politics, Shafer and his committee had been determined not to present any detailed figures until they were ready to sell the contract as a whole. The leak of information then knocked the ground out from under them. The subject was hotly debated in the meeting, and the committee had a rough time of it for a few minutes. However, the issue was so complex that emotions exploded in all directions, and only a part of the general resentment was directed against the committee. Furthermore, this was counterbalanced by the general recognition that the committee had already won substantial benefits in other parts of the contract.

The members applauded this progress and the tension eased. But, when Shafer described the deadlock on the arbitration issue and gave his advice, there was no more good feeling. Several rank-and-file members got up to say vehemently that this was the key to the whole contract, and the union could not accept management's terms here. The people voted unanimously to strike unless management gave in on this point. The touchy nature of this issue, together with the leak, combined to make this a militant meeting. Emotions were at a high pitch. The strike committees were ready to act. If the next negotiation meeting ended in a deadlock, the workers would follow their negotiators right out of the plant.

The management men fully realized that a strike was imminent. But they were taken completely by surprise when the union negotiators came in to chastise management for the leak. This was the first the management negotiators had heard of it. Perhaps that was just as well, for, while the union men gave vent to their outraged feelings, it became obvious that the management people had known nothing of the leak and were as distressed by it as were the union men.

The management men offered no defense for the apparent breach of trust except that Gossett reported he had given strict orders to the foremen that nothing should be revealed to the workers. The immediate damage could not be repaired, but Gossett offered the apologies of management and gave assurances that firm steps would be taken to avoid any future leaks.

When management accepted the union's charges without argument, the anger of the union men dissipated itself. But the situation was still hardly propitious for the launching of the crucial tenth meeting.

At the start of the meeting Shafer proposed that they might seek a way out of the deadlock through applying some part of the basic steel agreement. Caples began shaking his head as soon as Shafer began stating his point. The argument then began again but this time with a difference. There were two aspects of the rate question: (1) the setting of rates on new jobs and (2) changes in rates due to changes in pre-existing jobs. Management was assuming that the union was primarily concerned with rate setting on new jobs, whereas the union negotiators actually were most keenly interested in the question of rate changes. Suddenly this point came out in the discussion, and things began to move. It happened this way:

Shafer: There isn't any question in my mind that management's position isn't substantiated.

Gossett: We are not changing any past practice.

Shafer: I talked to our people about it—it's a question of reduction of rates. I can see and respect management's statements, certainly there will have to be a curtailment some place. I feel that Mr. Novy will verify that we made certain commit-, not commitments, that we were going to do when these negotiations started. This Committee did an excellent job and it makes one feel pretty good when the Committee and officers got up and told the people there are certain responsibilities that they will have to assume. Here you have had a problem, prior to the present time, and to the best of my knowledge, it's still a problem. What are we going to say about now existing rates?

Caples: Of course, that isn't the question. Your question is on the new rates. The fact is that we have not cut rates as John said, we have no intent to cut rates.

Kaufman: I think you have a clause that covers it. Section 13 of Article VII.

"It is agreed where labor of employees is materially increased or decreased by change in operating or manufacturing methods, equipment or materials, consideration shall be given to an upward or downward adjustment in rate."

Hanes: Only you didn't have the "downward" in.

Kaufman: That's right, but the "downward" covers you. I don't think that the employees think that we are going out and cut them. That was one that we did agree on fairly promptly.

Caples: Remember we had a lot of discussion on the section in front of it.

Kaufman: You could revise Section 13 to use the words "job content." That's the section that binds both of us on it.

Caples: That's true, if there wasn't a change in that you could arbitrate that point under this contract. Not the rate itself, but whether or not you had your change in the operating conditions. Let's say that there has been a change in job content and your guys say there hasn't been a change, that's arbitrable.

Shafer: I don't agree with you because I feel that the arbitrator would say that the major issue in dispute are earnings in itself because it has its effect.

Caples: Let's assume that we go out and say we are going to cut this rate, that rate, etc., and you say on what basis, and we say change in job content and you know there hasn't been a change in job content. If there hasn't been, we can't move.

Shafer: You say it's arbitrable. If it is, let's say it in the agreement, if it is. I will go along with you on the job content.

Kaufman: I think it is arbitrable. I think I would say it was, but what you really ought to do is re-align Section 12 with Section 13 something like this:

"Where there are changes in parts, tools, special equipment, machinery or methods which result in increase or decrease of job content, consideration should be given to an upward or downward adjustment in rate."

Where a change in rate is made, where the Union questions if there has been a change in job content, that question should be arbitrable.

Shafer: This job content, we can be confronted with more grievances.

Kaufman: The point on it is that actually we work out better language in 12. I would be willing to use 13 but the language in 12 is better. I do think 12 is better than 13.

Caples: I can see the basis for that fear but I don't think it's well taken.

Shafer: I am not going to argue that.

(Mr. Kaufman began drafting the new section while the two parties discussed this new section among themselves.)

Shafer: If and when we consummate this agreement, I'd like to look at your operations.

Gossett: We would be pleased to have you. I think you ought to get in and look around.

Shafer: It helps your position quite a bit.

Gossett: I don't like the way you say, "if and when we consummate this agreement."

Shafer: No, I think we can do something soon.

At this point the tension was broken. While there were still adjustments to be made, it suddenly became clear that there would be no strike.

Shafer then brought up again the question of the leak and suggested that management reconsider its proposals regarding certain classifications in the Maintenance Department. Management agreed to study the situation.

A short time was spent in making minor adjustments in the contract to bring it in line with the Taft-Hartley Act, and then the parties agreed to establishing the new rates retroactive to a point six weeks after the expiration date of the old contract.

The negotiators approached the eleventh meeting, July 18, with somewhat different expectations. Management expected that the meeting would be a formality except for adjustment of several rates in the Maintenance Department. The union men thought they had an acceptable agreement, but they wanted to make doubly sure that the contract meant what they thought it did. Particularly on the rate question, their strategy was to get the management men to spell out their position in greater detail and to try to bring all of them into the discussion in hopes that one man might make a commitment beyond where his fellows were then prepared to go.

In the old contract, the guarantee of existing rates was implied but not explicitly stated. The section read:

It is agreed where labor of employees is materially increased by change in operating or manufacturing methods, consideration shall be given to an adjustment in rate for extra labor performed, or the Company shall add additional help to take care of the extra labor involved.

Earlier discussions had brought out that this clause did not cover cases in which the amount of labor was reduced, so the negotiators had covered this point by referring to changes in job content. Now, in the eleventh meeting, a new clause was tacked on to the start of the section guaranteeing existing rates. The final draft of the section then read as follows:

Rates in effect as to the date of the Agreement shall not be changed, except that where changes in parts, tools, special equipment, machinery or methods result in an increase or decrease in or of job content, consideration shall be given to an upward or downward adjustment in rate.

The clause on rate arbitration also underwent a change. The progression can most readily be followed in this manner:

old clause: The arbitration provisions . . . shall not apply to the determination of wages, wage rates or job classifications.

added 10th meeting: except that where a change in rate is based on a change in job content . . . the question whether job content was changed as provided therein may be subject to the arbitration provisions . . .

added 11th meeting: and if the arbitrator decides that job content was not so changed, the previous rate shall be retroactively reinstated.

There was just one more safeguard that the union sought. What would be management's standard in setting new rates? An example will show the cause for concern here. Let us say workers have been averaging 160 per cent on a certain job and that figure is in line with the general plant average for incentive earnings. Then management changes the job content and therefore has a right to change the rate. Does management seek to set a new rate on which the employees will continue to earn around 160 per cent? Or does management aim at a rate which will yield between 120 and 130 per cent, which some authorities consider adequate? If the latter practice were followed, management could, in effect, cut rates one after another until the whole rate structure of the plant was seriously reduced.

Management's position was brought out in this way:

Caples: . . . We don't contemplate any change in incentives except where changes occur in job content.

Love: On the new rate now. I asked a question this morning about the new rates, whether they are going to be set to something similar, to a similar job in that category. If you don't have something on them for insurance where the employee can point to some similar work, you are going to have a "beef."

Caples: Here's the thing on a new rate. If you are applying a uniform rating method, which is done here in this plant, unless there is some fault in the application of the method, your rate should come out similar. We realize as well as you do, you cannot pay two guys practically doing the same thing, you cannot pay them differently.

So the union got a statement of policy that new rates would be in line with old rates, and shortly after this Shafer offered to have the union pay to have the record of the last two meetings in order to have in writing commitments such as this, which were not spelled out in the contract. (These last two meetings were transcribed by Novy's secretary at no additional expense to the company, and Gossett offered the copies free to the union.)

The negotiators spent some time discussing interpretations to various clauses in the contract and then settled the Maintenance Department rates on the basis of additional increases in certain classifications. These management offered in order to make good the damage in the union's internal political situation that had been caused by the leak.

The membership meeting then ratified the contract without question.

Chapter 8

Consolidating the Gains
at the Top

A WRITTEN CONTRACT is not an end in itself. The meaning of the contract can be determined only through the actions of the parties.

The management negotiators came out of the bargaining sessions greatly cheered. After the contract signing, their only reservation was: This seems too good to be true. For the first time they saw a real, solid chance of working out their problems with the union. Still, they felt that other union negotiators had expressed interest in management's problems while they were trying to get a good contract out of management and then had not followed through after negotiations. Would Shafer be different?

The union members greeted the new contract with real enthusiasm. It looked so good to them, and they were so relieved to have avoided a strike, that Shafer was actually able to stand up before the meeting and tell them that they could trust John Gossett. Gossett had been the most hated symbol of management, but he was also the chief symbol of management. Shafer saw no possibility of selling the whole management group at once, but he was willing to make a beginning on the key man.

Shafer had promised in negotiations that, upon the signing of the contract, he and his committee would go right to work liquidating the problems still outstanding. In the three weeks following the signing, management was already beginning to see improvements, but it took Shafer's first grievance meeting to crystallize the new relationship.

Shafer announced that he wanted to try to clear away the backlog of fourth-step grievances. He mentioned also that he had one problem that was not a grievance. Counsel Kaufman suggested that they air the problem first, and there followed a general discussion of the Barrel Department situation. Shafer called on Love to tell the story, and he began in this way:

First, I don't like the thing, I don't like it at all. Right after the contract was signed, in keeping with our promise, we talked to the people to see that any bad feeling that existed be eliminated from their mind. I think we did a pretty good job of satisfying the people, in the Barrel Department in particular.

He then went on to detail an accumulation of small irritations that was running down the morale of the department. It all happened while Foreman Snyder was away on his vacation. Production was moving up nicely:

The contract was signed and the people felt good. There was enough help, and we could keep production going . . . Also, we did have a break on the orders [long runs on the same type of barrel]. I don't think anyone can take all the credit for producing those barrels in that period of time.

Love went on to say, "The thing that disturbed me most was the appreciation that was given for that production." He said that no one had given the men credit for doing a good job; on the contrary, several of them had received a written reprimand. At noon one day there were more than enough men on the job in the Barrel Department, and the extra men were asked to go to work in another department. They elected to go home instead. In the past they had always been free to exercise this option, but this time they drew the reprimand.

Then the group leaders and setup men and Love had been missing out on their regular 15-minute relief periods. If one of the lines happened to go down when their period was coming up, they were asked to stay on the line to get it back in operation. One group leader, he claimed, had not had a relief period in two weeks.

Finally, the nurse had been down to talk to the men, and she talked for 20 minutes—while they were all checked in on piecework instead of being checked out to get their regular hourly rates.

The real problem, Love said, was that the men felt some people were trying to take advantage of them in order to make a record for themselves. Those suspicions would have to be cleared up.

Gossett and Novy said they had not been aware of any of these problems and would see to them at once. Novy scheduled for the following day a meeting of Love, Production Supervisor Short, and himself.

After expressing his satisfaction with recent developments, Shafer went on to tackle the production problem:

> We feel now that we have the cooperation with top management, that we are in a position that we can help eliminate the stumbling blocks that we have had in the past. When I told you we are interested in production, that we are. Our full intent and purpose is to make this *THE* plant, and along with that it's going to require some close harmony. Not being too familiar with the incentives in this department, I raised several questions. Our people are going to increase their earnings as time goes on with production. We hope that there will not be any impeding of our earnings.

Gossett and Kaufman explained that this was a straight-line incentive: it paid the same amount per barrel, no matter how many barrels were produced. There was no such thing as a reduction in price beyond a given production point.

The union officers expressed their satisfaction with this explanation. In fact, Love added, "I have no complaint. That's something I couldn't say a year ago."

Shafer then brought in a new subject, and the discussion went along in this way:

> Shafer: . . . I am wondering whether or not management would be willing to accept suggestions on the part of the people. It may be suggestions that will be a time saving factor, and the steward on the job can get these from his people.

Novy: We will also pay them an incentive for it.

Shafer: It certainly isn't going to affect the present system because it's a new line.

Gossett: We had a suggestion system here. It was inaugurated just prior to the time Bob [Novy] and I came to Chicago, and it continued for the remainder of that year. But the usual suggestions that came out of the box were obscene notes and so on. Now if there's some desire for a suggestion award system, we will be glad to discuss and arrange a program for that.

Shafer: We don't want any award system or suggestion box. Here's where we can save a little time. Certainly Lucius should be in a position to call it to his foreman's or immediate supervisor's attention.

Gossett: If there's a sincere effort made in that direction, it will be conducted.

Shafer: We don't want any awards on it.

Gossett: We are certainly wide open to that.

Short: I might add to that, that Lucius has given us some suggestions on the barrel line that we have followed.

Gossett: Bob will issue written instructions along that line so it will not cause confusion.

They then turned to a discussion of production on the side line in the Barrel Department. Up to this time no new rates had been set for the side line, which operated infrequently. While they worked on that line, the men were paid on the basis of the average they had received before the 1946 strike. Love argued that production was now higher than that, and yet the ruling meant that, when the men moved over from the main or auxiliary lines, they had to take a cut in earnings. He asked management to set a higher bonus figure on the side line, in view of this increased production.

The discussion went along this way:

Gossett: . . . you just recently started to pick up production on the side line. What assurance would you offer that production will compare relatively to the Main and Aux. lines after we consider your suggestion? They won't look on the side line as a day of rest?

Love: I don't know what we could offer except that we have worked just as hard. There hasn't been any slowdown. I don't know what we could give you to guarantee that it will continue.

Gossett: You can't give me anything in writing.

Shafer: The only thing that we can say is that in the event that situation
   does bog down, they will have to go back to the old system.
Love: I can assure you that it won't.
Gossett: That's enough for me.

Note that last remark: here the union leader was giving his word
on an important problem, and the executive said, simply and without hesitation, "That's enough for me." Those words are a fitting
measure of the tremendous strides they had taken toward liquidating
the heritage of hatred and distrust.

Having worked through these problems, the men now turned to
the grievances. Here again the progress was remarkable. There
were 22 grievances on the agenda—enough to occupy several long
meetings in earlier years. This time they were disposed of in little
more than an hour.

Some were dropped, since they were covered in contract negotiations. On some, management made changes. On some, both sides
made adjustments. And some were dropped by the union. Shafer had
no hesitation in dropping a grievance at this point when discussion
with management convinced him that the union had no case.

The celebrated air-hose case reached its final settlement here. Novy
reviewed the figures. The job, he explained, came up infrequently.
Management had records of running the job only twice in 1945,
before the new rate, and three times in 1946, and five times in 1947.
The average earnings on the job were 86 cents in 1945 and (not
counting straight-time pay increases) $1.19 in 1946 and $1.20 in 1947
—an increase of 33 to 34 cents per hour.

Rose said that if he could see the earnings records in the Time
Study Department he would withdraw the grievance. Shafer added,
"That's for sure, it will be withdrawn."

So the case was cleared, with ridiculous ease. In two minutes
these men disposed of an argument that had geen going on for over
a year. Why did the hard problem suddenly become so easy? Was it
the introduction of the earnings figures that made the difference?
No. They had been aired in earlier stages of the grievance procedure,
but they had made no difference then.

We can understand this case only if we view it *symbolically*.
Before the adjustment of relationships, the air hose had been one

of the key symbols of the conflict. For the workers and union leaders the case had symbolized the hatred and distrust they bore toward management. It was evidence to them that management was unfair and ruthless. So long as they continued to believe that management was unfair and ruthless the case could have no other meaning to them, no matter what logical arguments were brought against them. But as soon as relations were reorganized so that the hatred and distrust were beginning to be dissipated there was no longer an emotional need to hold onto that symbol of conflict. It then became possible to treat the case in terms of facts and figures, and by that time it was hardly worth bothering about.

Having provided a firm foundation upon which to build up production, the parties, in their next meeting, worked out a plan to cut down on absenteeism and tardiness. Management considered these fairly serious problems at the time. This was also a matter of direct concern to the union, since the absentees and latecomers slowed down production and cut the earnings of workers on incentive.

It was agreed that the Personnel Department would take out the time cards of those employees who were late or absent on a given day and substitute red cards, which indicated that the employee would have to go into the Personnel Office to get his time card. If the man had a plausible excuse, he was allowed to punch his card without a reprimand. If the excuse did not sound plausible, the personnel manager was authorized, subject to a union review committee, to put a reprimand on the man's personnel record.

In the old days a union committee could never have agreed with management on discipline—and was never given the chance. But now Gossett reports that it was surprising how often the union committee agreed with management that the man had no good excuse. In only a few cases were there disagreements, and here no reprimands were issued.

In the first eighteen months of operation under this system only one worker was suspended (for a week) for absenteeism or lateness and no one was discharged. The record improved substantially, and there was no need for penalties.

Now there was no longer any question as to what was happening. These top-level relations were further cemented by a case which came up on the receiving platform. The steel used by the plant is shipped over from the Indiana Harbor Steel Works in trucks. Sometimes a truck may arrive so late that there is not time to unload it before the second shift quitting time at 1:00 A.M. In some cases, to finish unloading the truck might involve only 5 or 10 minutes overtime work, but, if the men are not willing to stay, the work of unloading the truck cannot even be begun and the truck must be sent back to the mill. This is costly and inconvenient for management. At that time the workers were refusing to take any overtime and management was unable to persuade them to do so.

Gossett and Novy took stock of their position. As they interpreted their contract and various arbitrators' decisions, they were convinced that management had a legal right to *compel* the working of overtime in such situations. In other words, they could discipline or even discharge a man for refusing to work overtime. In earlier years they might have met the problem in that way—but not now.

They called on Shafer and asked his help. They explained that they tried to avoid overtime, but it was not always possible. The plant was then hard pressed to get enough steel on hand to keep up with its production. A truck sent back to the mill might shut down a department, with losses to management and workers as well.

Shafer promised action. He took up the problem with Vice-President Don Hanes (Love being out of the plant on a leave of absence at the time). Shafer advised Hanes to call a meeting of the second shift in the Receiving Department and present the case to them. If they then felt that management was taking advantage of them, they were to lodge a grievance, and the union would take it up with management. But meanwhile they should work overtime when asked.

Hanes followed through. The unloading went on without interruption. And no grievance came out of the case.

Gossett and Novy had no idea how Shafer had solved the problem, but that made no difference. They had called on him, and he had come through. They were more than ever convinced now that they could work together.

The handling of management's retirement plan also strengthened the relationship. Management had worked out a retirement plan involving contributions both from management and from the workers. Management was convinced that this benefit plan was one of the most liberal in effect in industry. Management not only made more than matching contributions but established past service credit so that workers of over ten years' service began just as if they had already been contributing for ten years. The plan was to be put in effect if 75 per cent of the workers agreed to the necessary payroll deductions. The union officers went over the plan in 1946 and recommended that the workers not accept it.

Following the 1947 negotiations, Shafer looked into the plan himself and became convinced that it could be valuable to the workers. He persuaded management to reoffer the plan. He not only persuaded the union members to accept it, but put through a resolution commending management for its generosity in this matter.

A benefit plan is likely to have little influence upon worker attitudes unless it is dramatized in some way which puts it on a personal basis. This happened quite naturally in this case when the union took up the problem of Nellie Sharpe, a long-service woman worker who was troubled with arthritis. It had become apparent that she was no longer able to do her regular job, and her health was so bad that there would hardly be another job in the plant she could do effectively. The woman was going to quit, but friends were trying to have her fired instead, so that she would be eligible for unemployment compensation. The union committee asked to discuss the case with management. Gossett checked the personnel records and found out that Mrs. Sharpe had only a few months to go before she would have completed twenty years' service and be eligible for a retirement check. Gossett said he did not think it was right to fire an employee who had served the company loyally and conscientiously for such a length of time. She would be taken off her regular job but management would keep her on the payroll and find something that she could do. It did not matter if the work was of little material value to management. Management should not seek to sidestep its responsibilities in such a case.

This proposal was happily received by the union officers and by Mrs. Sharpe. When the 20-year period was completed, there was a little ceremony in the office of the vice-president and general manager. While Love, Shafer, and Novy looked on, Gossett presented the worker with her retirement check. The worker who had contributed nothing to the fund now received slightly over $1,000, all from management's past service credit. The presentation ceremony was photographed, and the picture appeared in the official publication of the United Steelworkers. Such favorable notice for management in a union publication would have been undreamed of only a few months earlier.

After presenting the check, Gossett said to Mrs. Sharpe that she would always be welcome in the plant and he would be glad to have her come back to see her old friends. He asked her if there was anything else he could do for her. She then said that she would like to say good-bye to her friends and have one more walk through the plant. So the retiring worker walked through the plant with her daughter, saying good-bye to all her old friends. It was a touching ceremonial, and it made a strong impression upon the workers. Their picture of the ruthless, autocratic management was fading fast.

In late 1948 management extended still further the scope of discussions with the union. Management's engineers had been developing new machines and processes that would considerably increase the productivity of the production lines. These changes were thought to be at least two years away, but when they came in they would involve a major reorganization of jobs and relationships.

Gossett described management's plans fully and frankly with the union committee. He also tried to anticipate how the technological changes would affect the employment situation. Fewer people would be required on the production lines, he said, but more would be needed in the Punch Press Department, stamping out parts for the increased production, and more would be needed in the handling of raw materials and finished products. The union people expressed the hope that the impact of the changes could be cushioned by transferring surplus workers from production lines into other departments. Management gave assurances that everything possible would be done to effect the changes with a minimum of hardship to the workers.

No detailed plans were made at this time. The change was still too far away for that. But the union people were taken on the inside of management's planning. They felt now that on major changes they would always know the score, and they would be able to combat the fear of the unknown among their members.

In early 1949 the relationship met its first test in facing economic adversity. As customers reduced their inventories, orders fell off drastically in certain departments. Management first curtailed hours of work so as to keep on the existing working force. Later, in consultation with the union, management returned to the 40-hour week with the layoff of some workers. When a new cutback was required, Gossett called in the union committee and offered two alternative courses of action: a continued 40-hour week with a further layoff or a 30-hour week in the affected departments, maintaining the existing force. Shafer and his committee chose the 30-hour week. And that was that.

Since this plant produces for four industries, each of which has a different seasonal peak, employment over the years has been unusually secure and steady. Crises of this nature may seldom occur, yet, when they do, it is significant to observe how management acts to meet them.

According to the contract, management was not required to consult the union either on technological changes or on layoffs. Nor does management intend that such problems shall become matters of joint determination. Nevertheless, management, while retaining the initiative in these areas, now carries out its plans in a close consulting and cooperative relationship with the union. Gone are the days when each new management move caught the union by surprise and prompted a fighting response.

Chapter 9

A New Pattern of Relations

*F*OLLOWING THE 1947 negotiations, the top-level understand-ing grew steadily more solid and far reaching. Could that understanding be carried down through the ranks in both organiza-tions? The handling of problems arising in the months after the 1947 settlement would give the answer to that question.

The major problems of interpreting the contract involved incentive rates. The union officers came out of the negotiations convinced that top management did not intend to indulge in rate cutting. However, they felt no such assurance regarding the Time Study Department, which was charged with the function of establishing rates. They looked upon Mr. Peterson, the chief of the department, with sus-picion and pointed out that he had held the same position in the days of family ownership. How significant his connection with the old days was, in making his reputation, it is difficult to say, since the attitude toward him is quite typical of that felt generally by workers and union officers toward time-study officials. In other words, this seems to be more a question of position and function than one of personality characteristics. The union people were also suspicious of Peterson's young assistants. The theory was that these men were ambitious to get ahead in management and sought to draw themselves to the attention of higher-ups by tightening up rates and thereby cutting costs.

The union's suspicions of the Time Study Department were particularly aroused by an event which took place in the fall of 1947. For each job that is on an incentive rate there is a card giving the rate and also the job description. These cards had formerly been available within the department so that a worker could check the cards at any time. They were suddenly all called in to the Time Study Department. The workers could no longer check them freely and when grievances arose and the steward or grievance committeeman saw the card in the Time Study Department he observed that in some cases penciled notations had been added to what had been previously on the card. Actually the cards were called in by management simply in order to effect a change in the cost-accounting system. The union was not informed of the purpose of the move and, therefore, it was natural for the union officers to suspect the worst: that the time-study men, with the cards now in their hands, would be able to effect rate changes which it would be difficult for the union to block.

The union people felt that they must be constantly on guard against the Time Study Department. For them the chief test of the value of the new contract would come in this field. If they felt the contract helped them to protect themselves against time study, it was a good contract; otherwise, not.

The first major case under this contract arose in the Steel Storage Department in February, 1948. The immediate issue seemed trivial and yet the case had wide implications that made it important to both sides.

This was not a time-study case, pure and simple. It also involved in important respects the relations between Mr. Clark, the foreman, Mr. Mason, the union steward, and the workers of that department. This was the department whose rates had been set by Craig simply on the basis of past performance. The job duties depended upon customary practices and upon the interpretations of those practices by the people immediately involved in the situation. Here management was at a serious disadvantage. The department contained many long-service employees who could cite years of historical precedents for any position they took. The foreman, on the other hand, was new in the department, having been transferred only a few months earlier from another department.

The workers had not yet decided how they were going to get along with this new foreman. They were, therefore, inclined to be somewhat technical in their dealings with him. This is a common situation in industry. If the workers like and respect the man they are working for, they will put out additional effort not strictly called for by written agreement as a favor to him. If they do not like the foreman or have not made up their minds about him, they are inclined to become technical and push for a strict interpretation of the contract.

The job at issue, in this case, involved lifting strips of steel up onto an edger (a machine that shears off the edges) preparatory to trucking them through the plant. This particular job came up perhaps once or twice a month and took not more than five minutes each time. Such a job could, therefore, not be important by itself but only in what it represented to the people in the case.

What actually happened here is impossible to determine. The accounts of the foreman and the steward differ on certain points but they at least give a general idea of what took place.

According to the foreman, the worker in question had done this particular job several times without protest, but seemed to be especially touchy on this occasion and lodged a grievance claiming that the job was not included in his rate. Clark then conferred with Mason, the steward for the department. In Mason's presence he telephoned to Peterson, chief of time study, to ask whether the job in question was included in the rate. The two men had a long conversation on the subject, but Clark felt that he didn't get any clear answer and hung up with the issue still unsettled in his mind. Later Clark said he called Short, general production supervisor, and got word from Short that the job was included in the rate. Short had no recollection of the conversation. When Clark was called up to explain his position before Gossett and Novy, he felt that he was charged with misstating Time Study's position on the issue. Gossett suggested that Clark needed to take some action to establish worker and union confidence in him. While Gossett felt he had gone easy on the foreman, Clark felt he had received a severe going-over by top management, which suggested to him that it would be wiser to seek to handle problems of this nature between himself and the steward. Clark felt better about the case when he observed

that Mason also seemed unhappy. Mason reported that he too had
been worked over, in this case by the top union officers, for his
conduct of the case. Clark then asked Mason whether he had the
confidence of the workers in the department, saying that he would
not continue as foreman unless he had that confidence. From
Mason's reply he felt satisfied that the workers did have confidence
in him and he was encouraged to believe that they would be able to
work out their problems better in the future.

According to the steward's report, Mason had done this particular
job for the foreman several times on the understanding that it was
simply a favor and was not required of him. Then one time Clark
ordered him to do the job and Mason stipulated that he would only
do it as a favor. Clark determined then that he must find out what
was actually required and put in his telephone call to Peterson.
Mason heard only one end of the conversation, but reports that when
the call was concluded Clark said that Mason had been right; the
job was not included in the rate, but would he therefore please do it
as a favor. Sometime later Clark again ordered Mason to do the
job and backed up the order with the observation that, since he had
been doing it before, it was part of his regular duties. When Mason
threatened to lodge a grievance, Clark said that he would clear up
the situation by getting a time-study man to restudy the job. The
time-study man was not immediately available, however, and Clark
did not want to wait. He reported shortly thereafter that he had
checked again with Peterson, who told him that the job was included
in the rate. Mason now followed orders under protest and lodged
a grievance.

The second- and third-step grievance decisions upheld the foreman's position that the job was included in the rate. The fourth-step
grievance meeting was more important for the way it was conducted than for the decision that came out of it. The union was
represented in this grievance meeting by Shafer and Love, Hanes,
the vice-president, Rose, the grievance committeeman for the first
floor, and Gary, the grievance committeeman for the second floor.
Management was represented by Gossett and Novy, and Kluck,
personnel manager, and Short, general production supervisor.

The first discussion period on the grievance seemed to get nowhere. Peterson brought in figures to substantiate management's

position, but the course of the discussion led Shafer to believe that
neither union nor management people had the information they
needed to know what was behind the grievance. He asked management's permission to declare a recess. The union representatives
then withdrew for approximately two hours. The union committee called in Mason to go over the case once again. The committee
members could not at first understand why so much fuss was being
raised over a job that required a trifling physical effort, and consumed perhaps ten minutes a month. Rose and Hanes did not at
first think that Mason really had a grievance and were ready to
drop the matter. Shafer and Love also were skeptical about Mason's
position but they encouraged him to talk the case over at great
length. Finally, Mason reviewed the part of his story in which the
foreman had first said that the job was included in the rate and
then had said that he was going to get a time-study man in to set
a rate. Mason argued that this was inconsistent. If the job had
actually been included in the rate there would be no reason to have
a time-study man make a study. The fact that the foreman called
for the time-study man indicated that the job was not included in
the rate. This convinced Shafer that the steward had a case. Mason
also objected to the way in which the order was given.

Shafer then asked a question: "Suppose the foreman asked you to
do the job to help him out? You wouldn't refuse him then, would
you?"

Mason replied, "Then I'd be only too glad to do it for him."

That satisfied Shafer. He asked the steward to wait in the hall
as the committee went back to meet with management. He then
asked and received management's permission to have the steward
brought into the fourth-step meeting. A steward had never before
been allowed in such a meeting. Mason was invited to tell his story
as he had told it to the union officers, and he emphasized the point
that had been convincing to Shafer.

When Mason finished, Shafer asked again, "Suppose the foreman
would ask you voluntarily to do that job to help him out. What
would your answer be?"

Mason answered, "Then I'd be only too glad to do it for him."

Shafer argued that this put the case in a broader perspective. It
indicated that the workers were simply afraid that a little would be

added here and there to their jobs and, while no particular addition would make any difference, if the process were allowed to continue it would, in effect, mean a cutting of the rates. The union needed reassurance on this point. The particular job was not important in itself.

Furnished with this background of the case, management was now ready to settle in a manner entirely satisfactory to the union. It was agreed that the duties in dispute should be considered as included in the rates. However, management added the following statement to the grievance settlement: "We wish to assure all personnel that we will not knowingly add any duties unless duly compensated for in the present existing practices in that department."

In a formal sense, then, the union lost the grievance, but the union people felt reassured by the full and sympathetic hearing they had received.

The steward felt elated at this settlement and was especially pleased at the opportunity he had had to put the case directly to top management. Still, he chose to kid the foreman along by putting on a gloomy expression and reporting that he had had a severe going-over from the union committee. Then when the foreman had had his session with management, he was able to feel that he and the steward were in the same boat. To the foreman's request for an expression of confidence from the workers, the steward made no direct answer. He reported later that the men were willing to expect the best from the foreman now and give him a chance to make good. In fact, relations between foreman and workers and union steward seemed to improve considerably following the settlement of this grievance. From this point on, the foreman was careful to consult with the steward on proposed changes and other important matters of concern to them both. This outcome, therefore, was satisfactory to both union and management at both levels.

The case is particularly noteworthy in the contrast it affords to the earlier way of doing things. If union and management had sought to handle this problem in the formal and legalistic manner that had prevailed only a short time earlier, it would never have been possible to determine the nature of the problem, let alone solve it. It was only when both parties became willing to take any necessary steps toward solving practical problems that they were able to adapt the grievance procedure in this practical manner.

However, we should not exaggerate what was accomplished in this case. Since the grievance involved only a few minutes of time a month, it was not important in any material sense. As in the air-hose case, we have to see it in a symbolic or symptomatic sense. It was a symptom of two areas of friction: that of workers and steward with the foreman and that of workers and steward with the Time Study Department.

The handling of the case resulted in a marked improvement of worker-steward-foreman relations. (It also strengthened union-management relations at the top and gave the steward increased confidence in top management.) But it did not really come to grips with that second area of mistrust: worker-steward-time study relations. Management's reassurance on rates for this department was welcomed, but it only restated what was written in the contract, and it did not spell out any new pattern of relations in that area, which would have put that reassurance upon a solid foundation. In effect, that was to be the next job undertaken by the parties.

The Punch Press Department also had its rate case.

This is probably the most complicated department to supervise in the entire plant. Except for one production line, all the workers operate individual machines and are paid individual incentive rates. This means that there is a rate for each one of the wide varieties of jobs done on each machine.

For several years the department was in a constant state of change and confusion. There had been a high turnover of foremen and also of stewards. Much union and management friction centered in the department, and both sides fought without solving many problems. In the fall of 1946, Roberts, a new steward, went to work vigorously on these complex problems. He reported that he found the department full of favoritism and discrimination in the allocation of jobs. He sought to push seniority as the primary basis for the allocation of the most desirable job and felt he was able to cut down considerably on favoritism in this manner.

In the steward's first months on the job, he put in a constant stream of grievances; in fact, he was so active that his superiors in the union were afraid he would be too technical and find problems

which never really existed. Nevertheless, he kept pushing his grievances and felt that he was beginning to make some impression on
the situation.

In 1947 Theodore Schmitz took over the position as foreman. He
had been in the department for five years as a timekeeper and
assistant foreman, and was already well liked by the people and,
of course, familiar with the work in the department. He had a
genuine interest in the people working in the department, and they
report that he had always been ready to listen to their problems
and act upon their complaints and suggestions when possible.

Under Schmitz production improved. Schmitz reports, in fact,
that relations moved along so well that some of the workers would
suggest little additional jobs that they might do when they had
time in order to show their appreciation for the cooperation they
had from the foreman. Schmitz took care to consult with Roberts
frequently, and the two developed an effective working relationship.

Such was the situation in the department when the annual inventory revealed that the workers in the Punch Press Department
had been paid for 160,000 pieces which had not been received by
management. (This was between 1 and 2 per cent of total production.) How could such a discrepancy arise? It is explained largely
by the manner in which the pieces are counted. Each machine is
equipped with a meter which records the number of machine
strokes. It is a simple and relatively inexpensive way to make a
record. To count the finished pieces would require more elaborate
equipment or additional personnel. This means, however, that the
number of machine strokes is never exactly the same as the number
of finished pieces. There are three principal sources of error. The
machine stroke may turn out a faulty piece, which must be discarded.
This happens particularly on the cover line where eighteen employees perform various operations in making the covers for small
drums. A punch press provides the first operation in this line, and
the entire line is paid according to the meter count on the punch
press although a piece may be turned into scrap at any one of the
subsequent stations on the line. Machine strokes in which no metal
is blocked out provide another source of error. Sometimes, as the
head of the press starts down toward the steel strip, the operator
notices he does not have the metal adjusted just right and, rather

than have the piece turned into scrap, he snatches it out of the machine and waits for the next stroke to put it in again. The work of the maintenance men, or die setters, gave rise to larger errors. When the maintenance man was called in to service a machine, he always had to run it a certain amount to test it out after he had made his repairs. He might run anywhere from one to one hundred meter counts, without turning out any pieces. Similarly the die setter, in getting his die in place and in adjustment, might also run a number of machine strokes before he would be satisfied that everything was ready to work.

Management had been aware of this problem before and in 1946 had promulgated new rules for the checking of production in this department. These rules had been put into effect twice but each time they had given rise to such disturbances that they were quickly withdrawn. Now, following the inventory count revealing the 160,000 missing pieces, management determined that the new system must go in.

A checker was assigned to the department to work with the timekeeper in making a record of the number of pieces turned out. It would have been more expensive than it was worth to count the finished pieces and thus avoid paying for scrap, and management could not expect to check up on the times when an operator pulled a strip out of the machine in order to avoid making scrap. But management was determined that it would not pay for pieces not turned out. The new checker had orders to check the meters before and after the maintenance man or die setter came on the machine. In such cases, the meters would be set back so that when the operator came on to do the job he would not get credit for what he did not do.

Management also took steps to avoid paying for pieces which were actually turned out but were not turned out by the operator in question. This could happen in three ways: Group leaders came in early to set the machines up and see that everything was ready for operation when the regular shift came on. In the process, they generally ran a number of pieces on each machine. The die setter, in trying out his die, also might run a few pieces. Or the maintenance man, after servicing the machine, might try it a few times, blocking out actual pieces. In such cases, the regular operator would either not be in the plant at all, or he would be getting day rates while the machine was made ready for him, or he would be operating another machine on incentive rates. In any case, management argued that he was not entitled to pay for pieces he did not turn out. The new checker had strict orders to check the counts much more closely than had been done before.

The worker and union reaction was immediate and heated. The new system was introduced without any consultation with the union officers. They knew nothing about the inventory count that had pointed to the need for closer checking. The workers simply felt that the new system meant they were not trusted by management. All this talk about closer checking suggested that management suspected them of cheating.

Furthermore, the workers felt that their rates were being cut. They were not impressed by any discussion of laxities in past practices. The tightening up meant to them simply that they were not being paid for things that they had previously been paid for.

The new checking procedure also gave rise to heated charges of favoritism. Even with an additional employee on the job, management was not always able to do the thorough checking that the new regulations called for. In cases where the checker was not able to get around to certain machines, some operators might be allowed to record their own meter count, whereas other operators were not given this freedom. Thus it seemed that the checker trusted some people and did not trust others.

Up to the time of the introduction of the new system the problems of the department were being so smoothly handled that grievances had almost disappeared. Now, between February 26 and April 5, 1948, Roberts introduced seven grievances. All of them were related to the new system, but a study of the grievance records in these cases is singularly unrevealing.

These cases grew out of the lingering distrust of management— and that could not be written on the grievance form. The distrust had been aggravated by management's withdrawal of rate cards to the Time Study Office in order to install the new cost-accounting system. And then management introduced this new set of cost-accounting controls for the Punch Press Department. But note that management's cost-accounting procedures are not directly matters for bargaining and are nowhere covered in the contract. Consequently, while such accounting changes might cause a major disturbance in union-management relations, no grievance could be written on the real issue. Instead, the steward had to do the job piecemeal, shooting grievances at the symptoms instead of at the underlying problem.

These changes in management procedures had, in fact, given rise to far-reaching changes in relations within the Punch Press Department.

They were a serious blow to the foreman's position. In effect, the Time Study Department simply moved in and took control over one of the major areas of the foreman's activity. This led to friction and confusion. Many times the foreman had to telephone the time-study authorities and carry on extended conversations to get a clarification in certain regulations before he was able to answer questions put by the workers.

The foreman found himself tied down for hours in his office discussing grievances and related problems with the steward and with other workers in the department. This part of his job became so time consuming that he felt he had no longer any clear idea of what was going on out in the department.

The foreman also noticed that the exchange of favors he had so effectively built up with the workers broke down as soon as the new system came in. No longer were they willing and even eager to do little additional jobs for him. Now they continued to do strictly what was required of them and that was all. It is remarkable that production did not drop off, but remained at a high level. That speaks well for the relations previously established in the department.

These changes did not mean that the workers suddenly took a dislike to their foreman. He felt that he was powerless to act upon the problems of major concern to them, and they also came to realize that until these problems were settled the foreman was simply on the sidelines.

The records show that each one of Roberts's seven grievances was settled before it reached the fourth step of top management's consideration. Nevertheless, as these grievances were processed, there was a growing realization among the union officials and by the production supervisor and the personnel manager that the real problems were not being grappled with. Short and Kluck felt that it would be impossible to solve any of these problems until top management had given careful consideration to the new checking system itself. As long as the union people saw a possibility of getting rid of the system they would keep pushing individual grievances indirectly against it.

Finally Shafer and Love asked to meet with top management to discuss the problems of the department, and management agreed. This in itself testifies to the far-reaching changes in the union-management relationship. In this case there was not even a grievance to be discussed. It was simply recognized on both sides that a troubled situation existed, and it seemed to make sense to sit down and talk it over. Gossett and Novy met with Shafer and Love, and here again the steward of the department was called in to tell his story at first hand. There followed a meeting among Gossett, Novy, Kluck, Short, and Peterson, chief of time study, and Wunder, Treasurer of the Company.

After this Gossett called in Schmitz, departmental foreman, to see whether the settlement that management was considering would be satisfactory to him and to get his version of the disturbances. The stories told by the foreman and the steward fitted together without any conflict.

Gossett and Novy then called in Love, Rose, the grievance committeeman for the first floor, and Roberts, the departmental steward, to work out the provisions of the agreement. It covered four main points:

1. Workers would not be paid for machine strokes of maintenance men or die setters when no actual pieces were turned out.

2. When group leader, die setter, or maintenance man operated a machine, and turned out actual pieces, those pieces would be credited to the regular operator as they had been in the past. Management agreed that refusal to pay for these pieces would be, in effect, cutting the rates.

3. In situations where the checker or timekeeper were not able to check all the machines, the foreman or assistant foreman could step in to do the job for them. This was designed to meet the union complaint of favoritism where certain workers were allowed to report their counts and others were not. The management people thought at first they

would have to assign an additional employee to the department to make sure that everyone was checked, but Love pointed out to them that it was only occasionally when a number of jobs finished at approximately the same time, that the checker and timekeeper were not able to cover the department. It would be a simple matter to have the foreman or assistant foreman step in to the situation. This union suggestion saved management the salary of one employee, and it also relieved the union of the necessity of having additional people around to check them.

4. It was agreed that the foreman should have final authority on all matters affecting the pay of employees. That is, it would be up to him to approve all meter counts and in case the worker raised a question on some decision of checker or timekeeper, the foreman would be able to make the decision on the spot without having to appeal it to higher authority. This served to reestablish the foreman as boss of his department and was welcomed by the steward and the workers as well as by the foreman himself.

The agreement was now to be communicated directly to the workers. Management drew up a copy of the understanding and submitted it to Roberts and Schmitz to make sure that both interpreted it in the same manner. They discussed the document and found that there was only one minor point on which they were not in agreement. Schmitz then went up to see Production Supervisor Short to clarify this point. This resulted in a complete understanding between foreman and steward. They then called a departmental meeting at which both foreman and steward explained and endorsed the new regulations.

The final outcome of this long series of moves was impressive. The steward was enthusiastic over the way the problems had been handled, and he reported that the workers also were highly pleased. The foreman felt that a great weight had been taken off his shoulders and that he would now be able to function as he had in the past.

While they settled this departmental problem, the union and management officers came to realize that a broader question was at issue: Just how should the Time Study Department fit into the pattern of human relations with workers, union officers, and production management?

In earlier years, the very presence of time-study men in a department was an unsettling influence and gave rise to alarming rumors about rate cutting. The time-study men were then completely free from the immediate control of the production organization. They could go into any department at any time and study or restudy any job. They were not required to give notice to the union concerning their activities, nor even to the foreman. The union could only protest or lodge a grievance when a restudy of a job led to a change of rates. Since the workers did not know what was going on, it was natural for them to view any activities of the Time Study Department with alarm. The foreman also found time-study activities a disturbing influence.

Now top management ruled that a time-study man could not enter a department for the purpose of making any observations or studies without the written permission of the general factories manager or the general production supervisor. Upon entering the department, he had to present this written slip to the foreman and explain the purposes of his visit. He then had to show his credentials to the steward and make a similar explanation. Only then was he free to go ahead with his observations or studies.

These new regulations have proved highly satisfactory to the union officers and to the production men in management. Management's legal rights to make time studies have not been affected, but the union officers are now in a much better position to know what is going on. If they feel that unfortunate changes are going to be made, they can consult with management and present their point of view before the changes go into effect. This is advantageous to management also. If protests arise only after a decision has been taken, it is a delicate matter to reverse that decision. It is much smoother and more efficient to handle such matters in informal discussions before one or the other or both parties are committed to a particular decision.

Before these changes came, the foremen often felt that they could get relations smoothed out in their own departments if only the time-study people did not come in and disturb the situation with their rate-setting activites. The foreman might agree privately with his workers that a particular rate was not fair, but there was nothing he could do about it. Under the present regulations, the rate set by the Time Study Department is not put into effect until it has been approved by the foreman and the general production supervisor. This enables the production men not only to make their views felt before rates are finally set, but also to take responsibility for those rates.

The rate situation has also been helped by management's willingness to explain the rate-setting process in full detail to union officers. Whenever the union raises a grievance charging an unfair rate, management holds a full discussion with the union people and presents them with all the figures involved in the rate-setting study. If the union people still feel that the rate is unfair, management agrees without question to have the job restudied, and the results of the restudy are similarly discussed with the union officers. In some cases this process has led to a revision of rates. In any case, it leads to a better understanding between union and management concerning the rate-setting process. (This procedure was introduced shortly after Gossett and Novy came to Chicago, but it had little effect until it was accompanied by the various other changes I have described.)

The union people are generally well satisfied with the rate situation. There is some mention of certain rates which are said to be "tight," but there is surprisingly little concern over these. In general, the workers seem to feel that the rates are liberal and allow them to make good earnings. The fear of rate cutting has also been greatly minimized. The union officers feel that the contract plus the grievance decisions discussed earlier, plus thorough discussions with management on rate setting, give them a high degree of security in this field.

Top management and the other production men in management also are well satisfied with the present situation. While they still do not expect new rates to be accepted without question, they recognize that the incentive system itself is better accepted by the workers than it has ever been before. The production records, to be discussed later, are perhaps the best evidence of a healthy situation. Furthermore, the time-study men have no complaint over these changes and are finding their jobs much easier to do.

These changed relations showed their results in various and impressive ways.

We have no measure here for changes in sentiments, but the

changes have been so profound that we cannot fail to observe them. The change in sentiments toward Gossett is particularly marked. He speaks of walking through the plant during the period of conflict. Workers would turn sullenly away as he came near. And, as he passed on, he could feel their eyes drilling into his back, projecting their hatred upon him. After 1947, he could walk through with a nod and a smile, and they returned his friendly gestures.

In reviewing his term of office before a union meeting, Lucius Love highlighted two incidents. The first was the time when he met John Gossett and Gossett refused to shake hands with him. The second was the time when another manufacturer, having heard of the plant's achievements in production and cooperation, was invited to walk through the plant with Gossett—and with Lucius Love. To Love, those incidents were fitting symbols of the old day and the new.

This good will toward top management has been steadily spreading toward lower levels. In 1949 Bob Novy suddenly collapsed in his office and had to be rushed to the hospital. The word spread rapidly through the plant that Novy needed blood transfusions. Management was swamped with volunteers, and many times the amount needed was offered. The local union also sent a large basket of flowers to the hospital. The men and women who had hated Novy so intensely only a few months earlier now were competing with each other to express their good will.

The top union people have full confidence in Gossett and his top management. Lower-level officers also are convinced of the change, although in 1948 they were inclined to hold certain reservations. These two comments may serve as samples:

I am of a sceptical nature myself. I don't think a leopard can change his spots. But so long as management wants to deal the cards on the table, I'll deal them that way myself. If they begin to pull some fast ones under the table, I can palm the cards too.

Before, you was suspicious of anything management wanted to give you. You had to figure out what angle they was trying to get at with that thing. You'd want a week to talk things over before you took anything off of management. Now it's different. If they offer you something, you might say, "Let me sleep on it," and you'll tell 'em the next day.

If we can sum up those expressions, they seem to come to this. The union officers are all happy over the change. They are now willing to expect the best of management. But they will continue to examine critically anything that management proposes. They will do their own thinking. And why not? Cooperation certainly does not imply that one party to the bargain shall lie down and take on faith anything that is proposed by the other party.

On the management side the changes are equally marked. Strong feelings against the union leaders have given way to a friendly regard and wholehearted respect. Management once had quite uncomplimentary views of the workers in the plant. They seemed an extraordinarily contrary lot, lazy and irresponsible. Now the management people are happy to think of these same workers as fellow members of a team. The managers are genuinely proud of the production job the workers are doing, and they have gained a much more friendly interest in them as human beings.

The foremen have been among the chief beneficiaries of these changed relations and sentiments.

Before, the foreman was an unfortunate bystander directly in the line of fire in the union-management battle, with little control over his own situation. He was always on the point of quitting and, as he watched other foremen come and go, he often asked himself what was holding him to the job. He knew that management had little confidence in him, that the workers disliked him, and that the union officers would do their best to make his job more difficult. Today, he feels in control of the situation. He feels that he knows what is going on and that management has confidence in him. He enjoys the growing respect of workers and union officers.

His improved status is recognized in various ways. He no longer has to punch the time clock as he did years ago. He belongs to the Foreman's Club, and attends the monthly meetings for dinner, beer, and discussion. While the club was started upon the suggestion of Personnel Manager Kluck, that in itself seemed a sign of increasing management recognition. And since that beginning the foremen have taken over and made this club distinctly their own.

The changes in the foremen's role are summed up in this way by one foremen as he contrasts the situation before Gossett and Novy with that which prevails today.

Before the people would come to the foreman and ask for something, and it didn't matter whether the foreman believed in it or not, there wasn't a damn thing he could do about it. He could just go upstairs and management would tell him no. Then the steward would get going and the union would put on the pressure; and if they put on enough pressure management would give in to them. That made the steward Jesus Christ in the department and the foreman was just——. No wonder he couldn't get any respect from the people. Now it's different. When we go upstairs, we get action.

The improved situation showed itself in measurable form on the production lines. The rates in the Barrel Department were finally accepted in early 1947, and production began to move up there— very tentatively. The 1947 negotiations, followed by that fourth-step grievance meeting, cleared the road so that workers could at last feel that it was all right to increase production.

While the conflict was going on, management could offer no incentives that would have made much difference. Now that the road was open, management acted with skill and understanding.

Until late in 1947 the Chicago plant was far behind the New Orleans and Jersey City plants in its production. New highs of daily, weekly, or monthly production in these other plants were recognized by letters and congratulatory telegrams from the general factories manager. Management saw to it that the people in the Chicago plant were aware of what the other plants were doing, but before 1947 this had no effect. As the workers began to take an interest in production and moved up to higher levels, that change was immediately recognized. The foreman would receive a congratulatory letter from Novy, together with a bottle of whiskey from Short, and the workers at the end of shift would receive soft drinks all around and cigarettes. New records were also publicly posted next to the production lines. Management would put up a plaque with the record figure on it together with the names of the foreman and the assistant foreman, and all the workers on the line. As the workers in the Chicago plant came within hailing distance of Jersey City and New Orleans, management saw to it that the comparative figures were always available. Management also sought to stimulate competition between production lines doing the same work. In some cases such records went back and forth several times. Over a period of less than six months the Chicago plant moved from third to first place in production.

How did the workers react to this sort of stimulation? To give an accurate picture would require the sort of survey that I was not able to conduct. All the workers, of course, received more money as their production went up, and that was certainly rewarding. Did the records mean anything in themselves? Some of the union people say that it was only the money that was involved. However, there is clear evidence that the group leaders, who have some supervisory responsibilities but work on the lines and are union members, took real pride in the production records their lines were making, and were stimulated to put out increased effort. And there were also a certain number of workers who took an interest in production records because I heard from other workers or union officers criticism of certain individuals who were too strongly interested in setting records. Furthermore, we should note Love's complaint in the grievance meeting following the 1947 contract that the men were getting no recognition for their work. Management now was providing this recognition. The union's position seems to be that good production is a good thing, but that competition between workers or even between production lines or between plants is not something to be encouraged. There is no doubt that the goal of production does not mean nearly so much to the workers as it does to management. Nevertheless, it is a great change in union attitudes for high productivity to be accepted as a good thing, even with reservations.

Chapter 10

Beyond the Grievance Procedure

THE GRIEVANCE procedure has taken its place as only one among several channels for the solution of union-management problems. New forms of activity, undreamed of a few years ago, have grown up and are still evolving.

The preceding chapters have been based primarily upon research done in the spring of 1948. No comparable research has been done to analyze the changes that have taken place since 1948, but certain developments seem so significant that they must at least be sketched here.

In the years 1948–1950, we see two interrelated trends. An increasing area of activity is being handled *jointly* by union and management officers working together. And more and more people in both organizations are becoming actively involved in the cooperation process.

The union-management program for the Maintenance Department marked the beginning of a new stage of development in both respects. The beginning was described in this way by Novy:

For a long time the finger of top management had been on me on account of the costs in the Machine Shop. We had known all along that the costs there were way out of line. Of course this is an old plant and our equipment is quite old. We have to expect some breakdowns and some overtime work to get things back in shape. Even so our costs were way out of line compared with other plants. Now over a period of months I tried everything I could think of with our supervision. We changed this thing and that thing and the other thing, but nothing seemed to do any good.

I kept looking at those figures and beating my brains out, trying to think what we could do. And it had to be done quickly. I knew I couldn't do it alone. Finally I called Jake. We got together for lunch on some other matters and at that time I asked for Jake's help. Of course Jake agreed to cooperate, as usual, so he went right to work on it. We spent about three hours that first day laying it all out. I gave him all the facts that I knew.

Novy's invitation did not catch Shafer unprepared. He had been concerned about the department for some time and had been discussing it thoroughly with President Don Hanes. (Lucius Love became an international representative in August, 1948.) They wanted to cement maintenance and production workers together in the union. They found morale and efficiency exceedingly low in the department. They felt that there was friction between workers and foreman, and they saw that the foreman and his supervisor were not working effectively together. Men were not assigned to jobs that made the most effective utilization of their skills—which could be attributed to either favoritism or supervisory inefficiency. They also found discipline exceedingly lax, with violations all the way from overstaying the relief periods to working on personal jobs on company time without permission. As some men disregarded the rules, without being punished, others were discouraged from doing a conscientious job.

Shafer and Hanes had been building up a systematic picture of the department's problems and had been wondering how they would approach management on these problems. Therefore they welcomed Novy's invitation.

Novy put the problems to Shafer on May 5, 1949. Immediately after this meeting, Shafer looked up Hanes and went over the Novy-Shafer meeting in detail. The following day Novy and Shafer spent two and a half hours together discussing plans. Following this, Shafer again checked developments with Hanes. Later in the same day Novy and Shafer had a 15-minute session with Gossett. The purpose of the meeting was to inform the top executive that a new program was being developed and to get permission to go over with Shafer confidential figures on the operation of the department. Novy was proposing to lay all management's cards on the table.

Gossett asked for no details at this time. He believed in delegating authority and responsibility, and he gave this new program his wholehearted endorsement.

Still later in the day Hanes met for three-quarters of an hour with Shafer and Novy. From this point on, the circle of participation steadily broadened. For management, Novy, Paul Jones, assistant general factories manager, Tom M. Dwyer, chief of engineering, O. A. Thomas, departmental supervisor, and Joseph Kluck, personnel manager, all participated in the meetings with the union. At one time in the middle of the program of meetings Novy spent an hour reviewing progress with Gossett, and Gossett sat in on the final 2½-hour meeting.

Besides Shafer and Hanes, Art Marshall, the grievance committeeman for the department, and Al Wagner, the department's representative on the negotiating committee, made up the union's team in the meetings with management. Hanes, Marshall, and Wagner sought to keep in constant touch with workers in the department throughout the month in which the discussions were proceeding.

Management's notes on these meetings provide us with the barest outline of developments. We cannot trace how the various decisions evolved in discussion, but at least we must record some figures giving the magnitude of the program.

There is no record of meetings within the union on this program —only Shafer's comment: "We met constantly." Novy's record for the period May 12–June 13 shows 23 meetings jointly with the union or within management. Fifteen of the 23 meetings were joint ones. These meetings consumed 50 hours, 15 within management and 35 joint. If we had figures on the time spent within the union, the total would be considerably larger.

What do the figures mean? They certainly show that straightening out a tangled situation in a large department is no simple matter. It takes time, and the management not prepared to spend many hours in discussions had better not get involved in such a program at all.

Let us also note the comparison between the time spent within management and in joint discussions: 15 to 35 hours. That comparison is as good a measure as any of the progress in joint activity.

Decisions in this case were detailed and far reaching. For the June 3 all-day meeting, Novy's notes list 29 items that were gone over in discussion.

The discussants worked out a complete reclassification of jobs in the department to make for greater efficiency and increased earnings for the men. They found that the department was overstaffed, following this reorganization, and two workers were laid off. Management decided to discharge the foreman. The union expressed confidence in the ability of a certain group leader, and management was glad to appoint him as its new foreman.

Both supervisor and foreman had worked on the day shift, and there had been only six men under a group leader on the night shift. It was now decided to increase the night crew to sixteen and place the foreman on that shift. The supervisor would then be in charge of twenty-four men on the day shift. The new arrangement was designed to enable the maintenance men to do more of their work at a time when the production machines would be shut down. It would also make it possible for the supervisor to work more closely with his men, and thus was expected to eliminate some of the difficulties that had arisen with two levels of supervision on the day shift.

The discussants also worked out a joint statement upon departmental rules and discipline. This was thoroughly discussed at a departmental union meeting on June 9. The union leaders argued that the rules were only reasonable requirements for effective operation. They pointed out that management had made far-reaching changes in response to suggestions from the union, and they urged that the workers do their part in obeying the rules. The joint statement was then posted on the bulletin board in the department.

What have been the results? The management men report that costs have been cut substantially. Increased efficiency shows up especially in a sharp reduction in the amount of overtime hours— even with two less men. Novy and Thomas also feel that worker-management and union-management relations in the department have been greatly improved. Morale seems to them much better.

The union leaders are equally pleased with the outcome. They did not like to see two men laid off, but they felt that the program had actually saved jobs in the long run. They recognized that costs were unreasonably high. If they could not be reduced, management could save money by contracting out most of the work and keeping only a skeleton force sufficient to keep up with the immediate repair work. In that case, most of the men in that department would have lost their jobs. Management, of course, was reluctant to make such a move, but Novy felt it had to come if all other efforts to reduce costs failed.

The reclassification of jobs resulted in an increase in earnings for some of the men. Furthermore, it seemed to improve relations among the men and between the men and the rest of the union.

The Maintenance Department program worked so effectively that it has since been extended to other departments. Wherever there seem to be complicated problems that do not yield to grievance discussions, union and management people now sit down together to develop a joint program. As in the Maintenance Department situation, separate discussions of union and management people have been tied together with joint meetings. One new element has been added to the picture as the program has been extended to other departments. When the union and management people, meeting together, decide they don't have enough information upon a particular problem, they ask each other, "Who might be able to help us on this one?" A foreman or a steward may then be invited to join the discussion. And there have been several occasions when rank-and-file workers have been asked to tell their story.

This is an unfamiliar sort of situation for workers. When they come into the meeting, Shafer and Novy assure them that there will be no reprisals for anything they may say. They are asked simply to give their honest opinions on the problem under discussion. Some men have confined themselves to meaningless generalities, but others have made useful contributions to the discussion.

This new development provides further evidence of the strength of the relationship. Of course, people on both sides still discuss separately what proposals they will make in the joint meetings— and such preliminary discussions will certainly continue to be necessary. But the parties have accepted the problems as common problems to such an extent that they can call for testimony on a problem without advance knowledge of what the witness will say. There is no longer any need for carefully rehearsing the individual so that he will support the union's line or the management's line. If a man makes any thoughtful comments at all, they are fitted into the general picture and serve in shaping up the decisions.

The joint program has led to interesting changes within the union. The discharge of a foreman may be an unpleasant task for management, but no question of authority or departure from past practices is involved. The problems are more complicated on the union side.

Take the case of a group leader in one department where joint discussions were going on. Management felt that the group leader was not doing an effective job. The union people agreed. Since the men working under the group leader were all on a group incentive, his inefficiency was costly to them. The foreman was convinced that if he demoted the group leader and put another man in his place he would have a grievance on his hands, since all group leaders are union members. Instead, he put the problem to union Vice-President Columbus Gary. Gary proposed a line of action to Steward Ed Kohlheim. Kohlheim then pointed out to the group leader that he was holding back his men. He suggested that the group leader step down for a trial period to see if someone else could increase earnings on the line. The new man did increase earnings substantially. Kohlheim then told the former group leader that he could have his old job back—but he would be expected to match the performance of the new man. The former group leader decided to stay where he was.

The ineffective steward presents a much more difficult problem. In one case, the union leaders became convinced that a steward was not doing an effective job. They felt he was using the position as an excuse to avoid doing physical work and that he had changed certain customary practices in the department (by agreement with the foreman) in such a way that his close friends were getting undue advantages. But a steward is an elected official. He cannot be told to quit his job. Instead, Shafer, Hanes, and Gary encouraged the men to discuss the problems of their department, and that discussion pointed more and more at the shortcomings of the steward. Then a departmental meeting was called. Hanes talked with the steward to see if he wished to resign before facing such a general meeting. The steward declined, but when he found that sentiment in the meeting was predominantly against him he stepped down, and another man was elected in his place.

Such a joint program requires an understanding on both sides that problems will be thoroughly explored. Regardless of customary patterns of management prerogatives and union rights, there will be no reservations against discussing any points that may have a bearing on the problems of the department. This does not mean that the union will demand, "You must fire that foreman," or that management will insist, "You must change that steward." While the parties often argue their points vigorously, they proceed with a general understanding of what each party can and cannot do. They seek to deal with situations without changing personnel whenever possible. But when personnel changes are indicated, that comes out in the discussion without either party's making any demands upon the other. It is then up to the leaders of each organization to devise the best ways for carrying out the personnel changes.

This discussion of joint programs for several departments should not suggest that most current union-management activity is of this large-scale and somewhat formal character. Relations between the parties have become so easy that union and management officers right down to the foreman and steward level feel free to call upon each other for help on a wide variety of problems. The steward calls on the foreman. The general production supervisor calls in a foreman, a grievance committeeman, and a steward. And so on. Such discussions may crop up at any time on any sort of problem.

For example, take the scrap problem in the Punch Press Department. Novy was particularly concerned about this because it threatened to lose the company orders. Let us say that the plant had an order for 10,000 barrels. It would be a punch-press job to stamp out the bottoms and lids for the barrels. If 200 lids were turned into scrap there, the order would be 200 barrels short. While the customer would not be paying for what he did not receive, such short orders would be a nuisance to him and might prove costly in good will.

Novy first discussed the problem thoroughly with President Hanes. Then, for several days Novy made a point of walking through the department, looking into the barrels of scrap and picking up pieces for inspection. While he said nothing to anyone about this, he noticed that the volume of scrap seemed to drop while he was checking it. But he felt it was still too high. Then one day he asked Vice-President Gary to walk through the department with the foreman and himself.

As they walked through, Novy explained his concern over risking the loss of orders and asked Gary's cooperation in reducing the scrap. Novy argued that it was not fair for management to be paying for these faulty pieces.

Gary agreed in general, although he added that, since he did not work in the department himself, he was not sure just what could be done. Immediately after leaving Novy, Gary looked up the steward and asked that a departmental meeting be called. He reports that 80 per cent of the workers turned out for the discussion that afternoon after work.

After the steward opened the meeting, Gary took over and presented the problem to the workers. He stressed the danger of losing work for the department. He urged the workers to do a more careful job and proposed that, from this point on, they not be paid for scrap.

This aroused a storm of protest. The workers had two arguments. To eliminate scrap, they would have to slow up so much that they would lose earnings. And, they said, sometimes the scrap was caused by a faulty machine, which was management's responsibility.

On the question of management's responsibility, Gary said that whenever they found the machine faulty they should notify the foreman. If he ordered them to work nevertheless, management would pay for all scrap in that case.

On the question of earnings, he replied simply, "Let's give it a try." He suggested that the workers do the best job they could for a trial period. If they had to slow down so that their earnings were cut, in their efforts to reduce scrap, he assured them that the union would get together with management and work out a new rate to restore their former earnings. But he argued that neither union nor management leaders could know what adjustments needed to be made until the workers had pitched in to show what they could do.

The discussion continued at some length. The workers did not believe that they could substantially reduce scrap without at the same time losing earnings, but eventually they were willing to go along with Gary's proposal on a let's-give-it-a-try basis.

The results were striking. The next afternoon Gary walked through the department to check the scrap. He reports he found just two *pieces,* whereas the day before it had piled up in three barrels. At the same time productivity was at the usual pace. The foreman expressed his enthusiasm for the improvement, and Gary in turn told all the people that they should be proud of what they had accomplished.

While a scrap total of two pieces is certainly exceptional, the monthly scrap totals in the department have shown a sharp and sustained reduction, compared with previous records. Since earnings have been maintained, there has been no need to discuss the rates with management.

This case is especially interesting for two reasons. A glance back at developments in the Punch Press Department in the spring of 1948 furnishes us with an interesting comparison. At that time management had unilaterally made certain changes which affected rates and other aspects of the department. The accounting and checking changes gave rise to strong resentment that smoldered over a period of several months. Finally management and union got together to work out an agreement on these problems. At that time even a suggestion that management wished to discontinue paying for scrap would have aroused a storm of protest.

Two years later management approached the problem differently. Management called upon the union to ask for help. Adjustments were then made first within the union structure—with the assurance that, if the workers lost money, management in turn would have to make adjustments. In this way a major change in procedure was carried out in a few simple steps in a few hours' time.

Note also where the action began in the union structure: with the local vice-president. Shafer and Hanes were kept informed, but they encouraged Gary to carry the ball. This was as it should be, Shafer felt. He had been urging the local officers right down to the steward level to make their own decisions, and he considered it a healthy sign when they felt able to do so.

What have these developments since 1948 meant to the people

in the plant? Union and management leaders unanimously believe that the relationship has improved and is still improving. They feel that their satisfaction is widely shared throughout the plant.

At the same time they recognize that the new pattern of relations brings with it certain problems of adjustment.

What of the foreman? Where does he stand when union and management work together on the problems of his department? How do foremen feel when one of their number is discharged as part of the union-management program in one department?

Management recognizes that these new activities may give rise to anxieties among the foremen. In fact, when the foreman was discharged in the Maintenance Department, Novy immediately called all the foremen together to go over the case with them thoroughly, in an effort to reassure them upon their own positions. Still, we should not assume that the joint meetings present a threat to the foreman's job that did not exist before. A resourceful union leadership has many ways of making a foreman's job untenable, without ever challenging him directly—as this union demonstrated so thoroughly in the period of conflict. The new program simply brings into open discussion problems that were earlier fought through indirectly in grievances, slowdowns, stoppages, and so on. Turnover of foremen is now much lower than it was in the conflict stage.

What of the steward? Will he be able to develop his initiative if he knows that joint discussions may show up his shortcomings? Will he try to play it safe simply by following his superiors in the union?

I have no answers for these questions on foremen and stewards. Nor can I speak for research upon the morale of the rank-and-file union members in 1950. These are large questions to which a new program of research might well be directed. But the story must be cut off somewhere, if the book is ever to be written.

While there is much still to be learned about the sentiments of people at various levels in the two organizations, the record of sustained and increasing production from 1947 to this writing provides impressive evidence of union-management achievements in human relations.

Week after week, in department after department, new production records were made. By late 1948 daily production on certain lines had gone higher than the maximum estimates of the engineers who had set up the lines. This is not so fantastic as it sounds. The engineers know the maximum speed possible for each machine, but their estimates also include an allowance for down time. On some lines the workers have run at top speed and have cut the down time below the engineering estimates. There is no more "encouraging" machines to break down, and now, when a machine does go down, the workers don't sit back and wait for a maintenance man. They first jump in to see if some minor adjustment will put the machine back in action. Only if they find that a more substantial or skilled job is needed do they ask for maintenance help.

But records alone do not make profits and good worker earnings. They depend upon *sustained* production at a high level—and here the achievement has been particularly impressive. At this writing it is just four years since the men went back to work after the 191-day strike. In that period there have been no stoppages or strikes. Even in the industry-wide strike of 1949, which shut down nearly all organized plants, the Chicago plant of Inland Steel Container Company continued to operate—by agreement between union and management.

Impressive as these achievements are, I see no inclination of union and management leaders to rest upon their oars. Perhaps the healthiest sign in this case is the widespread recognition that life does not stand still. The leaders recognize that new ways of meeting situations necessarily create problems of adjustment among all people affected by the changes. They are alert in recognizing such problems and skillful in meeting them. They are not simply aiming for a relationship in which cooperation is decreed from the top. In the past two years they have made tremendous strides in extending active participation in the co-operation process to more and more people in both organizations. This effort holds rich promise for the future.

Part II

Analysis of the Case

Chapter 11

A Scheme for Analysis

NOW THE STORY has been told. I have found the case extraordinarily interesting, and I have tried to transmit that interest to those who read the book. But interest alone is not enough. What can we learn from such a case that will be helpful in analyzing and dealing with other cases?

If we simply look at the events in this case, the outlook is not promising. I can hardly claim that the case is "average" or "representative." For example, the old family management was probably one of the most ruthless managements ever to perform upon the American scene. To be sure, many of the incidents of the case, at all stages in its development, can be duplicated (in general terms) in the history of labor relations in this country. On the other hand, no single incident is ever exactly the same from case to case, and when we take series of incidents together the differences become so impressive that we despair of finding any laws of human behavior along this route.

We cannot advise executive Jones, "To meet your problem, do just as John Gossett did on August 5, 1947." The effectiveness of an action by Gossett or Shafer, Love or Novy or Caples depended upon the way in which it fitted into the then-existing pattern of union-management relations. For this reason we cannot prescribe any cure-all that will be effective, regardless of the situation.

But our failure to find answers in such specific incidents need not force us to give up the search for general conclusions. If we cannot deal with specific events in ordinary terms, we need to break down those events into abstract terms, which will make it possible to compare and contrast incidents from case to case.

That is the method of science. The scientist does not observe and analyze his data in the common-sense terms of everyday observation. He deals with abstractions such as atoms, electrons, protons, and so on. Some items such as these he has never even seen, but they are vital to him nevertheless. Working with such abstractions, he has learned to predict and control some of the processes of the physical world.

That is the test of whether the abstractions are "real" or not. To what extent do they enable us to predict and control behavior?

Similarly, we need to work with abstractions in the world of human relations. That is another way of saying that we need to work with a theory.

A theory is important to us for two basic reasons.

First, it points out some of the important items to be observed, described, and analyzed. None of us can observe or cope with all there is to see in any situation. Inevitably we observe some things and neglect others. If that selection process is left to chance, we have no way of comparing one man's observations with those of another and no systematic analysis can be undertaken. A good theory tells us what items are to be observed, described, and analyzed. Then two men, working on two different cases, will bring in their findings in the same terms, so that one study will add to the value of the other. When observations are made in different terms, the findings do not add up, and science does not grow.

Second, a theory can tell us how to relate the items of observation to each other so that we can predict and control behavior on this basis. We often hear people say that they will "let the facts speak for themselves." That is an illusion. The world is infinitely complex, and the facts about it, even in a narrow area of activity, are without number. Furthermore, a fact has meaning for people only in so far as it is fitted together with other facts. The facts of observation must be organized, and the facts themselves do not suggest how they should be organized. We can organize them according to our unconscious preferences. Or we can organize them in terms of a theory. Then at least we know what we are doing and why we are doing it.

If he thinks back over the story of this case, the reader will find that I have presented some observations in great detail, while others have been sketched in briefly for background material, and many that might have been made have been left out entirely. To be sure, the human interest I found in some incidents has led me to take them up in greater detail than would be justified by pure scientific considerations. I would like people to read this book. But, in the main, the selection of observations has been dictated by a theory of human relations. That theory has so far been only implied in the discussion. It is now time to exhibit the tools of analysis and show how they are used on this case.

By theory I do not mean a polished and final statement of relationships. The field of human relations in industry is little more than two decades old. Theories in this field will necessarily be crude and imperfect. What I set forth here must be looked on as tentative. My only claim is that this theory (which is original with me to only a minor extent) makes it possible to understand and explain behavior of union and of management people somewhat more effectively than can be done without the theory. Nor do I ask anyone to take the theory on faith. I shall present it in specific terms so that anyone can make his own observations in these terms and thus show the need to modify it—or even abandon it in favor of some more adequate theory.

The terms to be used in analysis do not cover all the world of human behavior. They select certain aspects for emphasis and leave certain others out altogether. That is always the way with theoretical schemes. They are to be judged not by their inclusiveness but by their workability: to what extent do they enable us to account for the behavior we are seeking to explain?

The theory is based upon four abstract terms. These are not remote from us like the unseen electrons of the physicist. As befits the primitive state of human relations, the terms are close to the field of our experience. They are *interaction, symbols, activities,* and *sentiments.*

Interaction refers to contacts among people. Various aspects of such contacts could be studied. For our purposes, we shall concentrate upon those aspects which are most open to objective observation: the frequency and duration of contacts, and the origin-response ratio of such contacts. How often, in a given time period, do A and B interact? How long do their contacts last? How often does A originate action for B compared to B's originations of action for A?

A researcher who is on the scene when the events take place can directly observe and measure these aspects of interaction. Where, as in this case, the researcher comes on the scene after the major changes in human relations have taken place, such observations are not possible. However, where the changes in the pattern of interaction have been substantial, we can determine the nature of the changes through interviewing the men who participated in the events we are studying. In this case, a comparison of the accounts of the experiences of various people draws for us a definite and coherent picture of the pattern of interaction at different periods in the case. There may be disagreements on minor points, but there is no doubt about the nature and scope of the changes.

Symbols are words or physical objects that *stand for* relations between man and man, and between man and physical objects. Here the words "stand for" are of particular importance.

For example, we are not concerned with dollars and cents simply as physical objects. In this book money is considered as a symbol—or set of symbols. It stands for the relations between man and the things he can buy with money. It places man socially in relation to other men. Worker A, who has a more highly paid job than worker B, is likely to be accorded higher status by his fellows in the plant community. Money is also used as an incentive designed to affect man's productive effort on his machine.

A large part of our behavior in an industrial society is channeled through the use of money. There is no question here as to the importance of money. The question is: just how is it used and what effects upon human relations does it have—in this particular setting?

The words that we use in conversation, discussion, speeches, and writing make up another important category of symbols. They are the primary means we have of relating ourselves to each other—of describing friends or foes, people we look up to or people we look down on, and many other aspects of human relations. When union and management bargain, they are engaged in a interchange of verbal symbols. The way those symbols are used can make the difference between strike and settlement. It is our task to explain the impact of these symbols in collective bargaining.

Activities refer to the things that people do. In that broad sense it could cover limitless areas of behavior. For our purposes, we shall use the term to cover a limited range of behavior that can be observed and, in some cases, measured. We will examine productivity: why do men produce little—or much—at their machines? Why do they keep the machines going—or encourage them to break down? Why do they stay on the job? Why do they walk out on strike? There are many more questions to ask under this heading, but these are the activities we are particularly concerned with explaining.

Sentiments refer to the way people feel about themselves, other people, their work, their organization, and so on. We cannot observe sentiments directly. We infer them from our observations of what people say and do. For example, a union officer tells the members that he would like to hang John Gossett out of his office window, and the members cheer him. Now, we cannot measure the degree of feelings expressed, but certainly we are safe in saying that the people do not like the executive. Similarly, Jake Shafer tells the members that they can trust John Gossett, that relations with top management are working out in a favorable manner—and the members cheer him. From one incident to the other we can confidently infer a considerable change in sentiments.

It is such changes in sentiments that we must explain. When we say about the key people in this case, "They learned to trust each other," we describe a change in sentiments, but we do not explain anything. Such changes in sentiments do not take place in a vacuum nor do they happen at random. They take place, in an orderly fashion, in response to changes in interaction, symbols, and activities.

I am tempted to say that changes in sentiments are merely the resultants of prior changes in the other categories. If we examine the process over a longer period of time, that does not appear to be strictly true. For example, changes in interaction, symbols, and activities at time A lead to changes in sentiments at time B, but the sentiments existing at time B may be a necessary condition for further changes in interaction, symbols, and activities at time C. The process is endless. Furthermore, people bring into the organization sentiments already formed through experience outside of the organization. For example, the sentiments toward his union, toward himself, and toward management that Jake Shafer brought with him to the first bargaining meeting in 1947 were not the product of any experience obtained in connection with Inland Steel Container Company. Of course, once he began interacting with his local union and with management, his sentiments underwent modification, but his initial sentiments were an important force in setting the stage for change.

The same point can be made concerning activities. To explain changes from conflict to cooperation, from low to high productivity, we look for preceding changes in interaction, symbols, and sentiments. But as we see activities change for one group we must recognize that that very change can serve as a stimulus to other changes on the part of another group. In this case the changes in worker activities led to changes in interaction, symbols, and sentiments on the part of management.

As I see it, interaction, symbols, activities, and sentiments are mutually dependent upon one another. That means that a change in any one of the four categories leads to changes in the other three. That is a general statement. It is our job to make its meaning more specific and precise through examining the data of this case.

Let us first examine briefly certain events simply in order to illustrate the meaning of mutual dependence. Take the developments in the Barrel Department following the settlement of the 1947 contract. The eleven long negotiation meetings marked a considerable change in the interaction of the negotiators. At the same time they were learning to express a new set of symbols toward one another. This process resulted in a change in sentiments on the part of the participants.

Lucius Love followed up by calling the Barrel Department workers together and urging them to put forth greater production efforts. (Change in interaction and symbols.) The men responded, and productivity went up. (Change in activity.) But this change in activity did not bring the response people customarily expect for a good effort. As Love reported later, the men were not given "recognition" for what they had done and they experienced increased instead of relaxed pressure from management. In other words, the anticipated changes in interactions and symbols did not follow upon these activity changes. The men then complained to Love, and he and Shafer brought their complaints into the meeting with management. This led to a further union-management meeting on the department's problems, following which management made changes in supervisory behavior in the department. (Here we see a sequence of interactions from foreman to workers to local union officers to international representative to plant management and back to foreman and to workers.) Following these changes in interactions (accompanied by the expression of a new set of symbols), we find the workers again putting in more productive effort and feeling more cordial toward management (changes in activity and sentiments).

That series of incidents illustrates the interdependence of these items of behavior. Interactions, symbols, activities and sentiments vary together. But when change comes, where does it strike first? There is no answer to that question because the life of an organization is a continuous process, and the beginning point we select is just a matter of convenience. For example, we could start with the change in activity (producing more) following the 1947 negotiations and show how interaction and symbol changes followed upon that. But then we ask, what gave rise to the change in activity? To explain that, we would have to go back to the negotiation process and examine the changes in interactions, symbols, and sentiments that developed there.

Life would seem much simpler if we could deal in simple, cause-effect relationships, if we could say that interactions are the cause of activities, or vice-versa. Research men in the natural sciences long ago abandoned simple cause-effect thinking, and there is no reason to believe it can be any more adequate in our complex social world. We have to deal with mutually dependent variables, such that a change in any one leads to a change in the others. We cannot yet measure all these variables precisely, but we can describe them roughly. And we can also show how they vary together.

The present chapter should not be considered a full statement of a theoretical scheme. It has simply defined the main terms to be used in analysis. It has presented a general statement concerning the interrelations of these terms. It is now our task to put the theory in more precise terms through applying it to the data of this case.

We shall begin in the next chapter by showing how the pattern of interaction changed markedly through different time periods and how changes in symbols, activities, and sentiments accompanied these interaction changes.

Two chapters dealing primarily with symbols will follow. The chapter on "The Collective Bargaining Process" analyzes the verbal symbols used to show how they contributed to the other changes we noted following the 1947 negotiations. The chapter on "Incentives for Productivity" examines the role of money as it affects activities of workers, interaction of workers and management, and the sentiments of workers.

The next three chapters, then, can be taken to represent the best statement of theory that I am now able to present. The later chapters present further applications of these theoretical ideas.

Chapter 12

Patterns of Interaction

W E ARE ALL aware that an organization has a structure. But
what exactly do we mean by "structure"? We don't mean the
organization chart, for any experienced person knows that the chart
explains little or nothing about the relations among the people in the
organization.

It is those relations which must be analyzed, for, as the structure
of relations changes, we observe changes in other aspects of behavior
within the organization.

Let us examine patterns of interaction here and note the activities,
symbols, and sentiments that are associated with the interactions.

I am limiting the discussion to the period from 1940 down to the
present time. I have broken those eight years into three time periods.
The first diagram represents the period of 1940–1944 up to the time
Gossett and Novy came in. The second diagram represents the
period between the Gossett and Novy entrance and the 1946 strike.
The third diagram represents the picture at this writing.

To make the point more readily understandable, the actual situations have been considerably simplified. I have limited the diagrams
to four levels in the company: top management, middle management, foreman, and worker, and to the corresponding four levels on
the union side: top union, grievance committeemen, stewards, and
workers. Middle management is intended to be the level of the
general production supervisor, while top management includes the
general factories manager and the vice-president and general man-

ager. Top union includes the international representative and the president of the local. To keep the diagram simple, I have omitted the staff organizations of management. Direction of the arrows

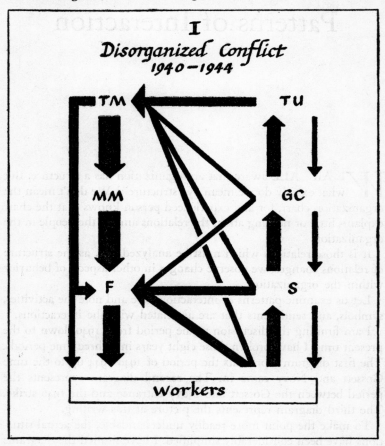

I

Disorganized Conflict
1940–1944

TM   TU

MM   GC

F   S

Workers

indicates the origination of action and their relative thickness suggests the frequency of such origination.

Diagram I represents the following situation:

A. Within the management's structure, origination of action proceeds in one direction only, from the top down. Suggestions or complaints of subordinates are not acted upon.

B. Top management frequently originates directly for foremen or workers, by-passing middle management or foremen. The channels of the organization are not observed.

C. Management does not originate action directly for the union as such. It acts upon the workers only through orders passed down the management structure.

D. The union originates action for management with a rather high frequency and these originations are not channeled in the usual manner. The foreman is acted upon frequently by workers and stewards. Middle management seems to be ignored. Everybody in the union, from bottom to top, is able to get action from top management when the action is pressured by a mass demonstration.

The diagram needs no other general description than its title: Disorganized Conflict. I cannot compare this with any other case, since I have seen none like it. However, it is not difficult to see how a pattern of interaction such as this is necessarily accompanied by hostile sentiments toward management and all sorts of activities which express that hostility. Since the foremen were unable to get action on their problems up the line in management, there was no possibility of adjusting problems and lessening pressure on workers through this channel. When the union people found that they could get no action through the grievance procedure—and could get action through work stoppages and group demonstrations—it was natural for them to express their hostile sentiments and take action as they did.

The situation in Diagram II can be summarized in the following manner:

A. Origination of action from top down in management is increased in frequency, but for the first time the channels of upward communication are open and subordinates are able to get action on at least some of their complaints and suggestions.

B. The channels of communication within management are much more closely observed.

C. The foreman is still under pressure from all sides.

D. The union's originations on management are now channeled in the orthodox manner. They are also reduced in frequency, and the union members must seek other methods for solving their problems. Exactly as in Diagram I, managment never originates action for the union as such.

To get action from workers, top management simply passes its orders down the management structure.

This pattern of interaction is common in labor relations today. Where we find it we also find management people much concerned

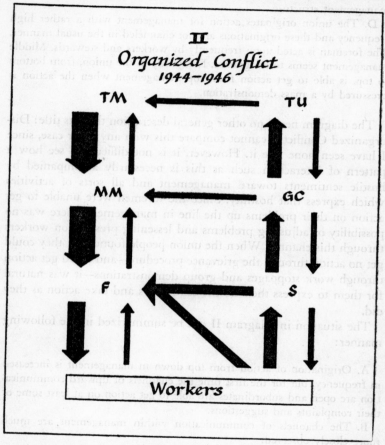

II
Organized Conflict
1944-1946

TM ← TU

MM ← GC

F ← S

Workers

over their powers and prerogatives. They tend to look upon the union only as a watch dog which has a right to challenge management when management fails to follow the contract. Between contract bargaining sessions, it is felt that the union should function only to raise such contract questions, and management tends to try to hold the union down to the specific wording of the contract. Management would like the union leaders to discipline their members for failure to observe the contract, but management asks no help from the union, as such, in the actual production process.

Since every meeting of union and management representatives involves demands by union upon management, it is natural for management to look upon the union in negative terms and seek to contain its aggressive tendencies by drawing a line beyond which the union is not to advance.

If management is willing to exercise countermeasures when the union oversteps the line, it may be possible to hold the line. But it does not seem possible, with such a pattern of interaction, to get the union to accept such a line of demarcation.

The union people feel blocked and checked, and they seek to break out of their confinement. The grievance procedure is open to them, but, as we have seen in this case, they have many problems that cannot be handled within the narrow, legal limits of grievances. They try to force those problems to management's attention through hurting management wherever management can be hurt—and especially in production. These pressures tend to move management toward further disciplinary measures, and those in turn move the union people to seek new ways to hit back at management.

If management is firm and consistent in its discipline, we do not have many of the wildcat strikes that marked the 1940–1944 period. Union resentment is bitter nevertheless and, when a strike does break out, the members show a remarkable staying power. While the struggle for power goes on, such strikes can be long and costly to both sides. In this case we have seen the union carry the 1946 strike almost to the point where the plant went out of existence as an operating unit.

From 1947 on, the situation may be described in the following way:

A. Pressures from the top down in management have eased up and subordinates are able to get action from superiors on their complaints and suggestions with a greatly increased frequency. The work of the factory is done much more on the basis of talking things over than on the basis of ordering people around.

B. The union is able to originate action for management with a frequency greatly increased over Diagram II. For the first time, management is originating action directly for the union. This happens at all levels, particularly at the top level, and at the foreman level. Management

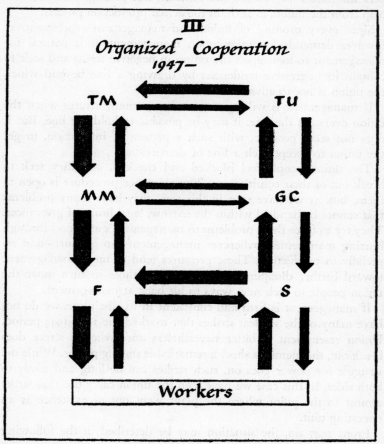

is now utilizing two channels in order to get things done, and the previous account has indicated how much more effective these two channels are than the one utilized in Diagram II.

C. The foreman's position is greatly improved. He is under less pressure from above and can originate more frequently up the line. He is also easing pressures by getting action from the steward.

D. The union officers are now originating action for their subordinates with greater relative frequency than heretofore. Throughout the period of conflict, the key officers maintained an unusual stability in their position. Nevertheless, pressures felt by rank and file workers were so intense in the conflict period that the leaders had constantly to act in response to those pressures. They could channel and direct the activity, but often they were in a position of carrying out activities that they would have preferred not to have underway at all simply because some actions were demanded of them. This did not mean that the officers did not want to lead the fight against management. It means that they were in a position of capitalizing on activity that was springing up all over the plant instead of being able to plan and organize it according to their own designs. Now as the union officers get action from management with increasing effectiveness and thus bring back rewards for the membership, they are in a greatly improved position to plan and control the activities of the rank and file.

This chart also represents something that is observed with increasing frequency in union-management relations. Wherever we have relations which are described by the parties involved as harmonious or cooperative we find that the picture looks approximately like this when it is reduced to a diagram. There may be variations in detail but the key points to observe are these. In all cooperative relations, management is not simply in a position of responding to the union. Management also originates action directly for the union, calling in the officers, offering responsibility, and asking for help on certain problems. Cooperation also depends upon an effective system of communication, up and down within management and within the union. Of course, these areas of interaction are not independent of each other. We are talking about a social system made up of interdependent parts, such that a change in any part leads to changes in other parts.

When relations are organized in this manner, we find that the people are no longer seriously concerned over powers and prerogatives. The management people invite the union to play a constructive role in furthering the welfare of the enterprise. The union leaders accept that invitation—in fact, they ask for opportunities to show the contributions they can make. No longer do all the contacts originated by the union involve demands upon management. Witness Shafer's urging management to accept the union as a channel for suggestions to increase productivity! Furthermore, since management is now getting action out of the union on its problems, the management people no longer feel on the defensive against the union. Drawing the line seems unimportant when you are getting as well as giving.

People on both sides now recognize that they are dependent upon each other. They determine their division of roles and functions according to the problems they must work out together.

Putting the patterns of human relations in diagram form has practical as well as theoretical use. Management and union officials both are concerned with influencing the sentiments and activities of workers and of each other. Sentiments and activities cannot be dealt with effectively in speechmaking or in written communication. They can, however, be changed strikingly, as they have been in this case, through changing the patterns of interaction.

Let us assume, then, that the pattern of Diagram III is the goal of union and management people who are seeking cooperation. The diagrams themselves do not tell us how we get from II to III. We need to study that process of change in order to show how others may be able to achieve the relations pictured in III.

How did behavior change in this case? People sometimes change their behavior when they find it unrewarding, when they find themselves unable to reach the goals they seek. The man who bumps into a stone wall is inclined to look for a different path before he goes into action again. On the other hand, a punishing experience alone is not enough to point out a new path. People may be blocked and punished again and again and still be unable to find the way out. The continuing frustrations on both sides may have made people receptive to change, but that alone was not enough.

The turning point in this case came in the 1947 negotiations. Certain essential changes had come earlier, to be sure, but those negotiations provided the transition to cooperation. Perhaps, if we analyze those bargaining sessions, we will learn more about this process of change. We will never have a full explanation of what took place in those negotiations, but the next chapter should provide some important clues. Here we will be paying particular attention to symbols—the words spoken by the negotiators—as they relate to sentiments, activities, and interaction.

Chapter 13

The Collective Bargaining Process

*U*NION AND MANAGEMENT people both say that the negotiations of 1947 marked the turning point in the case. Why so?

Does a comparison of the 1946 and 1947 contracts explain the change? Let us put the question in another way, and the answer will become obvious. Suppose that the top management of the parent corporation and the top officers of the union had negotiated the 1947 contract, without the participation of the local union or the plant management. Suppose, furthermore, that these negotiators had come out with a contract which was *identical* with that which was actually negotiated. Would the results have been the same?

The case clearly shows that certain contract clauses were of vital importance to the people involved. But their importance cannot be grasped simply through reading them. They can be understood only against the pattern of human relations into which they fit. The relations among the negotiators changed significantly during the bargaining process.

Collective bargaining is more than a legal or economic activity. It is more than a logical exercise. Collective bargaining is a social process. It involves people *emotionally*. It can change decisively the way people feel about each other—for better or for worse. Unless we understand how the sentiments of the bargainers toward each other changed in the course of the 1947 bargaining sessions, we do not fully understand this case.

It is sometimes said that the emotions must be kept out of the bargaining process. That is nonsense. The emotions people feel cannot be simply ignored or suppressed. Unless channels are provided for their expression, they will break out in destructive and unpredictable fashion.

Here the emotions ran high on both sides before the bargaining began. And everyone was involved. The rank-and-file workers participated in the prenegotiation meetings, joined in the work of strike committees, and put up their $5 contributions toward the strike.

One cannot read the negotiation record without seeing that on every page people were expressing the way they felt as well as what they thought. The emotions did find expression, and yet they were so shaped and changed as the process went on that they came out quite differently.

How did it happen? I cannot claim to present an entirely satisfactory answer, but perhaps I can pick out some of the main points.

CONTROL AND UNITY WITHIN THE UNION

We tend to take it for granted that management people will stick together and follow a policy set at the top. The union's problem is more difficult. If the union negotiators make a commitment to management, will they be *willing* and *able* to get the members to carry out that commitment? Management's estimates of the situation will depend in large measure upon the answers they give to that question.

Here management observed almost incredulously the control that Shafer exercised over his committee. This was a marked contrast to previous negotiations, where the situation seemed always to get out of hand. The managers could hardly fail to be impressed by the man who had such a firm command of the organization that had up to now seemed well-nigh uncontrollable.

So Shafer was in control of his committee, but what of the relations between the committee and the membership? Here too there were indications of a leadership that management had not seen evidenced before. In the period of intense strife, Love and his fellow officers had given ample proof that they had the membership behind them. Now, in the year preceding negotiations, there were certain indications of unity in a cooperative direction. Love had worked with management to solve the problems on the barrel line, and production there was beginning to come up—though slowly and tentatively. The officers had also been working on the problem of absenteeism, and we see management giving them some credit during negotiations. Perhaps the most encouraging point of all was Gossett's observation that the most difficult union-management clashes of the preceding year had cropped up when Love was out of the plant on a leave of absence. When Love was on the job, there was no such evidence of people in one department or another running with the ball without union backing—or with the union leader just jumping in to take up a cause because he did not dare to tell the people they had no grievance. So Love also might be counted on to use his very considerable influence in a cooperative direction—under proper circumstances.

Given the delicate situation that prevailed in this case, it was also important that the committee was able to negotiate freely without having to report back to the members until the deadlock was reached. The difficulties that arose from the Maintenance Department leak suggest that it would have been impossible to reach an agreement if the members had been kept informed and in a position to exert pressure on all parts of the contract. This is not to suggest that the contract was railroaded through. The members had two opportunities to discuss it thoroughly, and they participated fully in the prenegotiation stages, but negotiation itself is necessarily a committee matter demanding a freedom of action that could not have been provided otherwise in this case.

People, Problems, and Prerogatives

The negotiators did not concentrate exclusively upon the phraseology of the contract. Instead, they explored the problems that lay behind the phraseology. Shafer took the initiative in placing discussions on this broad plane. As Novy comments:

At first we didn't know how to make him out. He was quiet, he didn't raise his voice. Sometimes he seemed to go off on a tangent, getting into discussions on general things instead of a particular clause

of the contract. We finally got the idea that he was encouraging us to
discuss our general point of view on something, so we could get to
know each other better. After several meetings, it seemed that he was
laying the cards on the table, face up, so we began doing the same.

This sort of procedure was one of Shafer's great strengths. There
appeared to be nothing slick or sharp about him. At first he seemed
to be just a simple, good-natured rube, who had little idea of where
he was going. That impression led management to lower its guard
and to discuss problems in a more relaxed manner. Kaufman
commented to Caples, "The man jumps all over the place. You
can't pin him down." By the time the management men had learned
that the "confusion" was all part of the plan, the advantage had
been gained—for both parties. Instead of confining the talk to
the sharp points of disagreement, Shafer broadened the field to a
discussion of background problems. And he helped to provide
opportunities for the men to establish the personal understandings
that must necessarily go with a mutually satisfying bargaining relationship.

The negotiators constantly sought to relate the words of the
contract to the observed and anticipated behavior of people. In
many cases they were not simply disagreeing on a clause but rather
were seeking to explore for each other how the words would be
translated into action.

This approach contrasted sharply with the practices of previous
bargaining sessions in this case. In the earlier period one party
would bring in a proposal to change a certain clause and the other
party would immediately argue that the particular clause had
served well enough in the past and should therefore not be changed.
The people defending the clause would soon find that they were not
really discussing the merits of a proposal; instead, they were
saying to themselves that if they conceded on the point, that would
be a sign of weakness.

In that atmosphere the people were really talking about *power*
all the time, no matter what else they talked about. When people
think in terms of power, it seems to them that one party can only
gain at the expense of the other. In other words, there is just so
much power to go around, and, if you gain some, you must be

taking it away from me. Naturally, then, I'll fight to avoid giving in on anything.

People who concentrate attention on power in this manner are really pursuing an illusion. For example, management may win the power to require acceptance of certain orders. But those orders are designed to further certain objectives in terms of productivity, costs, and so on, within the plant. The very manner in which management wins a power argument may make it impossible for management to reach its economic objectives. Those objectives can only be attained through the effective working together of workers and management, and arguments focusing on power destroy the basis of cooperation.

In the 1947 negotiations, both parties broke out of this power framework. When management proposed a contract change, the union negotiators did not immediately take up a defensive position. Even when they were satisfied with the existing clause, they were willing to consider fully management's reasons for proposing the change. Unless they saw compelling reasons for refusing to change, the union people were willing to make an adjustment that would meet the problem as seen by management. Management met the union proposals in the same way. On both sides of the table attention was focused on problems, and the people made dilligent efforts to cut through words and phrases to make the adjustments that were required on either side.

Even on the deadlock clause the pattern finally worked out in this way. First this appeared to be one of those irreconcilable clashes between a management prerogative and a union right. As the issue finally worked out, the management people felt they gave the union no rights that were not assumed to be theirs by management under the old contract. Even if that is the case, it does not mean that no contract changes were needed. It was vital to provide the words that would make the union negotiators feel that they had these rights, regardless of the way management felt about it. Only when the negotiators divided the problem into its various parts did they see the extent to which they could get together by spelling out appropriate procedures.

On the prerogative level the union wanted full rights to rate arbitration and management adamantly refused. The settlement gave the union a written guarantee that existing rates, which were recognized as high, would be maintained and that new rates would be adjusted to this high-rate pattern. The union also secured the right to arbitrate the question as to whether there had been sufficient change in job content to justify a rate change. That clause would have made the celebrated "air-hose case" arbitrable. Thus the union got spelled out far-reaching protection to the rate structure.

On the other hand, management retained the right to set new rates and institute rate changes. Management avoided also the risk of having an arbitrator's decision on one rate appear to throw many other rates out of line. The sort of safeguards that the union won were simply the safeguards that are necessary to give the workers confidence in an incentive system and stimulate them to produce under it. Thus union and management won at the same time.

The parties discussed concrete, practical problems, but their discussion was not limited to these issues alone. People who simply discuss their disagreements continue to disagree. The specific problems must be placed in a more general framework. There are at least two frameworks ready at hand:

1. Abstract principles.
2. The experience of people with each other.

If the parties seek to resolve their disagreements in terms of abstract principles, they move the argument into an area where people have strong, conflicting sentiments, quite unrelated to the immediate bargaining situation.

If the parties choose the second framework, they are continually evaluating proposals in terms of past experience, current experience in negotiating, and anticipated experience. They recognize that what they believe depends upon the experience they have. If they are to change their sentiments so that they can agree on certain proposals, they need to reshape their relations with each other so that their experiences also will be changed. This is, in fact, what happened in this case.

THE ROLE OF THE MAN WHO ISN'T THERE

It is said that the successful negotiator will avoid personalities. If that means he will refrain from cursing his opponents and discussing their personal characteristics, the statement is sound. But it only tells what *not* to do and even leaves out important points there. For a man can be antagonized by an attack upon his policies or his organization almost as readily as by an attack upon himself personally. If you can't talk about such matters, what is there left to talk about?

That is where the man-who-isn't-there serves a useful function.

For example, the union put great emphasis upon improving grievance procedure. To substantiate their points, the negotiators brought up for discussion certain current or recent problems. They might have saddled the men across the table with responsibility for these problems—but they didn't. Instead, they talked about the foremen, who were apparently not following management's policies in some cases. The management negotiators could agree that these matters needed to be clarified without feeling that they personally were under attack. With this approach, the union was able to obtain its major objective in the grievance procedure, and the decisions worked out to the mutual satisfaction of the parties.

Management followed exactly the same procedure. Whether it was rest periods, absenteeism, or some other problem, management would attack the "small minority" of workers who were abusing their rights and demand contract changes to cope with that situation. If management had attacked the workers in general or had charged the union with responsibility, the union negotiators would have felt themselves under attack and would have fought back. Instead, they were able to agree that a "small minority" was out of line and constituted a problem to union and management both. But, they argued, let's not have universal rules to cope with this small minority; if union and management work together, we can cope with this mutual problem. The result might be a compromise change in the contract or no change at all, but in any case it would lead to the union's offering to assume more responsibility to clear up these problems and with management pleased to have events move in this direction.

On some occasions Gossett felt that one or another of the men across the table (not including Love) did actually bear a load of responsibility for the problem under discussion. Then he might face that individual as he talked but always without charging him with responsibility or even mentioning his name. The man so addressed might know that the remarks were meant for him, but there would be no need for him to defend himself directly.

We often talk of face-saving as if it were a peculiarly Oriental phenomenon. The skillful negotiator recognizes that that is not the case. He knows he cannot establish a reasonably harmonious relationship if he causes the men across the table to lose face. He may argue vigorously, but he will always seek to project his arguments outside of the room so that the people whose agreement he must get do not feel themselves under attack.

SAFETY VALVES

Shafer began negotiations with a statement that he expected his committee and management to carry on the discussions without any emotional explosions. This accorded well with management plans, but a firm resolve on both sides would hardly have been enough in this situation. The parties needed to have some specific ways of keeping tensions from arising as well as safety valves for blowing off steam harmlessly.

Even with Shafer in control on the union side, there were dangerous tensions to contend with, but Shafer would head off crises by taking the negotiators on his hunting and fishing expeditions. Since these discussions were all off the record, they do not show in the transcript, and we cannot see just at what points the expeditions came in. However, the management people themselves testify to the effectiveness of this tactic.

In negotiations there is always a danger that the parties will take themselves and their problems so seriously that every issue becomes a matter of principle that cannot be yielded. If some of the participants can lighten the atmosphere with a kidding remark or a little joke, an impending deadlock may be avoided. The interchange between Caples and Shafer on the question of who knew Caples's mind provides an illustration of this point, and other examples could readily be cited. It is not important that the joke be hilarious; if it eases tension, it has served its purpose.

THE DEAD HORSE

Said Shafer: "Don't kick the dead horse, because the more you kick it the more it stinks."

The union sought to rule out discussions of the bitter history of relations. The management negotiators felt somewhat limited by this, since some understanding of the past was necessary to their current argument. However, even in bringing up the past, management did not seek to lay the blame, but simply indicated the types of problems that suggested the need for certain contract safeguards. When management did not insist on constantly raking over the past, the union was willing to accept responsibility for current problems.

It is impossible to bargain without making reference to the past, for proposed contract changes make sense only in terms of the experience of the parties. The past may be surveyed in order to illustrate the importance of a problem. But if the negotiator allows himself to lay the blame for a problem, he immediately throws the argument back into the past and scrapes old wounds. The skillful negotiator knows that there is nothing to gain from laying the blame.

A FULL HEARING

When a man states a point of view on which you disagree, there are two contrasting ways of meeting the situation:

1. You can immediately bring in counterarguments to show him that he is wrong.

2. You can express interest (not approval) in his point of view and ask him to tell you more about it. Why does he feel the way he does? What is behind his thinking?

These two moves lead in opposite directions. The first move leads to increasingly sharp disagreements, marked by briefer and more rapid interchanges, more interruptions, and rising emotional tension.

The second move leads to relaxed tension and makes agreement possible. The man does not feel under pressure to get out his statement in a hurry and prepare for counterattack. He is able to talk to the subject and around it, in an informal, exploratory manner. You are able then to size up possibilities of getting together.

If we review the negotiation record in this case, we find many instances of this second approach. That was Shafer's way of meeting management's arguments.

For example, take the first argument over rate arbitration. Kaufman introduced the subject, suggested that the union speak first on it, but then opened up with a management statement. After Novy had commented, "That's putting it very mildly," Shafer came in with this remark: "I am interested in Mr. Novy's statement. You say, 'That is putting it very mildly.'" Now here was the crucial issue of negotiations. Management was opening up with strong pressure on this issue. It must have taken self-control for the union not to rush in with a counterattack at the first opening. Yet here was Shafer sitting back and simply asking management to talk more fully and freely on the subject. The result was that the management people did go on at length to lay out their position. They got the satisfaction of a full hearing. Only when they had had their say did the union open up with its arguments. At that time Love talked at length, and management gave him a full hearing.

This brings us up against the most puzzling problem of these negotiations. Somehow during the course of negotiations John Gossett decided he could trust Jake Shafer. When did it happen? We don't know. Probably it was no sudden decision but rather a slowly growing conviction. Why did it happen? No one point will give us the answer, but this point seems to be of considerable importance.

Gossett decided that Shafer had a sincere interest in management's problems. What did Shafer say to get that point across? Was it enough simply to say that he was interested in costs and productivity? Hardly. If union men could win the confidence of management men simply by saying, "I am interested in your problems," the situation (for the union) would be far simpler than what we actually find.

This is what we see in research. If I am discussing my problems with you, I am not satisfied with a statement of your interest. It does not matter whether the statement is a short sentence or a long and eloquent speech. I will only feel that you are interested *if you act interested*. And you can act interested only by encouraging me to explain my problems to you. I will only feel that you understand me and my problems if you help me to explain them fully to you *as I see them*.

I am suggesting that, in negotiations, listening is just as important as talking. In part, Shafer won the confidence of Gossett through listening to him, through giving him a full and sympathetic hearing.

DISAGREEING WITH RESPECT

Listening is not enough. After you have heard the other man out, if you still disagree, you must have a way of stating that disagreement. Here again there are two contrasting ways of doing it:

1. You can say, in effect, "I think you are wrong. You are wrong for the following reasons:"—and so on with a systematic "proof" of the other fellow's stupidity.

2. You can say, in effect, "Well, I see why you feel the way you do. In terms of the experience you have had, that is a reasonable point of view. But on the other hand, our experience has been different, and we have different problems." You can then go on to describe your experience and problems in order to show why the proposal is unacceptable.

The first approach leads to people trying to outsmart each other. The "winner" of such an argument simply humiliates his opponent in such a way as to make agreement impossible.

The second approach moves the argument into a field where agreement becomes possible. Relating sentiments to experience is sound science as well as sound strategy. We know that people at different positions and with different functions in an organization have different experiences which naturally build different sentiments. We cannot expect the executive and the union leader to have the same body of experience. But they can ask each other how their experience can be reorganized so that a given proposal will be acceptable to both parties.

In effect, this was the pattern followed on the critical issues in these negotiations. The steps went something like this:

1. An expression of respect for the other fellow's position.

2. A discussion of the body of experience that makes it impossible to accept his proposal.

3. A *joint* exploration of ways in which the proposal can be changed and/or of the ways in which the experience of the two parties can be changed so as to make such a proposal acceptable.

When negotiations are conducted in this way, mutual respect grows, and the parties actually come to grips with the economic and human relations problems of the plant. They do not get lost in abstract arguments over principles.

PATTERNS OF AGREEMENT

Bargaining seems to run in a pattern, with one disagreement leading to another or with one agreement leading to another. If that is true, then it is important to build up a pattern of agreement early. Even if the accord is only on minor matters or points that seem irrelevant, it helps to provide the atmosphere that leads to a resolution of major issues.

For example, take Shafer's hunting and fishing expeditions. Their function was not limited to serving as safety valves. Novy commented:

> It's been my experience that whenever you run into a real sportsman, you'll find that he is a pretty regular fellow. He's a man you can deal with straight from the shoulder. That's one of the things that sold me on Shafer.

Such things as hunting, fishing, and the war the men could discuss in a friendly, man-to-man manner, without any danger of emotional clashes. It helped them to feel confidence in the man across the table and served to break down the stereotypes of the aggressive-irresponsible union leader or the grasping, antisocial manager.

This does *not* mean that the chief point of bargaining is for both parties to discover that the people across the table are a "good bunch of fellows." In the 1947 sessions the negotiators developed a wholehearted respect for each other—which they openly expressed —and yet they were still prepared for a strike on the rate issue.

A real settlement of differences cannot be made on the basis of personal adjustment alone. On the other hand, such a settlement cannot be achieved without a personal adjustment. In other words, the personal adjustment paves the way for and makes possible an agreement on issues.

We would not expect the personal adjustment to take place readily in meeting the major issues, for it is precisely at those points that the parties feel themselves farthest apart and most challenged. The personal adjustment may be made possible through the injection of matters (like hunting and fishing) which are logically irrelevant but which allow the parties to agree with each other and embrace a common interest.

As they evolved this personal adjustment, the people could move ahead more effectively to find areas of agreement on contract issues. Both sides began with certain objectives that they felt were worth the risk of a strike and other objectives that they would try to achieve short of a strike. The pattern of agreement began to evolve on these nonstrike issues. The parties deliberately brushed past the strike issues in the early sessions.

By the time they had to work through these strike issues they had already found a basis of personal adjustment and had developed an effective pattern of meeting the lesser issues. Once again they searched for an area of common interest. It was a close thing; they almost failed to find it—but find it they did.

I am not suggesting that the interests of union and management are the same and that the people need only to search in order to see this light. The parties appear to oppose each other at many points, and the adjustment does not come easy. Nevertheless, we cannot escape from one fundamental fact: management and union are dependent upon each other. The two are so closely tied together that they cannot function without seriously affecting each other at many points of contact.

The skillful negotiator recognizes this interdependence and also recognizes that he can get help in solving his own problems only if he gives help in solving the problems that are felt on the other side of the table. That was the approach these men took to the problems of productivity and incentive rates.

The Union Assumes Responsibility

A manager can hardly develop cordial relations with union officers if their organization functions only to demand concessions and to question and resist his decisions. That way his experience with the union is always punishing. He never has the rewarding experiences that give rise to a cooperative attitude.

In the past management's experiences with the union had been largely on the punishing side. Now Shafer was saying again and again that the union would assume its responsibility on certain problems, such as productivity and absenteeism, which were of serious concern to management. Love and Shafer were both pointing out that the union had already taken action on the absenteeism problem. The management people readily gave credit for these efforts, even though they felt the results were small up to that point.

The management negotiators listened to these union responsibility discussions with some reservations. Other men had said that the union would take responsibility on certain problems, and nothing had happened. Still, there was a difference here. Shafer did not just say the union would help management on its problems. He encouraged management to lay those problems out on the table for a thorough discussion. This was much more than a mechanical statement of intentions. It encouraged the management negotiators to believe that Shafer and his committee meant to follow through.

Following Through

The bargaining process is not finished when the negotiators reach agreement on all points. Subsequent relations will depend upon the first steps that are taken in putting the contract into effect.

In this case the negotiators on both sides held meetings with the members of their organizations to explain the contract—and to discuss the *spirit* of the contract. They said that they had established the basis for a cooperative relationship. They urged their people to expect the best from the other party, to move ahead on the assumption that cooperation was going to develop.

Specifically, Shafer, Love, and their committee urged the members to show management the values of cooperative union relationship through putting out a little more effort on the production line. The people were glad to take their part in this process. They did not go all out at first, but they did enough to show the possibilities.

The first fourth-step grievance meeting served to tie the negotiation process right into the day-to-day relations within the plant. Shafer said he came in to clear away the backlog of problems and to make sure that people were moving ahead together on productivity. The problem he brought up was not even a grievance, and yet Kaufman suggested it be aired first. And the discussion of the first problem demonstrated again to the people around the table that they were really moving forward together. As we read the record of that meeting we can see the structure of cooperation going up before our eyes.

The men felt their way through the negotiations toward a tentative understanding. Following negotiations, they fitted the structure together and began to strengthen it. There was much work still to be done, but a solid structure for cooperation had taken definite shape.

Chapter 14

Incentives for Productivity

T HE PRODUCTIVITY achieved in this plant has been one of the most impressive aspects of the case. We may well ask: Why do the workers produce so much?

Compared to other workers, these men and women are doing well for themselves financially. Can it be that the money accounts for this performance? No, for we have to observe that productivity has risen tremendously while there has been little change in the incentive rates. themselves.

Perhaps, then, the change in human relations gives us our explanation. For a specialist in human relations, that is a tempting answer, but it is clearly not the whole truth. Interviews with workers and union officers clearly show the lure of more money. The incentive rates, then, do have some drawing power.

If we follow this either-or approach we shall never get an answer. It is not money *or* human relations. The problem is to fit them together into an effective combination.

It has been traditional to assume that money is the chief motivating force for workers. The man who talked in terms of money was a hardheaded realist, while the man who suggested other possible incentives was considered an impractical dreamer. But now the tide has turned. The Western Electric Company research program and many others that followed it have demonstrated beyond question that productivity fluctuates with changes in human relations.

There may be a tendency now to push money into the background and say that human relations are *the* thing. Let us not allow the pendulum to swing too far.

In science we no longer search for *the* cause for a given phenomenon. We recognize that there are always a number of factors involved. We don't try to determine which is *the* factor or even which is the most important factor. Instead, we try to discover how the factors fit together to produce the results we observe.

That will be our procedure on this problem.

We start by considering incentive rates as symbols. We make no assumptions about how men respond to these symbols. Our problem is to find out how they do in fact respond through observing their behavior. The explanation to be given is not based on this case alone. It has developed out of a number of other studies also.

We focus on four major aspects of the problem. They are closely tied together, but we can separate them for purposes of analysis.

THE PRICE OF WORK

How much can a man make on a job? Let us suppose the man is making a dollar an hour when he is not on incentive. It is well recognized that he won't put out his best on incentive if the rates are set so that his top performance will only bring a slight increase over his regular hourly rate. Why work hard for $1.05 when you can take it easy for $1? The size of the financial reward is certainly of importance. How big must it be really to motivate a worker? Incentive engineers suggest that the worker should be able to make 120 to 130 per cent of his basic hourly rate. Any such figure is arbitrary, for behavior will vary from case to case, but that figure is probably as good an estimate as any.

In those terms, the price of work at the Inland Steel Container Company is high. In 1948 and 1949 incentive workers averaged about 140 per cent of their hourly pay. (See Appendix B for summary of earnings.)

From the worker's standpoint, management has set a good price on these jobs. At least, so it appears today. A few years ago workers did not look upon the rates in that way, but we cannot explain this changed viewpoint from looking at the rates alone.

CAPACITIES OF MEN AND MACHINES

Obviously we cannot tell how attractive a price has been set until we know the capacities of men and machines. At first glance this would seem to be a problem that could be solved on the basis of good, systematic measurements. Measurements can give us part of the answer, to be sure, but they do not tell us everything.

Even with machines, there are elements that elude precise measurement. Management may know just how fast a machine can go, but how can we estimate how often the machine will break down and how long it will take to put it back into action? That will depend in part upon the machine itself. But, as we have seen in this case, it depends also upon the men who operate the machine. They can encourage breakdowns by carelessness or by tampering. They can minimize breakdowns by the care they take of the machine. And similarly they can prolong or shorten down time.

Furthermore, there may be "bugs" in the machine which prevent it from operating at its estimated capacity. Often these bugs are well known to the man on the production line but are not readily observed by management. Whether the necessary improvements will be made depends, therefore, upon the relations between workers and union and management. In this case we have seen how working the bugs out of the barrel lines in early 1947 depending upon bringing about these human relations changes.

Even as we measure the performance of machines, we cannot escape from human relations. And, of course, the problem of measuring worker performance is much more complicated than that.

A man's capacity to do work is not just a physical phenomenon. We are not simply measuring how fast he can operate a machine for a short period of time. We want to know how fast he can go eight hours a day, day after day, year after year, without injury to his health.

We cannot consider fatigue from the physical standpoint alone. Research has amply demonstrated that fatigue has important emotional aspects. A worker may perform 100 units of work in one situation and feel completely exhausted. He may perform the same 100 units of work in a more favorable social environment and feel reasonably fresh at the end of the day. Nervous tension can add greatly to the fatigue of any job. There is no need to labor the point on this case. The workers today are doing more concentrated work than they did in earlier periods, and they report that they feel less tired at the end of the day.

Of course, the capacities of men and machines are not unlimited. Even under the best of conditions there is always a point beyond which they cannot go. But we cannot estimate those maximum possibilities simply through studying the machine or measuring the performance of the man. Those observations give us only a rough guide. Beyond that point, we have to ask what is meant by "under the best of conditions."

GOALS FOR PRODUCTION

The rate itself does not set a production goal. Let us assume that the rate is a penny per piece. That determines how much a worker will make for 150 or 175 or 200 pieces in an hour, but that rate does not determine whether a worker (or a group of workers) will shoot for 150 or 175 or 200.

What difference does it make? Recent experiments have shown that workers increase their productivity when they get together to set themselves a goal. In other words, men produce more when they say to each other, "Let's see if we can make two hundred an hour" than they do when they set up no target.

That target or goal is an important symbol—and one often overlooked by incentive engineers. Perhaps it tends to be overlooked because the goal cannot be set by management alone. The manager or the foreman can say to a work group, "Fellows, let's make two hundred an hour," but that 200 does not become a goal for the group unless it is accepted by them. And research has shown that people do not accept goals that are just handed to them. They are moved much more strongly toward the goals they themselves have had a part in setting.

While management cannot do the job alone, management can help to provide the symbols and to give them meaning. Production records would not have existed in this plant, so far as the workers were concerned, if management had not publicized the records of the other plants. Then management helped to make the goals attractive by giving recognition to the groups that set new records.

Clearly, the great increase in productivity did not just happen. Union officers and workers got together to decide that they would raise their sights. I know of no occasion when they got together to decide that they would aim at a particular figure, but they did decide the direction in which they would move.

We can't tell, without much more interviewing at the rank-and-file level than I have done, to what extent these production records really became goals for the workers. It certainly did not happen on the basis of a conscious decision of the whole group. On the other hand, it appears that group leaders and a number of other workers as well took these records seriously and took pride in setting new records. Management then acted with skill and understanding to provide recognition to support that interest.

Actually individuals and work groups are always deciding how much they will do, but we usually think of that behavior in terms of quotas rather than in terms of goals. It becomes an accepted standard of the group that x pieces constitute "a fair day's work," and people will generally not go beyond that, regardless of the incentive or the exhortations of management.

If people set a higher goal for themselves, then they do go higher. That sounds obvious enough. But, granted that a goal of itself is important, what leads workers to raise their sights and shoot at a higher target? Again we ask: Under what conditions do men operate machines at their highest efficiency?

PATTERNS OF INTERACTION AND SENTIMENTS

Under what conditions do workers think it is *a good thing* to increase productivity? What reward is in it for them? "More money" is the obvious first answer where we have an incentive system. But how far can we go with that single reward?

We must remember that management also is rewarded by increased productivity. There is no secret about it. Workers all know how interested management is in productivity. So each additional piece they turn out helps management at the same time that it pays off for them. But suppose they don't want to help management?

When workers hate and distrust management, they feel that it is both wrong and dangerous to themselves to help management. They look upon the man who produces beyond the "quota" of the group as a self-seeking individualist—a "rate buster" who would sell out his fellow men for a few extra dollars. While most of us set a high value on money, we also look with scorn on the man who would sacrifice the interests of his fellow men for money.

So, when there is such hatred and distrust of management, the worker is pulled in two directions. He would like to have more money, to be sure. He needs it for his family and community life outside of the plant. But money is something he can't do anything with inside of the plant. And let us not forget that the life within the plant is very real to the worker. A factory worker once made this comment while he was working at his machine: "This is where we really live. We spend more time in this plant than we do at anything else except when we are home in bed." And the worker spends more time with fellow workers than he does with anyone else within the plant. He may want money—they all do, in varying degrees—but he also wants to be liked and respected by the people he works with. An extra dollar and a pat on the back from the foreman are nice things in themselves, but they can hardly compensate (in most cases) for eight hours a day of ostracism from the work group. So most workers will go after the bonus up to a certain point, and then they will pull back. They are constantly weighing the lure of the money against the requirements of living within the social system. Under those conditions, they work inefficiently and under nervous tension.

Several studies have shown that where such worker-management hostility exists, less than one in ten of the workers will do the production job he is capable of. Management may reward that tenth man, but the real problem is with the other nine, for it is they who determine whether the plant average is high or low.

What can management do in such a case? Suppose management tells the workers that the rates will not be cut, no matter how much they produce. That is, suppose management tells the worker that his high production will not injure other workers or himself. What then? Managements today give such assurances over and over—but without effect. We must realize that we are dealing with sentiments here. If the workers hate and distrust management, why should they believe anything management tells them? Their sentiments change as their relations with management change, and relations do not change when we simply tell people something.

For good production to be accepted as a goal by workers, their sentiments toward management must change. The hatred and distrust must give way to respect and confidence. Only under those circumstances can it become a good thing for workers to take actions that help management, while they help themselves. If the pattern of interaction is reorganized, those sentiments necessarily change. Then workers are no longer pulled in two directions. They can make money and still be accepted by the work group. They can have the respect of the foreman and of fellow workers at the same time. They can turn their energies all in one direction instead of constantly balancing the pull of management and money against the pull of fellow workers.

In this case the workers held back their production at great financial loss to themselves through the months and years when they were fighting management. Because of the way they felt toward management, they thought that was what they had to do. But then in 1947 and thereafter the pattern of interaction underwent far-reaching changes. In this process the sentiments the people bore toward each other also changed strikingly. For the first time, stepping up production became a good thing to do—from any point of view. So the workers went out and stepped it up. They went after the money—to be sure—but only when it fitted into the proper social setting. Money has only limited drawing power in a social system shot through with conflict and distrust.

This change in the pattern of interaction affected the agents of the incentive system as much as anybody else. The time-study men tend to be a focus of conflict in industry. Generally they have never been production workers themselves, whereas many foremen have. But this white-collar status and difference in background is only a small part of the story. Time-study men are looked upon by workers as agents of change. They are not working *with* the men; instead, they are constantly checking the men. The stop watch and clip board stand for mysterious operations that are beyond the knowledge of the worker who has not been trained in time study.

In most cases it is always the time-study man who originates action for the worker—never the other way around. And every action of the time-study man seems to threaten a change in the established order of things.

In such an atmosphere neither worker nor time-study man can do an effective job. If the time-study man moves in and out of each department freely and on his own, neither his contacts nor the nature of his job enables him to make the personal adjustment that is possible to an effective foreman who works with the same people every day. Furthermore, while the foreman develops a regular pattern in his contacts with his workers, the time-study man's contacts are not only less frequent; they are also more sporadic and unpredictable. Contacts of this nature always have an unsettling effect upon people.

In 1948 the place of the time-study man in this social system was markedly changed. No longer did he move about completely on his own. Management now directed him to have the signature of the general factories manager or the general production supervisor before he went into any department. Then, immediately upon entering the department, he had to explain to the foreman what he intended to do and how he planned to do it. Next he had to give a similar explanation to the steward. In this way he could be introduced to the workers through regular and well-established channels of interaction. He could fit himself into the existing pattern of interaction rather than to disrupt the established routines.

In this way the workers and steward and foreman would all have advance notice of contemplated changes. If one or more individuals thought that the change would be unfortunate, they could take this point of view up, informally, through the established channels before a management decision was made. In this way management gained a much better opportunity to assess the probable effects of a decision than was the case when the time-study man simply moved in on his own. It is not easy to reverse a management decision, without unfortunate effects. If an unwise decision can be avoided in the first place, both union and management are that much better off.

This does not mean that management will refrain from making any decision that is opposed by the union or by the departmental

foreman. It simply means that management has a better understanding of the situation and a better chance of winning over opposition before a definite decision is reached.

These observations upon the time-study men can be applied to
other staff officers also. Generally, the interactions up and down
the line of authority are much more frequent than those occurring
at any point between staff and line. The staff officer can function
most effectively if he fits himself into this existing pattern of
interaction in the line of authority and in the union. He will be a
source of friction unless he fits himself into these channels.

When all these changes had taken place in the relations of union
and management and in the relations of time-study to production
management and to the union, we observed that the symbols of
the incentive system took on a greatly altered meaning. I have
described the change for the incentive system in general. The point
can be made more specifically if we review once more the air-hose
case.

The rates in this case became an exceedingly important symbol
to the union. They didn't mean simply so many pieces per hour
on such-and-such a job. The job came up so seldom that this literal
meaning was of minor importance. At the time when the case
first arose, the union people hated and mistrusted management.
From these sentiments it followed that any change management
made was probably a threat to the union. When management made
a change that could be interpreted as rate cutting—the gravest
threat of all—it followed naturally and inevitably that management had done a terrible thing. Under the existing pattern of
interaction and sentiments, no logical arguments offered by management could have persuaded many of the union people to view
the case in any other light.

But then, in the time that it took the case to get from the first
to the fourth step of the grievance procedure, the pattern of interaction and the accompanying sentiments had markedly changed.
Necessarily, then, the symbol took on a different meaning. The
union people no longer needed that symbol to stand for their distrust
of management. They were therefore able to look at it simply in
terms of comparative earnings before and after the change. On
that basis they could be satisfied that they had not been cheated.

The point can be stated in more general terms. A symbol should not be considered in an absolute sense. Whether it is an incentive rate, a profit, or a cost figure—or any other symbol—people's interpretations will be influenced according to the sentiments they feel toward those who set up the symbol. Therefore, where management is hated and mistrusted, management wastes its time and energies putting out logical arguments on wages, prices, profits, and so on. It does not matter how sound those arguments may be in economic terms. They will be accepted or rejected primarily in terms of the pattern of interaction and sentiments that has developed between union and management. In fact, the economics of the enterprise cannot be considered in objective and realistic fashion until the relations between the parties are so adjusted as to create sentiments of mutual confidence.

Chapter 15

The Problem of Prerogatives

MANAGEMENT PREROGATIVES are today one of the most difficult issues in industrial relations. Many people feel that the parties can find peace only when they are able to agree on an allocation of functions so that some are recognized as joint responsibilities while some are granted to management exclusively and others are reserved to the union. Can such lines be drawn?

Developments in this case point out a possible answer to the question. It remains for us only to spell out what is already implicit in the description and analysis.

We find that unions and managements that are able to work together harmoniously have, in fact, developed a general understanding of their individual functions and of the way those functions may be fitted together. Can that understanding be arrived at through prior discussion or can it only evolve on the basis of the experience of the parties? That is the central point at issue.

When we seek to draw the lines on the basis of prior discussion we immediately get into difficulties. In the first place, as we survey the industrial relations scene we find a variety of adjustments on this prerogative issue. We can pick out two contrasting adjustments of this issue and find in both cases that the union and management people are well satisfied with their situation. A search for a "natural law" of management prerogatives inevitably breaks down when faced with this variety of experience.

In the second place, we must question whether an issue of this sort can ever be resolved on the basis of a discussion of principles. When we discuss what management should do in a specific case, we are dealing in concrete terms. When we discuss, in general, what management's functions are, then we are in the abstract realm of principles. Many observers have noted the difficulty of solving issues in those terms. Principles are precisely those things which people hold to with the greatest emotional heat. We often find that groups of people are able to work together when they give their attention to practical problems but are unable to get along when they discuss the principles underlying their relationship.

That experience is well illustrated in this case. We have seen that it was one of the great strengths of the negotiators on both sides of the table that they were able to avoid discussions of abstract principles and instead concentrated on specific problems. Furthermore, the parties were able to adjust their functions somewhat differently from step to step in the process of acting on these problems. They evolved a different relationship and a more mutually satisfying one on this problem-to-problem basis. We can be confident that they would not be where they are today if they had sought in advance to reach a general decision on the division of functions and responsibilities.

Adjustment on this issue apparently must come through an evolutionary process. But does that evolution involve management's constantly giving ground to the union? That is the fear of many management people, and that fear quite naturally impels them to try to draw the line somewhere and take up a strong defensive position behind that line.

Such a point of view is a product of our recent history in industrial relations. Unions in the mass production industries of this country are still a relatively new phenomenon. They sprang up with aggressive attacks upon management and proceeded to whittle away management's prerogatives in one field after another. The executive naturally views this process with alarm and wonders where it can end.

An equilibrium has been achieved in many cases, but it tends to arise in terms of a rather general understanding among the parties as to how they fit together rather than from any specific line of demarcation. This sort of equilibrium has one basic characteristic we have already noted in this case. Management originates action for the union directly. Management does not remain in the defensive position of simply responding to the union's demands.

Reciprocity develops between union and management. Management is able to get help on its problems through the union. The union assumes some responsibility for the welfare of the enterprise.

To be sure, this brings the union into certain areas which it would not otherwise enter, but does that in itself weaken management's control and leadership? Let us put the question in terms of examples from this case. On the basis of discussions with the union, John Gossett directed certain changes in cost-accounting and checking procedure in the Punch Press Department. On another occasion he offered the union leaders a choice between layoffs and a shorter work week. Both areas are strictly within the province of management, as defined by the management clause in the contract. By consulting the union leaders and even working out plans with their help, did Gossett weaken the position of management?

Or consider a more far-reaching example. Management and union worked through the complex problems of the Maintenance Department on a joint discussion basis. Did that weaken the position of management?

What do we mean by strength or weakness in labor relations? It is true that management's area of unilateral action has been reduced, but is this a loss to management? In this case (and in many others) we see management unable to gain its economic objectives when it relies on unilateral action. Through consultation and joint action, we see management reaching goals that the management people themselves say would have been impossible on a unilateral basis.

By taking the union leaders into management's confidence on important matters, management increased the confidence the members and leaders had in management. Consultation and joint action greatly strengthened the economic effectiveness of the management organization.

Either in business or in political life, it is difficult to govern without the consent of the governed. Men who are preoccupied with the extent of their powers are inclined to overlook the problem of building up willing consent among subordinates in their organizations. Without such consent, power becomes an illusion.

Those on either side who seek to confine the union to a "watchdog" position overlook some of the essential requirements of a harmonious union-management relationship. According to the watchdog point of view, the union's functions should be limited to the grievance procedure and the annual round of collective bargaining.

The grievance procedure is certainly a key part of any union-management relationship and no relationship can be satisfactory to the parties unless grievances are being effectively handled. However, we must not expect of the grievance procedure results that cannot be obtained through those channels. We must emphasize some of the limitations of the grievance procedure.

In the first place, the grievance procedure involves one-way origination of action from union to management. It is an essential counterweight to the originations of management upon the workers and assures the workers of a channel of upward communication. But we have already seen in this case—and many others could be cited—that relations began to improve only as management began to originate action directly for the union. This does not happen if the union-management relationship is confined strictly to the handling of grievances.

Where union-management relations are shot through with conflict, it becomes impossible to treat grievances effectively simply as grievances. In this case we have seen how at least half the grievances pushed by the union, for many months, were simply parts of a pressure move against management. When the relationship changed so that such pressure seemed to the union no longer necessary, the pressure grievances dropped out. Only then could management take up a grievance with confidence that a study of the grievance might clarify some underlying problem.

We have seen how the air-hose case completely changed its meaning when the relations among the parties changed. That suggests that the manager who hopes to cope with the union primarily through the grievance procedure is setting himself an impossible task.

The manager or union leader who seeks cooperation should be primarily concerned with disturbances in the pattern of human relations, for it is these which give rise to grievances and other manifestations of discontent. He should recognize, then, that the grievance procedure covers only a part of the area that can give rise to such disturbances. For example, accounting procedures are generally considered as exclusively a management function and are thus ruled out of the area of bargaining or grievances. But in this case we saw how management's changes in its accounting procedure in the Punch Press Department gave rise to serious human relations disturbances. These led to grievances, but, since the actual source of the disturbances was outside the scope of the grievance procedure, the grievances had only an indirect bearing upon the real issues. All they indicated was: there is trouble in the Punch Press Department. The manager who sought to meet that trouble on a grievance basis alone would never have got to the heart of the problem. It was only when management and union sat down together to discuss the underlying disturbances that they were able to take effective action.

Finally, grievances deal only with the past. We often find that uncertainty over the future disturbs the relations between the parties. When changes are constantly introduced by management without prior discussion with the union, workers and union people come to feel insecure and feel a need to fight for their positions. More and more executives are recognizing that they can build a more effective organization if they help everyone involved to anticipate and prepare for the changes that must come in the future. Gossett's discussion of proposed technological changes presents a statesmanlike example of this line of action.

This is not an either-or question. The grievance procedure is vital, but it must be supplemented by discussions focused upon the underlying disturbances to the system of relationships. These discussions do not have to take place in separate and special meetings.

It is not the form but the substance that counts. These human relations problems can be taken up at grievance meetings or at other meetings—so long as they are taken up. Management will find that the discussion of such problems actually makes it easier to settle pending grievances. For example, take Shafer's first fourth-step grievance meeting following the signing of the 1947 contract. Shafer announced that the union had a number of grievances and also a problem to discuss. Kaufman seized the opportunity by suggesting that the problem be aired first. Disposing of the problem first seemed to clear the air and make it easy to run through all the grievances. If management had decided that the grievances must be disposed of first, it is doubtful whether they could have been so easily worked out. And what if management had said that it would not discuss the problem until it had given rise to grievances that had worked their way up to the fourth step? Such a decision would have lost for management all the gains that had come out of the bargaining process.

In effect, Shafer was saying: We have a problem that is threatening to disrupt the new relationship we are building. In effect, Kaufman was responding: Any problem that threatens this relationship must be met at once; let's get into it.

This analysis points to the necessity of broadening the area of a union-management discussion beyond the specific points of the contract. But that does not mean that the broadening must necessarily be done by making new areas subject to the joint determination of collective bargaining. Operating a business successfully requires the exercise of professional skills and initiative. There are many decisions that cannot wait upon the process of joint determination. And there are also decisions that must be taken even when full agreement of all the parties cannot be secured. But, if there are limitations to the possibilities of jointly negotiated decisions, there is a tremendous area where management may retain the initiative but still proceed with the advice and consultation of the union.

What should be the area of joint determination? On what problems should management act without discussion with the union? Where should management retain the initiative but act only following consultation with the union?

Those are questions on which no definite answers can be given. When we have studied the experience of people in various other union-management relationships, we may find that certain sorts of problems are more effectively handled by one type of procedure while other sorts fit better with another procedure. But in the present state of our knowledge we must trust to the imagination, patience, and intelligence of leaders on both sides to work out satisfactory adjustments on a case-to-case basis.

Now we can only point to two guideposts to action:

1. Union-management adjustment grows out of the solution of specific problems. It cannot come out of a general discussion of powers and prerogatives.

2. Cooperative sentiments and actions depend upon an appropriate pattern of interaction. Without spelling out that pattern in full, we can note that it requires management to originate action directly for the union. Only in that way can management get away from its defensive frame of mind. Only in that way can the union leaders play a responsible role in the development of the enterprise.

Chapter 16

What Are They Getting Out of It?

PEOPLE IN UNION and management say they like their new relationship. More than that: they are proud of it.

Let's look at it now from their point of view and ask: What are they getting out of it? If we are to apply the findings of this case to other cases, that is an important question.

It is not easy to break out of a pattern of conflict and establish a set of harmonious relations. It takes all the ingenuity, skill, and social understanding possessed by the leadership on both sides. Is it worth the effort? What rewards may a union or management man expect to gain if he sets out upon the difficult road from conflict to cooperation? What satisfactions are there for people in a cooperative relationship that they do not find in conflict?

We often read about the "objectives of management" or of the union or of the satisfactions gained from some action by union or management. It is as if the writer were talking about an individual possessing all the emotional and thought processes of other human beings. Actually the union or management is an organization made up of many people. The union or management as such does not think or feel or act. It is only its particular members who think and feel and act.

Sometimes we speak of management or union in a shorthand sense. We say "management takes a stand" because it is too cumbersome to say, "certain individuals in the management organization take a stand." But useful as such a shorthand term is, we must not allow it to mislead us when we are discussing the problem of motivation.

When successful action is taken by management, there are particular people carrying out the action and getting their satisfactions from it. To be sure, they may gain a sense of satisfaction from serving as effective members of an organization, but those satisfactions they experience individually.

For example, it does not matter how economically advantageous a particular arrangement of relationships is to the company, as such. Unless its individual members feel rewarded in their day-to-day activities, they will not support and develop that relationship. We come back necessarily to the question: What satisfactions are these people getting out of the new relationship?

It is generally thought that union and management people get quite different satisfactions out of a cooperative relationship. There are differences, of course, but, in this case at least, each of the six points I shall list involves satisfactions that have been achieved by both sides.

1. Economic Gains

Let us take the most obvious point first. As the company grows more prosperous, the earning possibilities of members of management increase. The sale of the plant that seemed imminent in 1946 would, of course, have meant the loss of jobs for many members of management and lower salaries, in many cases, in new jobs. Furthermore, the profit-and-loss statement has an important symbolic significance as a yardstick for successful performance of a management job. When the profit-and-loss statement shows losses (at least in generally profitable times) the executive may lose confidence in himself, and he may lose some of the respect of other business people. The statement shows that he is not a successful businessman. On the other hand, a good profit picture increases his self-confidence and adds to the respect with which other businessmen regard him. By the profit yardstick, these management men have shown themselves to be highly successful.

To the workers, the new relationship has meant the assurance of continuous earnings and high earnings subject, of course, to changes in customer demand for the products. The union officers, having had a part in these developments, can feel their own positions more secure in the favorable earnings opportunities enjoyed by the rank and file. They can also take pride in helping to make these high earnings possible.

2. Satisfactions of Achievement

The rewards of work are not paid off in money alone. There is deep satisfaction in knowing that you have done a good job and that you are doing an increasingly good job. Satisfaction does not come simply from *taking;* men want to feel that they are *contributing* their physical and mental energy toward getting the job done.

Management's gains here are obvious—and so are the union gains, up to a certain point. But note the great change in worker contributions. In the conflict period the workers gave little thought to ways of making the plant more economically efficient, and they felt that management was not interested in their ideas. Now they are not contributing their physical energy alone. Through their union they are playing a creative role in building up the economic effectiveness of the plant.

Nor is the sense of achievement confined to the economic sphere. People on both sides gain satisfaction from the strides they have taken in learning together. They recognize that the task of bringing cooperation out of conflict is one of which they can all be proud.

3. Status and Personal Recognition

The most obvious gains here have come to the union. In earlier years the key to all the union complaints was that management did not respect the union officers. We may recall, here, the statement of one union man that he wanted to hang Gossett up outside his office window until he would promise to give the respect that was due the representatives of the men. This was considered an acute problem. If management did not show respect for the union officers, it must mean that management would be glad to get rid of the union. This seemed to threaten the position of every worker in the plant.

In a 1948 union meeting, in reviewing his experiences as president of the local, Lucius Love gave a major emphasis to this point. He began with the story of his first meeting with Gossett when the executive had refused to shake his hand. And he contrasted this with a recent experience in which an executive of another company, interested in union-management relations at the Chicago Container Plant, had been shown through the plant. On this occasion Love had been invited to walk through the plant with Gossett and the visitor. He felt that this was a fitting measure on the extent of the change in relationships, and other union members seem to have accepted it as such. They seem to get an important vicarious satisfaction from seeing their elected representatives, their own people, accepted on an equal footing by members of top management.

The local union has also gained in standing outside of the plant, compared with the old days when the WLB censured it as an irresponsible organization. The members can now stand up before the community and speak with pride of their organization.

Management has made a similar gain in this field. In the days of conflict few union members had respect for any member of management. Today that respect is present and it is growing. It is a hard job for a man to direct an organization with a knowledge that most of the members of that organization hate him and will hurt him if they can. Gossett reports that winning the respect of the union officers and members has given him one of the greatest satisfactions he has ever enjoyed. Other members of management feel the same way.

The gain in status and respect achieved by the foremen is particularly impressive. In earlier years they had no standing with the employees and little confidence in themselves. There were even some employees who were offered promotion into supervision and turned it down. Today the foreman is no longer by-passed in union relations, nor does he feel disregarded by management. The foreman feels increasingly that he is running his own department and has the respect of employees as well as of management.

This is not a case of one man's gain being the other man's loss. Each side has profited from the gains achieved by the other. One union man puts it this way: "I feel much better now. A man wants to have respect for the man he's working for. I didn't have no respect before."

4. SECURITY OF POSITION AND FUNCTION

In the earlier period union and management were struggling to frustrate each other. Management was not seeking to destroy the union, but Gossett and Novy broke up the old patterns of activity, which had been effective in getting action from management, and provided no new channels through which the problems could be solved. The union leaders, being unable to solve problems sitting together with management, could only maintain their positions and represent the feelings of the rank and file through trying to prevent management from doing its job. Running the plant and the union became a contest. The object was to predict what the other side was going to try to do and then to take steps so that, whatever it was, it would not be accomplished. The contest was carried on with great effectiveness by both sides, so certain satisfactions were gained from frustrating the other party, but those were more than counterbalanced by the feeling of being frustrated by the opposition.

Now both parties have developed a pattern for carrying out activities in a mutually supporting manner. An exchange of services has developed throughout the organization. The exchange is seldom directly mentioned, but it is there beneath the surface. The union officers know that if they do something for management, the service will not go unrewarded. At some later time management will do something that will help them to carry out their functions more effectively.

Whether he is a union officer or a member of management, a man can do his job now. This is particularly striking in the case of management and can be illustrated in terms of the amount of time spent on union-management problems. Novy estimates that in the conflict period he and Gossett were spending 80 per cent of their time wrestling with problems in union relations. Only one-fifth of their time was then available to carry on the other important activities of management. Today, while they are ready to devote whatever time is necessary, they estimate that less than 5 per cent of their time is taken up with labor relations problems in the Chicago plant. Furthermore, even when they spent 80 per cent of their time, they always had the feeling that they were not quite reaching the real problems at issue, whereas now 5 per cent of the time serves to raise real problems and bring about their solution.

5. Predictability and Peace of Mind

In the conflict period workers and union officers were living in what social psychologists call "an unstructured situation." No one ever knew what to expect. The future was unpredictable; the only thing that was certain was that a new crisis was always around the corner. Each crisis involved serious risks for the union people. You had to stand by your union and fight management, but if you did so, management was out to get you and you might be disciplined or discharged. The union would protect you when it could, but you had to watch your step or you would find yourself in a position where management, according to the contract, had a right to punish you and the union had no right to protect you. Management was especially interested in finding ways of weeding out the most aggressive union people. Love himself was told once that he was being fired, but in that case further investigation apparently convinced management that it did not have a strong enough case against him. This sort of situation placed heavy responsibility on the shoulders of the union officers, not only to protect themselves but to be constantly on the alert, to see to it that some of their strongest members did not get themselves out on a limb where they could be chopped off by management. Several people were eliminated in such a way that the union could not protect them.

The change in this situation is well illustrated by the comments of two union people. One rank-and-file worker, when asked what she was getting out of the new relationship, said:

It gives you peace of mind. You can go about your business without worrying all the time what is going to happen next. Before there was always something being cooked up. You'd see people talking together and you'd want to know what was going to happen next. It took your mind off your work. You'd get careless and wouldn't pay no attention.

A union steward made this comment:

I think the main thing is that we can relax now. That doesn't mean that we can go to sleep. We still have to watch things, but it isn't tense like before, and you can enjoy your work. Before we had so many problems it was hard to know what to do. Many times I've laid awake in bed thinking about a problem until two or three o'clock in the morning when suddenly the answer would come to me. Then I'd have to get up at six o'clock to get ready for work. Now when we go home at night, we can really get some rest.

Management has experienced the same change. I have already cited Novy's observation that, in the conflict period, he and Gossett could sit down and figure out nine possible actions the union might take and could only be sure that they would hit upon the tenth, which management had not anticipated. The nervous tension within management was extreme.

Furthermore, constant anxiety and uncertainty forced management to live on a day-to-day basis. There was no use in making long-range plans, even if you had time for such activity. Why plan something new when you were struggling hard to cope with the problems you already had? That situation has changed completely. Gossett and Novy can devote a large part of their time to the planning activity that is so essential at that level of the organization, and their subordinates also have time to plan at least a little ahead and think beyond immediate emergencies.

What this change has meant is well expressed by one member of management:

Now I look forward to coming to work in the morning. I have a wonderful time on this job. Before I just had to drag myself to work. I'd wake up in the morning and think to myself—do I have to go to work again? You'd dread it coming in to work. You didn't know what would happen from one day to the next, but you could always expect trouble.

6. Accord with Systems of Belief

I am making no moral judgements of this point. I am not saying what is right or what is wrong. I am simply saying that people feel better when they are able to believe in the things they are doing. It hurts a man to have to do things which he feels are wrong, either on orders from higher authority or because, though he may believe in the general policy, the means of carrying it out are distasteful. A man can justify actions he does not believe in when they are taken to achieve an end that he does believe in. However, he will feel much more at peace with himself when he believes in both the means and the ends of his actions.

That expresses the situation I observed in this case. In the conflict period there were many times when members of management had to take actions that were personally distasteful to them because they were under orders or because those actions seemed justified by some larger goal that they did believe in. This same situation was found within the union. The men now freely say that they were cheating as they broke down machines and held up production. They felt that this cheating was justified because they felt that management had cheated them. The main purpose was to get back at management and anything that enabled them to do this was justified.

Now, by contrast, in large areas of union and management activities the people no longer have to justify the means by the ends. They no longer need to argue away their feelings of guilt. They can act with the confidence that comes from feeling that they are acting in accord with their beliefs (sentiments).

The Chicago plant has become an effective organization economically; it pays off to stockholders, managers, and workers; to its customers it gives better products and improved services.

Economic effectiveness is basic. Without it, all the other values would be in jeopardy. Nevertheless, the man who conceives of union-management cooperation in those terms is missing a large part of the picture. There is much more to it than goods and services and money. We cannot measure the personal satisfactions a man feels, as we can measure the money he gets, but those satisfactions are real and important to him.

The day is past when a business leader could justify his service to the community simply in terms of the profits his company made. Similarly, people are coming to doubt union leaders who can think *only* in terms of wages, hours, and working conditions.

More and more leaders of industry are talking about "business as a social institution." Most of the talk is still in rather general terms, but it does express a growing sense of social responsibility. These men are recognizing that their day-to-day decisions have a direct impact upon hundreds and even thousands of men. They affect men's pocketbooks; they affect men's whole lives.

In recent years, union leaders have gained a comparable strategic position in our economy. Many of them too are recognizing that increasing responsibilities go with increasing power and influence.

The power of management and union leaders extends far beyond human relations in the factory. That power can mean high or low prices, full employment or unemployment, prosperity or depression. But, as we ponder those questions, let us not forget the life that is lived in the factory.

Ours is an industrial civilization. People spend a large part of their lives at their machines or in their offices. Amerca's promise of "life, liberty, and the pursuit of happiness" will mean little to them if their lives in industry are fraught with conflict, tension, and frustration. The manager or union leader who can help to build a better way of life within industry gains the inner satisfaction of discharging one of the heaviest social responsibilities of modern man.

Chapter 17

The Role of the Union

SOME PEOPLE say that the union is what management makes it. There is an element of truth in that statement. There is also an element of untruth in it.

If we were to take the statement literally we would assume that the union leaders could take no initiative in shaping union-management relations, that they must simply react to the conditions management sets before them. Let us examine this assumption in terms of the evolution of the union in this Chicago plant.

The story of the birth and early days of the union certainly shows management setting the pattern. The strike was as close to a spontaneous response to management's actions as we shall ever find. And, once the union came into being, there was so much to do in clearing up past abuses of the old management that the leaders could hardly be expected to see beyond the immediate problems.

These men had to learn from experience. Love says again and again, "I didn't think I was qualified," but no one better qualified stepped forward, so Love went to work improving his qualifications, tackling the problems of the plant, and studying in night school.

In time the union developed its own organizational structure, so . that all business no longer went through Love in the first instance. But the top local leaders did not function in the settled manner of men who simply handle the higher steps of grievances and recommend policies to the membership. Since the union people felt that they were not getting action through the grievance procedure under the old management, the local union leaders became organizers of other forms of pressure upon management. Especially they became the leaders of demonstrations in the offices of management at various levels, from bottom to top. Many of these demonstrations they set up and organized themselves. Others were going to happen anyway, and the local leader could only come along as a spokesman.

The change in top management in 1944 brought a head-on clash between two different patterns of interaction. The local union leaders were accustomed to frequent top-level meetings in which all orders of problems were negotiated. Gossett, in Jersey City, had been accustomed to a pattern in which he met union problems at the top step of the grievance procedure. Since the Jersey City plant was small, he had other informal contacts with union people but nothing comparable to the negotiation meetings he was faced with at Chicago.

Eventually a pattern developed in which the grievances were processed in an orderly fashion but these channels were supplemented by top-level discussions of problems that could not be handled readily through the grievance procedure. For cooperative relations, this pattern was necessary, but it was not easy to achieve, and it took the intervention of a man from outside the local scene, the international representative, to help bring it about.

The local union reacts to management, to be sure, but the local union is also part of its international organization. As time goes on, those ties become increasingly important. Management still limits the possibilities of harmonious adjustment. There may be no steps toward cooperation the union can take unless management is willing to move also. But a skillful international representative can help management to make the necessary adjustments—even as he helps his own local to adjust to management.

We have seen, in analyzing the negotiations, how Shafer helped to set the stage for more harmonious relations. Throughout those negotiations, and in the follow-up meeting, he was, in effect, seeking to bring about a change in the pattern of interaction. He was insisting that the union take responsibility on certain problems that he claimed management alone could not solve. He was asking management to call upon the union for help. He was asking management to abandon its defensive attitude toward the union.

This did not mean that Shafer expected to be "easy" and not ask management to do things for the union. I have never heard it suggested that Shafer will drop a case he believes in so as to be nice to management. On the contrary, he pushes grievances and other problems hard. But even in the area where the union originates for management, he introduced an important new element. Up to this time the union had brought only complaints and grievances to management. In his first grievance meeting he also proposed that the union become the channel for bringing to management suggestions to improve productivity and efficiency.

The discussion of this point is of considerable interest. Management proposed that a suggestion system be set up so that individual workers might be rewarded financially for their contributions to the enterprise. Shafer said flatly that he wanted no system of awards; he wanted the suggestions to channel through the union. Management agreed.

Whatever Shafer's motives for taking this position, we must observe that his proposal would have quite a different effect upon the social system than could be expected for a suggestion-box plan. In the ordinary suggestion plan, the *individual* worker, as a worker, writes his suggestion on a piece of paper and places it in the suggestion box. If the management committee reviewing the suggestions finds it worth while, the individual receives an individual reward. Except for the presentation of the award, the whole process is done on paper. The winner is pleased to get the money, but the operation of the plan has no effect at all upon the pattern of interaction that determines whether we have cooperation or friction.

When the union steward or higher union officers bring suggestions on production to the various levels of management, these moves help to shape the relations between union and management. Personal interaction has far greater effects upon a social system than written communication.

It is one of management's tasks, in its union relations, to provide opportunities for the union to initiate action in a manner that will fit in with the goals of the enterprise. The management that wants no help from a union will always have difficulties with that union. It is one of the tasks of the union leader to show how this help can be given.

This sort of activity brings about a considerable change in the functions of the union. The functions of a local union, in relation to management, may be roughly divided into two categories: *protective* and *integrative*. As protective, we think of those functions which are carried out in holding management to the contract. They involve a recognition of differing interests and are essentially efforts to maintain or improve the position of the union as compared to management. As integrative, we think of functions in which both parties work together toward the same or related goals.

This is no either-or proposition. No union leader will dare to promote integrative functions unless he feels assured that the protective functions are taken care of. If these protective functions can be carried out effectively, then a whole new area opens up for the effective teamwork of union and management.

We do not know what this new type of activity has done to the union organization itself. Perhaps it is too early to say. It represents a change, to be sure. Those who measure the strength of a union in terms of the aggressive actions and sentiments of its members will consider the union weaker today. But those who measure strength in terms of the union's ability to get action from management to meet the needs and interests of its members will find the union immeasurably stronger today.

The development of this new type of activity requires adjustments on the part of union officers. Some who came to the fore in the era of conflict may find it hard to adjust to the new functions. But there are new functions to perform. An organization needs a set of activities to maintain itself. The observer who notes the dropping away of some of the old activities should also note that the union is taking on new ones.

There are dangers to the unwary in this cooperative process. Some cooperative relationships in the past have broken down because it was only the top union officers who were personally involved in the cooperation process. They found themselves separated from the rank and file in actions, interactions, and sentiments, and in time they were repudiated by the rank and file. That can happen, but it need not happen. It will not happen if the lower levels of the union are actively involved in the process. So far that seems to be the case in this Chicago plant.

If we return to the problem posed at the beginning of this chapter, we are forced to recognize the powerful molding influence management has upon its union-management relations. But we are also forced to deny that the union simply responds to these management pressures. There is still a wide field for effective action on the part of skillful and imaginative union leaders.

Chapter 18

The Problem of Bigness

DECADE AFTER DECADE we have seen industrial organizations grow bigger and bigger. More recently we have been witnessing the growth of big unions.

These large-scale organizations may have many advantages for society, and yet, at the same time, they bring with them some of the most troubling problems of our age.

As industrial organizations grow, in most cases, we see a trend toward increasing centralization of control. More and more of the decisions that are important at lower levels are made at the top.

Top management tends to strive toward consistency in its policies, so that a given problem may be handled the same way wherever it is met within the organization. Policies become rigid and inflexible. Individuals, groups, or even local organizations are lost sight of in the process of centralized policy making.

As the organization grows, the levels of authority between bottom and top multiply, and the channels of communication become clogged. Orders from the top down are sometimes sidetracked or distorted. Complaints and suggestions from the bottom up are blocked or lost in the shuffle.

The top executive in such an organization can get systematic records of productivity or costs or engineering developments for a given local unit, but how adequate is his information upon the human problems of that unit? Any research man who has studied a local situation and then gone to a top executive of a large corporation for his analysis of that local situation is likely to have great difficulty in relating what the executive says to what he has observed at first hand. It is often as if the two men were referring to two totally different situations.

This observation implies no criticism of the ability of the top executive. It is just extraordinarily difficult, in big business, for the top man to acquire the information necessary for an accurate picture of the human problems of a local unit. Of course, no one expects him to have the detailed knowledge of the foreman or plant superintendent. And yet, if his information is not accurate in a broad, general sense, some of his most important decisions may be based upon disastrously false assumptions.

We see in big business today some of the same rigidities that we condemn as bureaucracy when we talk about the government. And some large industrial unions, though they are younger and have had less time to rigidify, are already showing many of these same symptoms of bureaucracy.

We see large organizations becoming muscle-bound. As cooperation deteriorates, executives pile on new systems of records and controls, and the records and controls lead to a still further deterioration of cooperation, which, in turn, calls for new records and controls—and so on and on.

Perhaps I am painting an extreme picture, and yet there are large organizations for which that is an accurate portrait, and there are many others moving in that direction.

We must stop and take stock of our position. Is this an inevitable trend of our industrial civilization? Must man become a mere pawn of the organization—no matter how sincerely the top leaders wish to respect the dignity of the individual?

I do not know the answer. Certainly there is no easy answer. But perhaps we can find a way out if we discover large organizations which have avoided some of the ills I have described. Their experience may provide significant guides for those who are seeking a way out.

This case provides one such example. The parent corporation, Inland Steel Company, is only about one-tenth the size of United States Steel Corporation. Still, it has 25,000 employees, and it is a completely integrated company, from coal and iron mines and ore boats through steel production and into fabrication. Inland is big enough to experience many of the human problems of big business.

So our Chicago plant is just one unit of a big business, and yet it has been possible to tell the story of that plant almost as if it were a completely independent unit. How can this be? What is the nature of the control exercised by top management of the parent corporation? How can so much autonomy be granted to a local unit?

The president of Inland Steel Container Company (from 1944 to 1949) was a member of the Executive Committee and of the Board of Directors of Inland Steel Company. He was in a position to speak for the interests of the subsidiary. He was also president of the Inland Steel Products Company (formerly Milcor Products Company) and devoted most of his time to that position. For Inland Steel Container Company, he delegated the full responsibility to Gossett. Gossett called upon his superior for advice on various problems, and felt free to discuss the problems thoroughly with him. He felt at all times that he had the support and confidence of the president, but at the same time the president gave him full freedom to operate the business. Thus responsibility has been placed at the points where people are in close touch with the actual problems.

In industrial relations, the parent corporation does not determine policy for its subsidiary except in a few particulars. The Industrial Relations Department of the parent corporation, through Caples, serves in an advisory capacity. It is the department's function to keep executives throughout the corporation informed about significant industrial relations developments within and outside of the corporation. Caples is also called upon frequently for advice.

In the actual collective bargaining process, the Industrial Relations Department of Inland Steel Company has played a more prominent role. In both 1946 and 1947 Caples and Charles Kaufman, a lawyer retained by the corporation, were active in the negotiations. The 1948 negotiations were settled easily without any legal adviser. Caples sat in on one meeting mainly for the purpose of expressing to the union the satisfaction the parent corporation felt with the relationship that had been developing.

It is the policy of the parent corporation to settle collective bargaining contracts at the local level. It is up to the local management to determine its needs in order to run its plant efficiently. It is up to the Industrial Relations Department to help local management achieve these conditions.

However, the provisions written for the Chicago plant can serve as precedents for other plants in the corporation, and it is one of the functions of the Industrial Relations Department to see to it that a local plant does not commit the rest of the corporation to a policy that top management of the corporation would oppose. This restriction applies to only five points at the present time. These are as follows:

1. No contract may provide for a closed shop or a union shop. During the war, the Corporation had to accept maintenance of membership clauses, and these it is willing to continue, as in the Chicago plant. This point is considered a matter of principle which is not subject to argument in terms of the material advantages or disadvantages of the policy to the company. Top management people feel that a union shop requirement is contrary to the rights of individual self determination in our democratic society.

2. No contract may provide for the arbitration of wage rates. This, as we have seen, applies to incentive rates as well as regular hourly pay. Top management takes the position that wage questions should be settled in the annual bargaining meeting, and should not be open to negotiation and arbitration between times.

3. No contract may call for promotions, demotions, or layoffs to be handled on a strict seniority basis. Local managements are free to give whatever weight they feel desirable to seniority in such matters, and in the Chicago plant it has become the practice to follow seniority as a matter of course except where management feels that there are very compelling reasons for making a different decision. It is top management's belief that unless the management has the power to make exceptions to seniority, the efficiency of the plant will seriously deteriorate.

4. Each contract must secure to management the right to schedule work and men without having to have prior agreement with the union. The union has access to the grievance procedure where it feels that these powers have been abused, but management feels that the powers themselves are essential to efficient operation.

5. Management will not pay time and a half or double time for work on Saturdays or Sundays as such. The contracts carry the usual provisions concerning time and a half after eight hours on one day or after 40 hours in one week. Time and a half is paid on the sixth consecutive work day

in any week and double time is paid on the seventh consecutive day. Where every day is worked, the sixth and seventh day will be Saturday and Sunday. If, for any reason, the plant should be closed for one or two days during the week, the Saturday or Sunday work would be treated just as if they occurred on weekdays. In this plant, management agrees that the regular work week shall run from Monday through Friday, and that no work shall be scheduled on Saturday or Sunday except in emergencies. To management, this provision is strictly an economic policy. To pay premium rates for Saturday or Sunday work as such would add to the cost of operation in the plant where the contract was signed, and would put the rest of the corporation under pressure to accept similar provisions.

Local management is not free to deviate from any of these five provisions, and in case of a deadlock in any of them it has the backing of the parent corporation in accepting a strike. To accept a strike on any other contract provision the plant must first have the agreement of the corporation's Industrial Relations Department. The judgement of the local executives will ordinarily be followed in such cases, but it must be first cleared with top management.

In recent years there has been a strong trend toward industry-wide or at least corporation-wide collective bargaining, with master contracts subjecting all plants and all union locals to the same contract provisions. It might be argued that bargaining on this local basis tends to weaken the position of the union in enabling management to play off one local against another, and that it would make it more difficult to strike the entire company on some issue of major importance to the union. Let us examine this point of view. Certain plants of Inland Steel Company are organized by unions other than the United Steelworkers so that a uniform steelworkers' contract would not hold in these cases anyway. Most of the employees of the company are represented by the United Steelworkers, so there the issue would naturally arise. The most important point to note here is that the Chicago plant of Inland Steel Container Company has been going along with the wage pattern set by the United States Steel Corporation, and the United Steelworkers. As soon as this pattern was set in 1946, the Chicago plant management offered the $18\frac{1}{2}$ cents to its local and wages were never an issue in these negotiations, except in the question of incentive rates. In 1947, 1948, and 1949, local management similarly followed the industry pattern. To refuse to follow the pattern would be to invite a strike. Thus, on this key issue, the union maintains a united front and can hardly be said to be dissipating its bargaining power.

In contrasting a company-wide or industry-wide contract with one negotiated for a single plant, we must not forget that there are other possibilities between these extreme points. In some cases we find companies negotiating a basic general agreement for many or all of their plants, while the local units negotiate supplementary agreements to spell out the terms in detail as they apply to the local situation. In other situations, even though a master contract is negotiated centrally, we find different adjustments between union and management worked out on a local basis.

I am not saying that such decentralization is possible under all circumstances. I am only saying that the men in this case could never have worked through to the harmonious adjustment they reached if the terms of the settlement had been dictated from above. They had to go through the experience of working out their problems in order to establish a new pattern of relations.

That conclusion applies to human relations generally, inside industry or outside of it. Only a flexible, adaptive organization can function efficiently and serve the psychological needs of its members at the same time. Only the people who are close to a problem have the information needed for its solution. And the best way to get a decision accepted and carried out is to invite the people who must act upon the decision to take an active part in shaping it.

The people in this case have been highly successful in achieving a balance between central control and local autonomy. The distribution of functions here cannot be mechanically applied to any other case. Other executives and union leaders must seek to make their own adaptations.

There is, however, one general principle that can be stated. Decentralization of control in a large organization does not just happen. As the company grew, the top-management people of Inland Steel were constantly concerned over the dangers of building a rigid bureaucracy. They bent their efforts toward maintaining as high a degree of local autonomy as possible. Except on a few points, they did not worry about having different units meeting the same problem in different ways. On the contrary, they would have worried if they had found all units following the same policies.

The executive might well have this motto on his desk: Centralization will get you if you don't watch out. Centralization seems always to triumph in a large organization when the executives are so preoccupied with immediate problems that they fail to note the direction in which they are drifting. To build large organizations that are nevertheless flexible—to build organizations that are both efficient and adjusted to the needs of men—that task requires of American industrial leaders the same order of skill, imagination, and knowledge that has made our industry the most productive in the world.

Chapter 19

In Conclusion

W HAT CAN WE learn from this case?
The chapters of the analysis have pointed to conclusions on special problem areas. It remains only to draw certain general conclusions.

First, a word of caution is in order. Some will point out that the case involves only one plant of moderate size. Will the conclusions apply to the giant plant and to the giant corporation?

To that conclusion, there are two answers:

1. What do we mean by "apply"? If we mean that we want to carry over mechanically from one case to another specific contract clauses, policies, and actions, then of course there is no application. We do not prescribe the same treatment for every case any more than the doctor prescribes the same treatment for every patient.

The application is not a matter of specific gadgets. It is a general approach to problems, a framework within which we can think more effectively about those problems. That certainly we can apply.

2. The problems of giant plants and giant corporations are more complicated than those of this case. Some of what we have learned here can be applied there, I am sure. How much, remains to be seen. Here again we can turn to the field of medicine for an analogy. The doctor does not prescribe treatment without first studying the patient. Medical science is so far advanced that, in many cases, the study may involve only a few brief observations. The field of human relations is relatively in such a primitive state that much more study is needed

before we can draw conclusions. But certainly we cannot make progress with a patent-medicine approach. Research is called for—research in which the research man works closely with management and union men to profit from their experience, to explain the course of events, and to put conclusions into such a form that they can be used in other cases.

One general conclusion can certainly be drawn from this case: it takes time to build and maintain good relations. Of course, labor relations took much more of the time of Gossett and Novy in the conflict period. But even when relations are good, the executive must be prepared to spend time on them. The executive who looks upon labor relations as an intrusion upon more important duties will never do an effective job here.

For the union man, time is also a problem, especially at the level of the international representative. He deals with labor relations all the time, but often he has to represent so many local unions that he has no time to go thoroughly into the problems of any one of them. Shafer met this problem by devoting a far larger proportion of his time to this local than to any of the others he represented. He justified this on the ground that he was here engaged in an important experimental program. What he learned here could be much more valuable to the union in the long run than the day-to-day handling of routine problems. Certainly the far-reaching changes he helped to bring about could not have taken place without his painstaking and time-consuming efforts.

Discussions take time. Their results should be weighed in two categories:

1. Actions coming out of discussion.
2. Effects upon the relationship.

If we look at the first category alone, we will be impatient with the time spent. One man can make a decision faster than two, and two are much faster than ten. But in industry some of the most important decisions must be acceptable to tens and hundreds and thousands of people. A decision that is not accepted and followed through effectively is worse than no decision at all. That points to the importance of the second category. Where people discuss their problems together, there is greater likelihood of general acceptance of the decision reached, and the discussion process also strengthens the relationship so that future actions will be carried through more smoothly.

Finally, let us examine the common statement that union-management problems can be worked out if we just have some "mutual good will." There are two things wrong with that statement.

In the first place, where does the good will come from? Some people make the problem sound like a cookbook recipe: mix one part fair wages, one part good working conditions with three management prerogatives, add a dash of mutual good will, sweeten to taste—and so on.

The trouble is that people's sentiments cannot be changed by simply telling them that it is a good idea to change their sentiments. In this case, union and management people began with hatred and distrust, while now mutual good will prevails. But the good will was a late arrival on the scene. It only developed *following* far-reaching changes in human relations. That is the sequence of change we see, as a rule: first a change in human relations, then a change in sentiments.

The executive or union leader must know how to deal with the sentiments and emotions of men. He must recognize that he cannot change sentiments by operating on them directly: by urging people to change the way they feel. It is only as he changes the relations of people to each other that he can change their sentiments toward each other.

In the second place, the good-will slogan is a grave oversimplification. These are exceedingly complicated problems. They are not to be solved simply by trying to be a nice man. Many goodhearted people break their hearts in this field because they lack the social skill and the understanding of human relations necessary to make good intentions effective.

These problems call for ingenuity and experimental daring. Those qualities were present in this case on both sides. They are all too rare in labor relations today.

In other fields the American businessman is a brilliant experimenter. He is quick to try new machines and processes, new job methods and production layouts, new merchandising and advertising techniques, and so on. But this ingenuity is often discarded when he enters the field of labor relations. There he seems to seek out the security of the old ways of doing things. He changes. Events force him to change. But all too often he changes reluctantly, and so is unable to capitalize on new situations.

If the American businessman could turn his ingenuity and experimental bent toward the field of labor relations, then we might see many more cases to match the success achieved in Inland Steel Container Company.

The challenge to union leadership is equally clear. Since, in the mass production industries, union leaders represent relatively new organizations still moving into new areas of activity, they are less likely than management executives to try to stand pat on old ways of meeting problems. But these new areas themselves pose new responsibilities. The evolution of enduring and mutually satisfying agreements demands imaginative leadership on both sides of the bargaining table.

Appendix A

Research Methods

The conclusions from a study are no more reliable than the methods that were used to reach those conclusions. Therefore, the serious student will want to know just how this study was carried out. This is not the place for a full discussion of the field methods of the social anthropologist or sociologist, but at least I should present a brief account of how the study was carried out.

It began one day in the spring of 1948 when I happened to be sitting next to William G. Caples at lunch. In casual conversation he mentioned the remarkable change that had taken place in the Chicago plant of Inland Steel Container Company. I was very much interested. Earlier I had collaborated on a study of a striking change in union-management relations ("From Conflict to Cooperation," special issue of *Applied Anthropology,* Fall, 1946). From that experience, I felt that there was much more to be learned scientifically from studying a case involving considerable change in relationships than from a case in which relationships have remained much the same over a period of years. Where relations stay in the same groove, it is extraordinarily difficult to examine the forces that keep them there. Where relations change, we are able to get at the dynamic processes.

At my request Caples arranged a luncheon meeting for me with John Gossett and Robert Novy. Their account further stimulated my interest. Next they arranged to have a joint union-management meeting including Lucius Love and Lawrence G. Shafer to go over the union's side of the story. We spent most of one day at this.

At that time I was convinced that the case was well worth studying, but I was to remain in Chicago for only two months longer. The study would not be worth undertaking unless I had the fullest cooperation. On this point I got the most encouraging assurances—and subsequent performance surpassed my greatest expectations.

I was free to talk to anyone within union or management for as long as I wished in the privacy of the conference room. In the case of local union officers or workers, arrangements would have to be made, of course, to relieve them of their regular production work. There was never any difficulty on that score.

Novy urged the management officers to speak with perfect freedom about past and present problems, and the same advice was passed along on the union side. On such a short-term project no researcher can expect to penetrate the deepest feelings of the people involved, but this endorsement by the key officers on both sides speeded up my work immeasurably. Even in the first interview with some of the management people I began to get a full account of past frictions and conflicts within management. Under other circumstances I would not expect to get at such data until I had been around for several weeks.

In the two-month period I interviewed people at all levels of the management and union organizations. In the time I had I was able to cover only an insignificant fraction of the workers, but I got a large body of data from stewards and higher levels.

I was also given free access to all the relevant documentary materials. I read through the bitter bargaining sessions of 1944–1946 and the turning-point sessions of 1947. I went over the grievance records, including the transcript of the fourth-step grievance meetings.

As I was about to leave Chicago I discussed with Gossett, Novy, and Shafer my understanding and interpretation of the case. During the summer of 1948 I wrote a first draft on the case, covering everything I had except for an analysis of the 1947 negotiations. On that point I felt I needed further discussions. In September I went back to Chicago for a day-long meeting to discuss my draft with Caples, Gossett, Love, Novy, and Shafer. This suggested that I was on the right track but that some minor points and several major ones needed revision.

The next step involved working up the discussion of the 1947 negotiations. In the fall of 1948 Shafer spent two days at Cornell, and we put in long hours going over the record. Shafer gave a running commentary on the written record—why the union people talked and acted as they did, to the best of his recollection. He also sought to fill in what happened in recesses and in the "off the record" discussions.

In the early spring of 1949 Gossett and Caples visited Cornell and discussed their interpretations of those negotiations, together with other aspects of the case. In June, 1949, we all met again in Chicago to review my analysis of the negotiations. This again led to revisions on several points.

I next prepared a new draft of the case, including negotiations. This was discussed in a day-long meeting in Chicago in March, 1950. The meeting again led to revisions and a final draft to be submitted to the publisher. At this stage the revisions were of a minor nature.

Following this meeting I spent three days in Chicago to check into aspects of the case on which I was uncertain.

The data in the case are drawn largely from personal interviews. Ideally, the researcher should be able to observe interpersonal events, and I have done that in other studies, but observation is exceedingly time consuming and could not be used here extensively for that reason. I did attend one union meeting, but my observations went little beyond that point.

The interviewing was not based upon any set schedule of questions. I assumed that at first I did not know what were important questions to ask. My job was to get people to talk freely about the case. At first I guided them only to the extent of asking them to tell me about specific interpersonal events, as well as about their sentiments concerning the relationship. For example, suppose a steward said, "We used to be fighting all the time, but now we get along pretty good." I would draw him out to get examples of behavior. Who fought with whom in what ways at what times? Then what sorts of experiences did he have, which led him to feel that "we get along pretty good." I sought to develop the data in chronological order. The informant might jump back and forth in time in his interview, but each event I would seek to place approximately in time, so that I could examine the development of the relationship. An informant might comment, "We trust each other now. There was no mutual confidence before." A picture of the situation at the "no confidence" period or of the situation at the "trust" period would not explain anything to us. We need to understand how one situation evolved into the other, and that can be done only through getting interpersonal events in a time sequence.

As I began to fill in for myself an outline of the case I was able to ask more specific questions. For example, "I've been hearing about a grievance on an air hose in your department. I'm not clear as to what happened there. Can you tell me what the case was all about?" While this sort of question narrowed down the interview at the outset, the informant's answer would generally serve to suggest a number of related questions that had not occurred to me before.

I did not take notes during interviews, feeling that such a written record might make people self-conscious and hesitant about revealing some points. I took notes after the interview and later dictated from the notes as full a record of the interview as I could remember. While no one can expect to get a verbatim record in this way, long field experience helps one to come fairly close. In this case my chief informants checked over the parts of the case in which I had quoted them, and at least their memories came fairly close to mine.

(For a more detailed discussion of field methods in such a study see B. B. Gardner and W. F. Whyte, "Methods for the Study of Human Relations in Industry," *American Sociological Review,* October, 1946. Also Whyte's appendix on field-work methods in a forthcoming book edited by Morton Deutsch, Marie Jahoda, and Stuart W. Cook, *Research Methods in the Study of Social Relations,* Dryden Press.)

The uses of documentary materials in such a study deserve special comment. I feel strongly that such materials are next to useless *alone.* The student who read the grievance on the air-hose case or the grievances on the accounting changes in the Punch Press Department would not have had the slightest idea what was going on. A statistical study of various types of grievances would be equally unrewarding. The only time when there were enough grievances to make counting seem worth while, the grievances themselves were simply put in at any point where the union people felt they could get a foothold and exert pressure.

The transcripts of fourth-step meetings and of negotiation sessions seem much more meaty. They probably do tell fairly accurately what was said—within limits. In bargaining, what happens when we run into an "off the record" passage? And what happens during recesses? These discussions, which are not included, may provide the key to what is actually said at the bargaining table. And even where we have a full record of a lengthy discussion we can only put it in perspective if we know things that are not on the official record: What are the speakers trying to accomplish here? Why do they feel strongly on this issue? What experiences have they had on this point that have led them to feel this way?

On the other hand, let us not discard the documentary materials. When supplemented by interviewing they can prove invaluable sources of information. The interviewing provides the background material to make the record meaningful, and the record suggests many points of investigation that might have been overlooked in the interviewing.

Some of our human relations studies of plants go on for many months, perhaps for several years. This study, then, covered a relatively short period. Without any question, that is a weakness. The weakness is particularly marked at the level of worker and rank-and-file union member. So many people were involved at this point that I could not hope to cover an adequate sample without extending the study for many months more. The evidence on worker reactions is, therefore, largely indirect. On the other hand, union and management cooperation was such as to make up in part for the short time available for study. People "opened up" much sooner than they do in tension-ridden situations. Also, arrangements were so effectively carried through that I could spend all my day at the plant in interviewing, with only a few minutes' break between-times to make notes. In most situations the researcher has to spend a large part of his time waiting to talk to people.

No account of the study would be complete without a tribute to the cooperation given me by both union and management people. They were proud of what they had accomplished, as well they might be. They felt that what they had learned might be useful to others who faced similar problems. They recognized that, if the story was to have any scientific value, I would have to be completely free to get at any data I felt was important. They gave me the sort of cooperation that is the research man's dream.

Nor was this simply a passive cooperation: letting me do what I wanted to do. These men, I felt, had not only gone through remarkable experiences; they had also considerable insight into those experiences. It was not a question of my pumping them for information I would put together entirely on my own. They were collaborators with me in a real sense. They not only told me what happened; they also helped me to explain what happened.

The experience of going over successive drafts also was exceedingly valuable to me. Those conferences led to changes in the manuscript and additions to it that strengthened it considerably. I also appreciated the attitude of my collaborators toward these criticisms. On *factual* matters they would point out flatly where I had made mistakes. On matters of interpretation they took the position that the responsibility was entirely mine. They could advise me, and I sought such advice. But whether the explanations were good or bad they were my own.

The Record in Figures

PRODUCTION RECORDS 1942–1949
1944 = 100
Average Hourly Production

	Barrels	*Pails*	*Tons Per Man-Hour Produced*
1942	116	106	—
1943	120	92	—
1944	100	100	100
1945	115	126	107
1946	122	126	105
1947	146	132	125
1948	184	140	143
1949	168	131	128

Note particularly the sharp rise in productivity between 1946 and 1948 in the Barrel Department and in total tonnage produced in the plant. The tonnage per man-hour figure is probably the best over-all index of productivity.

Note also that productivity figures are lower in 1949 than they were in 1948. In the opinion of union and management people, this does not mean less effective performance. They explain the change in terms of a marked change in the types of orders going through the plant. The year 1949 marked a sharp drop in the number of long runs, on which top records can be made, and a great increase in the number of short runs and more complicated orders, on which it would have been impossible to maintain 1948 quantity levels.

Incentive Earnings 1945-1949

	Rates on Top and Bottom Labor Grade	Plant Average Incentive	Incentive Earnings	Increases Over Base Pay	Total Hourly Earnings
1945	.72	143%	1.03		1.03
	.86		1.23		1.23
1946	.72	147%	1.06	.185	1.245
	.86		1.26	.185	1.445
1947	.72	157%	1.13	.305	1.435
	.86		1.35	.305	1.655
1948	.72	165%	1.19	.43	1.62
	.86		1.42	.43	1.85
1949	.72	162%	1.17	.43	1.60
	.86		1.39	.43	1.82

In 1948 and 1949 incentive earnings averaged approximately 40 per cent of total hourly earnings (base plus increases).

Average Hourly Pay—All Workers

1945	$1.175
1946	1.2945
1947	1.4415
1948	1.6271
1949	1.673

Appendix C

Contract Comparisons, 1946–1947

It may be useful to present here a summary of the more significant changes from the 1946 to the 1947 contract. I will indicate in each case whether the change was proposed by union or by management, but a word of caution should be added here. I do not imply that one party either "won" or "lost" on a given issue. In this case it would be distorting the situation to speak in "won" or "lost" terms, for, to a remarkable degree, the 1947 contract proved to be a mutually satisfying document.

SUMMARY OF CONTRACT CHANGES
ARTICLE II
Union Recognition

1946 Section 1: "The Company recognizes the Union as the sole and exclusive collective bargaining agency for all production and maintenance employees, including floor inspectors, and excluding supervisors, foremen, assistant foremen, office clerks, timekeepers, and weight clerks.

"The above excluded employees shall not, except for the purpose of instruction or in cases of breakdown emergency, handle tools or materials."

Management asked more latitude for foremen in the form of a provision that they could work on production not exceeding 10 per cent of the time. Union argued this was unworkable. Agreement on adding clause "or when regular employees are not immediately available."

ARTICLE V
Prohibition of Strikes, Work Stoppages and Lockouts

1946 Section 1: "The union agrees that, consistent with the principle of a fair day's work for a fair day's pay, it is the objective of this Agreement to secure and sustain maximum productivity per employee and the highest level of employee performance and efficiency consistent with safety, good health, and sustained effort, and further agrees that neither the Union, its agents, or .its members, individually or collectively, will authorize, instigate, cause, condone or take part in any strike, work stoppage, sit-down, stay-in, slow-down, other curtailment or restriction of production, or any other action which interferes with the attainment of such objective. The Company shall have the right to discipline (including discharge) all employees taking part in violations of this section."

Clause concerning "fair day's work for a fair day's pay" was stricken on the grounds that it was meaningless. Management asked protection in the case of a possible jurisdictional strike. Immediately after the clause on "other curtailment or restriction of production," the following was inserted: "picketing in or about the premises of the Company, failure or refusal to pass through or otherwise respecting any picket lines in or about said premises." After that, the Section continues as in the 1946 contract.

ARTICLE VI
Hours of Work

1946 contract contained no explicit statement on employees' obligations. Management obtained the following section in the 1947 contract:

"Each employee shall be at his designated work place ready for work at his scheduled starting time at the beginning of his shift and after his rest period and his lunch recess. Employees shall not leave their respective designated work places for their rest periods until notified by their supervisor or their relief, or for their lunch recess or at the end of their respective shifts until their scheduled quitting times. Employees shall remain at their work places during their shift hours. Violations of this section shall be cause for discipline by the Company."

The union people felt that this section simply spelled out the obligations that should be common practice. Management was glad to have this spelled out.

Article VII
Wages

12-cent general increase, ½ cent for inequity adjustments. Management proposal. Union had demanded "a substantial increase." Industry pattern followed.

New employees in Maintenance Department to receive 5 cents under regular rate for probationary period of 60 days. Such period had been 30 days. Management proposed 90 days, compromised on 60.

On new piecework jobs, the 1946 contract had the following section: "When piecework jobs are assigned to employees and no rate has been established, the employee will receive his average piecework rate that he had received for the previous week while working on a rated job. After the new rate has been set he shall receive the rate of the job."

Management felt that this payment of average earnings provided no incentive and was able to obtain the substitution of the following clause: "When an employee is assigned to operations recognized as piecework for which no piecework rate has yet been established, such employee shall receive the base rate applicable to such job provided that, when the piecework rate is established, such rate shall be retroactive to the start of the job, and the employee shall receive any additional pay to which he would have been entitled had the piecework rate been in effect from the start of the job."

1946 contract provided that there be no interchange between male and female jobs except where there were "major changes in parts, tools, special equipment or machinery." Union sought to strengthen bars to interchange. Management agreed to substitute for the above clause the following wording: "unless there are changes in parts, tools, special equipment, machinery or method which result in substantial changes in or of job content."

Concerning provisions for changing rates, the following section appeared in the 1946 contract: "It is agreed where labor of employees is materially increased by a change in operating or manufacturing methods, consideration shall be given to an adjustment in rate for extra labor performed, or the Company shall add additional help to take care of the extra labor involved."

A "side letter" from management following the 1946 contract guaranteed existing rates, but this was not in the contract. Also, there was no mention of conditions under which rates might be lowered. Discussion led to the substitution of the following section (section 13): "Rates in effect as of the date of this Agreement shall not be changed, except that where changes in parts, tools, special equipment, machinery or methods result in an increase or decrease in or of job content, consideration shall be given to an upward or downward adjustment in rate."

Article VIII
Seniority

1946 Section: "It is understood and agreed that in all cases of promotion, demotion and increase or decrease of forces, within the bargaining unit, seniority shall govern providing the employee or employees have the knowledge, training, ability, skill and efficiency and physical fitness to perform the job, or jobs, in question."

1947 Section: "In all cases of promotion, demotion, and increase or decrease of forces within the bargaining unit, the following factors listed below shall be considered; however, only where both factors (b) and (c) are relatively equal shall length of continuous service be the determining factor:

      (a) Length of continuous service.
      (b) Ability to perform the work.
      (c) Physical fitness."

Management proposed the new clause except that seniority was listed as (c), which is in accord with the basic steel contract. The union accepted on condition that seniority be listed first, feeling this would strengthen its case in arbitration. Management's present policy seems to be to follow seniority without question except when the other factors seem to be of compelling importance.

Article IX
Furlough

Employee on furlough may have period extended by 2 thirty-day periods (instead of one). Union proposal.

1946 contract provided that any employee might be given a furlough not to exceed 3 months without loss in seniority except for time absent. No special provision for union officers. For 1947 management accepted union's proposal as follows: "The Company shall grant requests for leaves of absence not to exceed one (1) year for not more than two (2) employees certified by the Union to have been elected or appointed to full time positions with the local or international organization of the Union, provided adequate notice thereof is given. The Company shall also grant requests for leaves of absence not to exceed thirty (30) days for not more than five (5) employees certified by the Union to have been elected or appointed its representatives to attend conventions or similar Union functions, provided adequate notice thereof is given and the granting of such leaves of absence will not substantially interfere with production."

ARTICLE XI
Vacations

3 weeks after 25 years' service (instead of 2 for all having more than 5 years). Union proposal.

Employee who quits must give 2 weeks' notice to be entitled to vacation pay. Management added the 2 weeks' notice stipulation.

ARTICLE XII
Adjustment of Grievances

1946 contract began with this section: "Grievances are defined as differences as to the meaning and application of the provisions of this Agreement."

Union got the section stricken on the grounds that it was unnecessary and confusing. Section 2 in the 1946 contract then became Section 1 in the 1947 contract, as follows: "Should differences arise between the Company and the Union or its members employed by the Company as to the meaning and application of the provisions of this Agreement, or should any trouble of any kind arise in the plant resulting from an alleged violation of this Agreement, an earnest effort shall be made to settle such grievances through the following steps . . ." The 5-step procedure of 1946 is then retained.

U.S. Conciliation Service substituted for American Arbitration Association. Union proposal.

Arbitrator prohibited from amending contract. Management proposal.

Committeeman may enter another department to *investigate* as well as to act on grievance. Union proposal. 1946 contract allows such entrance only to process grievance.

Grievance committeeman on grievances has time off *without* pay. Management proposal. In 1946 time off was with pay. Now the union instead of management pays for the man's time.

No more than 1 member of 1 department to be absent at one time to process grievance. Management proposal.

Time allowed for processing grievances shortened. Union proposal.

1946 contract held that "the arbitration provisions . . . shall not apply to the determination of wages, wage rates or job classifications."

1947 contract added the following clause: "except that where a change in rate is based on a change in job content under Article VII, Section 13, the question whether job content was changed as provided therein may be subject to the arbitration provisions of Section 1, and if the arbitrator decides that job content was not so changed, the previous rate shall be retroactively reinstated."

This change is thoroughly discussed in the text.

Index

DATE DUE

HIGHSMITH 45-220